THE UNCOLLECTED LOUIS ZUKOFSKY

RECENCIES

RECENCIES SERIES:
Research and Recovery in
Twentieth-Century American Poetics

MATTHEW HOFER, Series Editor

This series stands at the intersection of critical investigation, historical documentation, and the preservation of cultural heritage. The series exists to illuminate the innovative poetics achievements of the recent past that remain relevant to the present. In addition to publishing monographs and edited volumes, it is also a venue for previously unpublished manuscripts, expanded reprints, and collections of major essays, letters, and interviews.

Also available in the Recencies Series:

Thinking with the Poem: Essays on the Poetry and Poetics of Rachel Blau DuPlessis edited by Andrew R. Mossin

"A Serpentine Gesture": John Ashbery's Poetry and Phenomenology by Elisabeth W. Joyce

Amiri Baraka and Edward Dorn: The Collected Letters edited by Claudia Moreno Pisano

Yours Presently: The Selected Letters of John Wieners edited by Michael Seth Stewart

All This Thinking: The Correspondence of Bernadette Mayer and Clark Coolidge edited by Stephanie Anderson and Kristen Tapson

Geopoetry: Geology, Materiality, Ecopoetics by Dale Enggass

Ingenious Pleasures: An Anthology of Punk, Trash, and Camp in Twentieth-Century Poetry edited by Drew Gardner

A Description of Acquaintance: The Letters of Laura Riding and Gertrude Stein, 1927–1930 edited by Jane Malcolm and Logan Esdale

Evaluations of US Poetry since 1950, Volume 1: Language, Form, and Music edited by Robert von Hallberg and Robert Faggen

Evaluations of US Poetry since 1950, Volume 2: Mind, Nation, and Power edited by Robert von Hallberg and Robert Faggen

For additional titles in the Recencies Series, please visit unmpress.com.

THE UNC
LOU

EDITED BY JEFFREY TWITCHEL

UKO
POETRY, DR

UNIVERSITY OF NEW MEXICO PRESS

DLLECTED

S ZU

'AAS AND MARK SCROGGINS

FSKY

MA, PROSE

ALBUQUERQUE

Library of Congress Cataloging-in-Publication Data

ISBN 978-0-8263-6878-2 (cloth)

ISBN 978-0-8263-6879-9 (paper)

ISBN 978-0-8263-6880-5 (ePub)

Library of Congress Control Number: 2025944341

Founded in 1889, the University of New Mexico sits on the traditional homelands of the
Pueblo of Sandia. The original peoples of New Mexico—Pueblo, Navajo, and Apache—
since time immemorial have deep connections to the land and have made significant
contributions to the broader community statewide. We honor the land itself and those
who remain stewards of this land throughout the generations and also acknowledge our
committed relationship to Indigenous peoples. We gratefully recognize our history.

Cover image courtesy of Louis Zukofsky Colletion, Harry Ransom Center,
    University of Texas at Austin

Designed by Isaac Morris

Composed in Nobel and Jenson.

All Louis and Celia Zukofsky materials © Musical Observations, Inc.
    Used by permission.

"Donna mi prega," by Ezra Pound, original by Cavalcanti, from *Translations*, © 1963 by
    Ezra Pound. Reprinted by permission of New Directions Publishing Corp.

"Canto XXXVI," by Ezra Pound, from *The Cantos of Ezra Pound*, © 1966 by Ezra Pound.
    Reprinted by permission of New Directions Publishing Corp. and Faber and Faber Ltd.

Permission to reproduce "The Gnat" by Carl Rakosi granted by Daniel K. Nordby,
    Literary Executor of the Estate of Callman Rawley (Carl Rakosi).

CONTENTS

A Preface and 18 Poems to the Future

Translations (1930–1943)

PART IV. Uncollected Prose

Uncollected Early Prose (1930–1936)

Uncollected Later Prose (1956–1973)

PART V. Musical Adaptations of *"A"* (1964–1967)

INTRODUCTION

Louis Zukofsky believed that the work of a poet's life, across all genres, forms a singular whole: as he puts it in "A"-12, "Each writer writes / one long work whose beat he cannot / entirely be aware of." His own work exemplifies the complexities and dialectical contradictions of that claim. On the surface, there is an orderliness to the considerable breadth of his writing: a methodical working through each of the major literary genres; the adoption or invention of strict predetermined forms; even the series of titles that imply a plan, such as "Poem beginning 'The'" followed by "A", or the alphabetically suggestive centerpieces of his canon: "A", *Bottom: on Shakespeare*, and *Catullus* (poetry, criticism, translation). Yet when one examines these big works in detail, one finds a seeming anarchy and playfulness, an openness to contingency that eludes any planning. The overriding impulse in all this work is invention, which intimately involves a persistent reflection on itself and its inheritances—its objecthood in a world of objects.

Most of Zukofsky's published writing in poetry, fiction, and critical prose has been collected. This volume represents an addendum to that corpus that aims not to change the shape of Zukofsky's canon, but to make available a number of texts that deepen our understanding of his achievement. *The Uncollected Louis Zukofsky* gathers a diversity of works in several genres: poems, a play, critical essays and notes, and less easily categorized writing. Some key items have been out of print for many decades; some, particularly early poems, were published in Zukofsky's lifetime but never made it into his books; others he considered publishing but for whatever reasons never followed through. These, however, are by no means scraps from Zukofsky's wastebasket: an inveterate condenser, Zukofsky never kept such materials.

Only a small number of the texts here are "new" discoveries from the manuscript archives. Zukofsky rarely failed to finish what he started, and anything he finished he almost always saw into print sooner or later. But while there are no undiscovered masterpieces among Zukofsky's papers, there are many minor gems and unexpected illuminations among the texts brought into print here.

· · · ·

Zukofsky's publishing career broadly mirrored the fortunes of formally innovative poetry in the United States over the course of his lifetime: a promising beginning, followed by long famine, then final feast. In the late 1920s and the 1930s, there is a flurry of periodical appearances; then a long period of only sporadic publication; and finally, in the last two decades before his death, a growing tide of small press volumes and trade collections.

Already steeped in the works of the first generation of modernist writers—T. S. Eliot, Ezra Pound, James Joyce, Marianne Moore, E. E. Cummings—the twenty-three-year-old Zukofsky brought himself to the attention of Pound in 1927. Pound published Zukofsky's first major work, "Poem beginning 'The,'" and connected him with his friend William Carlos Williams, who in turn recognized in Zukofsky a sharp editor for his own work. Those editorial skills stood Zukofsky in good stead when he was invited, at Pound's instigation, to edit what became the "'Objectivists' 1931" issue of *Poetry* magazine. The "Objectivists," a "group" that Zukofsky reluctantly invented at the behest of *Poetry*'s editor, Harriet Monroe, provoked little more than a ripple of publicity and controversy at the time, but it did actively project Zukofsky into the literary debates of the moment, where he fiercely argued on behalf of the kind of writing he believed in and practiced. Such advocacy would characterize his activities throughout the rest of the 1930s.

In some respects, his position was an isolated one. Although the importance of such modernist monuments of the previous decade as Joyce's *Ulysses* and Eliot's *The Waste Land* was increasingly acknowledged, there was a sense, at least in English-speaking circles, that formalist fireworks and experimentation had had their day, that it was time for a call to order. Eliot's poetry after *The Waste Land* was notably less adventurous, and over the 1930s, he practically ceased being a poet and instead established himself as a critical and cultural authority, projecting an immensely influential middle of the road aesthetic in his roles as editor of the *Criterion* and at Faber books. At the same time, for many others—especially the Leftist writers in Zukofsky's orbit, with whom he shared political convictions—the catastrophic economic and political developments of the decade demanded a more tendentious and accessible writing than the formally complex and sometimes opaque poetries Zukofsky championed.

Zukofsky was not, however, isolated during this time, either personally or in terms of literary involvement. He had abundant correspondence with Williams, Pound, Basil Bunting, Lorine Niedecker, and Carl Rakosi, was involved in at least one formal group, the League of American Writers, and irregularly did editorial work for *New Masses*. His major poems of the period—"'Mantis,'" "A"-8, and the first half of "A"-9—all found prompt periodical publication. Still, by the end of the 1930s, he had yet to publish a book of poetry and felt increasingly estranged from both Pound and the Left. The two collections he would publish in the next decade, *55 Poems* (1941) and *Anew* (1946), were small press productions underwritten at his own expense.

Beginning in the 1950s, Zukofsky's publishing fortunes would change, at first slowly and then quite dramatically, as younger emerging poets like Robert Creeley and Robert Duncan—figures associated with what would come to be called the "New American Poetry"—sought him out, wanting to reconnect with a more formally inventive and expansive modernist poetics that had largely been driven underground over the preceding decades. Journals and presses run by these younger poets would bring out a half dozen of Zukofsky's books over the later 1950s and early 1960s.

By the second half of the 1960s, Zukofsky's work had been taken up by such major publishers as W. W. Norton (whose poetry series was edited by Denise Levertov) and Doubleday/Paris Review Editions. During the last decade and a half of his life, Zukofsky would see all his very considerable new work, as well as most of his early work (both published and unpublished), brought out by established publishing firms. In the days before his death in May 1978, he was checking the proofs for the complete edition of *"A"* by the University of California Press and awaiting finished copies of the elaborate fine press edition of his final work, *80 Flowers*.

Since Zukofsky's death, the vast majority of his work has been brought out in readily available and reliable collected volumes: *"A"*, in a succession of editions; an expanded edition of *Prepositions*, his critical essays; the *Complete Short Poetry* (including *Catullus* and *80 Flowers*); the *Collected Fiction*; and a five-volume "Centennial Edition" of his more or less complete critical prose. These volumes from New Directions, Dalkey Archive Press, and Wesleyan University Press constitute the central canon of Zukofsky's writings; but although they present the primary texts of Zukofsky's work, they are by no means comprehensive. Overseen first by Zukofsky's widow Celia, then by his son Paul, they represent a series of admirable but piecemeal editorial and publishing efforts, rather than a unified "complete works."

The Uncollected Louis Zukofsky, then, is intended to address some of the gaps and omissions in these collections. In the present volume, we have Zukofsky's only play, *Arise, Arise*, long out of print; an elaborate presentation of *First Half of "A"-9*, privately mimeographed for personal distribution and never reprinted; a substantial number of poems, mostly early and mostly published in journals, but which did not make it into any of his collected volumes; a gathering of critical pieces, some unpublished, that were not included in *Prepositions*, or in a couple of cases were substantially truncated for that collection; and finally a set of musical arrangements of passages from that most musical of long poems, *"A"*.

The majority of the material presented here is from the 1930s, a period of Zukofsky's writing that has attracted a good deal of critical attention from scholars. For good reason: it was an extraordinarily active decade for Zukofsky, who was wading into various aesthetic, political, and aesthetico-political debates and tirelessly experimenting in a number of genres—verse, critical polemics, drama, and experimental prose. These previously unavailable texts present a more rounded view of his development as a young writer than can be gained from the texts Zukofsky chose to retain in his collections. The later, postwar works included are much thinner on the ground but stand as interesting illustrations of the mature Zukofsky's poetics.

I. Arise, Arise

Zukofsky recounts in his *Autobiography* that his "first exposure to letters" was drama, specifically the New York Yiddish theater, where his brother Morris took him as a child to see performances of Shakespeare, Ibsen, Strindberg, and Tolstoy. Given the mature Zukofsky's consuming interest in drama, evident most notably in his vast rhapsody on Shakespearean themes, *Bottom: on Shakespeare* (1963) and in *"A"*-21, an adaptation of Plautus' *Rudens* (*The Rope*), it is perhaps surprising that Zukofsky himself only wrote one play. *Arise, Arise*, composed in the mid-1930s, has been an unjustly neglected work. Not much is known about the circumstances of its composition, or Zukofsky's early hopes for staging or publishing it. Clearly, however, he valued the work, and when the opportunity arose, it was published and properly staged in the 1960s.

In 1950, Zukofsky submitted *Arise, Arise* to a Japanese journal, *Shigaku* (Tokyo), at the suggestion of Kitasono Katue. In a cover letter to the editor, Isaku Hirai, Zukofsky offered the following remarks as a possible preface:

> I conceive of *Arise, Arise* as an action which is at the same time a poem—a poem perhaps best defined by the integral

$$\int \begin{array}{l} \text{music} \\ \qquad \text{- and, as such, realized only in a dance of human bodies} \\ \text{word} \end{array}$$

that having weighted in their minds some valid ideas of the West can form them as movement on several parallel levels of art. Such craft the East, for example, has achieved in the Classic Chinese theatre and the Noh.

While this note is addressed to a potential Japanese audience, Zukofsky frequently remarked that ideally his play should be performed by Chinese actors; he had a lifelong interest in East Asian drama. Zukofsky was attracted to a theater of artifice and little interested in dramatic realism, whether of character psychology or action. He was familiar with Strindberg's dream plays and Expressionist drama (alluded to in "Poem beginning 'The'") and delighted in the absurd high jinks of Apollinaire's *Les mamelles de Tiresias* and Alfred Jarry's *Ubi Roi*.

Zukofsky, however, was temperamentally more low-key and grounded in the actual world than these models. After its first page or so, the action of *Arise, Arise* takes place entirely behind a dream curtain, projected as taking place in the mind of the Son, whose immediate reality is the fact of his dying mother. This latter is taken straight from Zukofsky's life, as his mother (who is directly addressed in much of "Poem beginning 'The'") died after a lingering illness in 1927, as is also the passing mention in the play of an elder sister who died when he was a boy. Parallels to the play's Father and Aunt can also be found in Zukofsky's life. But although at any given moment the play's presentation might seem ordinary, there is a persistent undercurrent of absurdity and non-sequitur in the dialogue—characters often speaking past each other. The play is interlaid with numerous quotations or paraphrases from a variety of sources, particularly Marx, unmarked quotations simply interpolated into the dialogue as if other voices are speaking through or taking over the characters.

Zukofsky stresses the artifice of the play's mise-en-scène: the prominence of certain recurring props, the frequent sounding of diverse music. What initially appears to be a typical family melodrama fails to lead anywhere; scenes and scenarios change without explanation; one character dies offstage and is resurrected later; the character of the Girl is unstable; the Mother mysteriously appears and disappears. The dream aspect of the play is less the projection of a distinct other reality than a license for imagining change and alternatives within the present, the taken for granted. This destabilization of the ordinary is also a mourning process wherein the remembered continue to live within the present, offering a path beyond the isolation of the self into a sense of enlarged community.

All this relates to a growing political emphasis, a social allegory that culminates, conventionally enough, in a marriage and dancing. The double allusion of the play's title gestures at its ambition: to Donne's "Holy Sonnet 7," in which the souls of the dead arise for the Last Judgment—"arise, arise / From death, you numberless infinities / Of souls, and to your scattered bodies go"—but also to the Socialist anthem the *Internationale*, with its exhortation to the workers of the world to shake off their economic bondage: "Arise, damned of the earth, arise, convicts of hunger." On both the subjective and social levels, it is the recognition that the dead remain actively alive within us and the world we inhabit that is the revolution in consciousness offering a possibility for a radically new and more equitable order.

II. First Half of "A"-9

"A"-9, a complex adaptation of the medieval Florentine poet Guido Cavalcanti's canzone "Donna mi prega," is commonly taken to represent the culmination of Zukofsky's pre-World War II work. Its intricate formal joinery and conceptual ingenuity have long attracted attention and have often been taken to be, for good or ill, quintessentially Zukofskian. The poet and his wife Celia published *First Half of "A"-9* in 1940, in a mimeographed edition of fifty-five copies. Zukofsky's own poem takes up only a few pages. The rest is occupied by what amounts to a presentation of Zukofsky's workshop: Cavalcanti's original Italian text; passages from Marx and contemporary physics texts that supply most of the poem's vocabulary; four translations of the canzone, in whole or part (two by Pound and two vernacular versions by Zukofsky and his friend Jerry Reisman); an explanation of the rigorous intricacy of Cavalcanti's canzone, along with a mathematical formula determining the distribution of "n" and "r" sounds in Zukofsky's final translation; and a prose restatement of the poem's content.

As this presentation highlights, in one sense "A"-9 is a response to Pound, who had placed his second translation of Cavalcanti's canzone as a major statement within his own epic-length poem (as Canto 36). There is an aspect of one-upmanship in Zukofsky's insistence on strictly adhering to the dizzying formal complexity of the canzone, which Pound, the master craftsman, had declared impossible to replicate. Furthermore, there is a sharp political rebuke in filling out the content mostly with material from Marx, as well as perhaps a repudiation of Pound's nostalgic medievalism in working in a bit of contemporary science.

First Half of "A"-9 should be read in the context of 1930s debates about literary modernism and the political; it exemplifies Zukofsky's conviction that the literature of the past is by no means irrelevant for a revolutionary era. Zukofsky can also be seen as translating Marx back into Cavalcanti's meditation on love. Cavalcanti is brought into the present by implying that "love" (the philosophical subject of "Donna mi prega") is at the heart of contemporary social and scientific discourses, that is, that representation of unseeable social and scientific laws draws on similar tropes. The colloquial renditions of the canzone by both Zukofsky and Reisman, on the other hand, counterpoint what often comes off as an exceedingly intellectual exercise to remind us that Cavalcanti's poem, as well as perhaps Marx and quantum physics, are after all about love and sex.

III. Uncollected Poems and Translations

From the mid-1930s, which marks the end point of the poems selected for *55 Poems*, any poem Zukofsky published would end up in one of his collections. There were, however, a significant number of published poems that never made it into that first book. The majority of these uncollected poems were composed in the 1920s and are coterminous with those in the "29 Poems" section of *55 Poems* (the "29 Songs" are from the first half of the 1930s). During this period, Zukofsky was still trying out a range of modernist possibilities, such as the irony and satire of "Poem beginning 'The,'" or the early movements of *"A"*, which have struck many as imitative of the *Cantos* but with a more autobiographical focus and relaxed manner. This would culminate in *"A"*-7 (1930), which can be taken as marking the beginning of Zukofsky's distinctive verse.

These early poems can be described as "pre-Objectivist" in that they usually maintain a readily identifiable lyric voice struggling to express a sense of phenomenological density, of the impress of the larger world on the subject. They also stand as Zukofsky's earliest attempts to write a politically conscious poetry that avoids tendentious declaration. In this regard, of particular interest is a largely unpublished sequence, "18 Poems to the Future," which Zukofsky sent to Pound for *The Exile* as a follow-up to "Poem beginning 'The.'" Pound found the sequence not up to the standard of "'The'" and only published its preface, with its fiery quotations from Georges Sorel.

Nevertheless, this work is of interest as Zukofsky's earliest known instance of a poetic sequence, a form that he would explore in most of his succeeding collections, as well as in "A" itself. Here, Zukofsky self-consciously attempts to break away from the nature-suffused verse of his early years and situate himself in the city, as part of a felt but largely unseen complex of technology and innumerable other lives. The individual poems are located at various points in greater New York City, and their political, even apocalyptic, implications are gestured at by epigrams drawn from John Bunyan's *The Pilgrim's Progress*. The mechanics here are rather crude compared with what Zukofsky would soon be capable of, but the sequence is an intriguing transitional work as he works his way out of the closed aestheticism of his student days.

• • • •

The modest gathering of later poems, from the 1930s through the early 1940s, offers glimpses of Zukofsky's diverse experiments: a found poem, a couple of collaborations, a pair of brief lyrics for William Carlos Williams's opera *The First President*, and a small cluster of alternative versions of published poems or outtakes that did not quite make it into one of Zukofsky's collections. All the unpublished poems presented here, including alternate versions, were at one point considered ready for publication; these are not merely discarded drafts. But they offer insight into Zukofsky's revising habits, which invariable involved condensation, often drastic.

The principle of collaboration, in its manifold senses, and the concomitant principle that all writing is necessarily rewriting, are central to Zukofsky's entire enterprise—whether works overtly written by several hands or to be included in others' works, reworking of poems by others, collage poems, found poems, responses to other poets, and of course translation. The mirror fugue on Carl Rakosi's "The Gnat," for instance, is a tribute to the two poets' interactive friendship during a period in which Zukofsky was offering Rakosi detailed advice on his draft poems, much of which was incorporated into their final versions.

After World War II, virtually nothing that Zukofsky wrote failed to end up in a book, but we include two late poems. "Julia's Wild," a series of rearrangements of a line from *The Two Gentlemen of Verona*, is a well-known work that Zukofsky performed at readings and allowed to be published in anthologies, but chose to leave in *Bottom: on Shakespeare* within its context as an exchange with and homage to his friend Cid Corman. The poem can be understood as a combination of both a found and a serial poem—there are a number of other notable examples of the latter, such as "Songs of Degrees 1 & 2" ("Hear, her / Clear / Mirror") and "A"-20. The final poem, "THE OVERWORLD," was written as an epigraph for *GAMUT: 90 Trees*, the project for which Zukofsky had been gathering notes for some years but had only just begun at his death. This is another found poem and radical condensation, carved entirely out of the final "After Scene" of Thomas Hardy's *The Dynasts*.

. . . .

Later in life, Zukofsky would gain some notoriety with his translations from Latin (a language he did not really know): the bravura "homophonic" translation of Catullus with Celia Zukofsky and the rendition of Plautus' *Rudens* incorporated into "A"-21. We present here a handful of earlier, more conventional translations from French, a language in which he did have a reasonable competence. These translations—of poems by André Salmon, Guillaume Apollinaire, and Alain Bosquet—were produced almost as byproducts of other projects: the Salmon for an essay for *Poetry*, the Apollinaire in the course of Zukofsky's work on *The Writing of Guillaume Apollinaire*, and the Bosquet for a projected wartime periodical, *La France en Liberté*. Zukofsky was intrigued by Salmon's "nominalism" as manifested in the long poem *Prikaz* on the Russian Revolution—a presentation of multiple discrete moments and perspectives without recurring characters or plot, which he compared with the cinematic montage of contemporary Soviet filmmakers. *The Writing of Guillaume Apollinaire*, ghost-written to boost his friend René Taupin's academic credentials, was not only about Apollinaire but was formally presented very much in an Apollinairean anarchistic spirit, and although Zukofsky persisted in expressing its personal importance to him, few others could make heads or tails of it. The "sequence" of snippets from Apollinaire poems offers a similar *jeu d'esprit* in miniature form. Decades later, Zukofsky would return to the French poetic tradition in "A"-19, where he performs some homophonic renditions from and improvisational dialogic somersaults on Mallarmé.

IV. Uncollected Prose

The earlier critical prose collected here, mostly from the 1930s, shows Zukofsky wearing his polemical hat. On the one hand, he is pushing back against voices calling for a more subdued and sober modernism, a retreat from formal experimentation. Zukofsky's brief review of the Japanese-American poet Bunichi Kagawa, for instance, is more interested in firing a few shots at R. P. Blackmur and Yvor Winters, two critical figures influential in subsequent decades in institutionalizing a conservative view of modernism—or in Winters's case, an elaborately dismissive one. On the other hand, there were Leftist writers and critics who took the literary itself as intrinsically contaminated by class elitism and bourgeois subjectivity.

Particularly in the later years of the decade, Zukofsky would advocate a politically relevant writing that nonetheless took full advantage of the long inheritance of literary forms and values. One such intervention was *A Workers Anthology* (1934-1935), which presented a historical selection of poetry from Ovid to Apollinaire to argue that literature of social critique was not incompatible with high aesthetic values, that in fact literary classics typically implied social and class criticism. This polemic is behind his unpublished review of Muriel Rukeyser's first book, *Theory of Flight*, arguing that a sloppy and imprecise poetic technique muddies her on the whole salutatory political stance. Along similar lines, he wittily skewers Wyndham Lewis's portentous polemic style as obfuscating whatever might be of value in his cultural criticism. In a more positive vein, Zukofsky succinctly highlights the distinctiveness of Basil Bunting's poetry in what is apparently the only review of his first book, *Redimiculum Matellarum* (1930). A couple of pieces on Pound's *XXX Cantos* can be read as augmentations of Zukofsky's long essay on Pound (later collected in *Prepositions*), which, taken together, represent one of the few extended and insightful early discussions of the *Cantos*.

In addition to various reviews and brief critical and polemical notes from the 1930s, this edition presents the original versions of two key essays: "Charles Reznikoff: Sincerity and Objectification" and "American Poetry 1920-1930." Zukofsky composed the former in early 1930 as a comprehensive critical introduction to Reznikoff's work, which he intended for *The Menorah Journal*, at the time probably the only venue that would consider publishing such an extensive discussion of this little-known writer. *The Menorah Journal* rejected it, much to Zukofsky's annoyance.

When he was invited to guest-edit a number of *Poetry* magazine, Zukofsky conceived of the issue as a snapshot of progressive tendencies in American poetry. He would have preferred to use "American Poetry 1920-1930" as his major critical statement, but the article had already been submitted elsewhere. So he retooled the essay on Reznikoff following Harriet Monroe's suggestions—deleting the sections on fiction and drama, bringing into greater prominence the terms "sincerity" and "objectification," and relegating Reznikoff to the subtitle. Thus were born the "Objectivists," as the February 1931 issue of *Poetry* would be titled. Given the historical importance this essay has acquired, it seems worth presenting in its full original form, which was intended to draw attention to an unjustly ignored poet and friend who himself was temperamentally averse to self-promotion. This version raises the question as to what extent the famous discussion of "sincerity" and "objectification" is specific to the example of Reznikoff's work.

When Zukofsky prepared *Prepositions* (1967), he drastically truncated the three main "Objectivists" statements—"Program: 'Objectivists' 1931," "Sincerity and Objectification," and "'Recencies' in Poetry," the preface to An *"Objectivists" Anthology*—presenting them together under the title, "An Objective." His purpose at the time was both to erase his historical relations with the "Objectivists" and to de-emphasize these documents in favor of "Poetry / *For My Son When He Can Read*" (1946), which he then considered a more significant statement of his poetic position. Less severely but for similar reasons, he considerably trimmed the more historical contextualizing elements from "American Poetry 1920-1930," blunting its polemic edge. Although this essay may strike us today as a competent tour of the major U. S. poets circa 1930 (with side remarks on some minors), Zukofsky has his eye firmly focused on where the technical possibilities of free verse, often referred to as "quantitative," have and have not been fully embraced—that is, whether or not poets have developed new ears beyond the strait-jacket of inherited meters.

The paucity of late critical pieces reflects Zukofsky's distaste for conventional critical prose after the 1930s. Aside from two attempts to summarize his poetic position in the years following World War II—"Poetry / *For My Son When He Can Read*" and "A Statement for Poetry" (1959)—he put all of his critical energies into *Bottom: on Shakespeare*, which started out as an essay on the playwright but grew into a sprawling, compulsive contraption, absorbing infinite topics and quotations. Although *Bottom* is routinely categorized as a critical study, Zukofsky himself suggested it could be read as a poem—or just about any other literary species. Indeed, in many respects, the work struggles mightily with itself: at its heart, it is an intellectual endeavor that would turn all thought back into its literal being on the page. This scepticism regarding the value of any strictly critical enterprise marks the sparsely scattered later reviews and statements collected in *Prepositions*, and the few pieces added here.

Zukofsky's review of Robert Creeley's *The Whip* is a tribute to one of his earliest champions among the new generation, the younger poet with whom he felt closest both personally and poetically. It is less a commentary than a florilegium of Zukofsky's favorite passages from Creeley's book. Zukofsky frequently responded to the younger poets crowding his mailbox by noting his favored passages from their small press publications. Jonathan Williams, another young admirer who had published an elegant edition of *Some Time* (1956), asked for a preface for his book *Amen/Huzzah/Selah*, so Zukofsky agreed he could use this letter, responding to Williams in his own off-beat, super-punning manner. These pieces hint at the considerable contact Zukofsky developed with up and coming poets during the later 1950s and 1960s, involving extensive correspondence and publication in their little magazines, as well as frequent visits to his home. The importance to Zukofsky of these younger poets' and publishers' recognition is acknowledged in many short poems and throughout the movements of *"A"* written during the 1960s.

Zukofsky's *Autobiography* (1970) consists largely of a selection of his short poems set to music by his wife Celia, and thus is exemplary of the couple's collaborative artistic efforts. These include the jointly-translated *Catullus* and *"A"*-24 (Celia Zukofsky's "L. Z. Masque"), an arrangement of four "voices" from the range of Zukofsky's writings spoken simultaneously over Handel's harpsichord pieces. The few brief autobiographical remarks Zukofsky added show his characteristic reticence—"I have always felt that the work says all there needs to be said of one's life"—but these statements lay out concisely what he felt to be important moments of his writing career.

V. Musical Adaptations of "A"

"A" begins with a performance of Bach's *St. Matthew Passion*, a composition that sets the last events of Christ's life to music, the words sung by a variety of voices and by a double chorus. From its very beginning Zukofsky conceived of "A" as a polyvocal work: as he puts it, "One song / Of many voices." It is hardly surprising, then, that Zukofsky would be attracted to literalizing his poem as musical performance.

While Zukofsky's early experiments in "musical" form are for the most part analogical, after his 1939 marriage to Celia Thaew, a classically trained pianist and occasional composer, he found himself blessed with a partner who could realize his ambitions to work in both words and notes at once. (Celia's knowledge of Latin was also crucial; their 1969 translation of Catullus was a fully collaborative work.) The most notable musical fruits of their partnership are the settings of the short poems in *Autobiography*; Celia's setting of *Pericles, Prince of Tyre*, published as the second volume of *Bottom: on Shakespeare*; and finally "A"-24 (Celia's "L. Z. Masque"), an arrangement of four "voices" from the range of Zukofsky's writings spoken simultaneously over Handel's harpsichord pieces. One might also keep in mind that by this time, young Paul Zukofsky was launched on his own career as a virtuoso violinist, so musical performance was very much a part of the Zukofsky family's everyday existence.

The two texts presented here, both dating from the mid-1960s, appear to have been inspired by this environment of collaboration and performance, which also included a staging of Zukofsky's *Arise, Arise* (1965) and a public performance of *Autobiography* (1971). Just what Celia Zukofsky contributed to these musical arrangements of "A" is unclear, but doubtless she had some hand in them. These musicalizations of "A" have not previously been publicly accessible and consequently have received no critical attention. For those who read Zukofsky with an ear to the musical implications of his poetry, however, they are of compelling interest. Not merely do they provide us with a glimpse of how Zukofsky imagined the realization of "one song" among "many voices," but they also provide a glimpse of the poet's own possible "Selected 'A,'" as it were. The succinct "'A' cantata 13 v" reveals the final section of that movement of "A" as a love song to his wife and collaborator.

· · · ·

For some time, this collection bore the title "Addendum," a nod both to its supplementary relationship to the body of Zukofsky's published work and to Zukofsky's own alphabetical titling predilections: *"A"*, *ALL*, *Anew*. It also nodded to Paul Zukofsky, who after his father's death assiduously worked to keep Zukofsky's writing in print and to make out-of-print texts available. Paul used to refer to the "Additional Prose" section of the expanded *Prepositions+: The Collected Critical Essays* as the "A-dum-dum." He would no more have approved of this collection than his father would have, but we believe that on some level, Paul would have recognized its value.

ARISE, ARISE (1936)

Arise, Arise

A Play in Two Acts

CHARACTERS

The Mother	The Nurse
The Son	Attendant with rag
The Father	Attendant with duster
The Girl	The Aunt
The Doctor	The Cousin

N.B.

The play requires two curtains: the familiar one of the theatre, and the dream curtain of dark, heavy indefinite voile back of the theatre curtain.

The actors should be dancers.

The costumes, not confined to a realistic locale, are essentially theatrical and as such never give the feeling of being anachronous: The Mother and The Girl in simple white suggestive of the Greek stage; The Son in black trousers and white linen shirt open at the neck; The Nurse in the contemporary blue linen outfit of her profession; The Doctor in a gray-black three button suit; The Father in afternoon dinner jacket and formal striped trousers; The Attendants in navy serge trousers and white jackets; The Aunt in Empire gown; The Cousin in contemporary business suit, rather nondescript.

Act I

Scene 1

(The whistle of a train passing over country is heard as the Theatre Curtain rises. Moonlight behind the Dream Curtain falls in the crack between its hem and the floor of the proscenium. The Dream Curtain remains lowered. Following the whistle of the train, the SON'S VOICE *reads:)*

SON'S VOICE:
    "At the round earth's imagined corners, blow
    Your trumpets, Angels, and arise, arise
    From death, you numberless infinities
    Of souls, and to your scattered bodies go,"

MOTHER'S VOICE: When I arrived in Canada the ground was alien. I was happy. Russians brought treelings to be transplanted. When a sailor with a basket of apples slung over his right arm offered me some, I slapped him with my left.

SON'S VOICE: You weren't bright, mother. Did you hear what I was reading?

MOTHER'S VOICE: They thought I was bright when I was a servant that half year, and left coins for me to find while I was dusting. I returned them. Though they felt I deserved them, it was more than I could accept and feel at home. They would often ask me to sit down and talk while the owner was writing letters in the morning.—Our ship had come after the war. There was a shortage of coal. Not enough had been stored aboard. The planking had to be used to sail us in. We would have drowned but for that. It mattered. I would hardly care now. Your father in New York sent for me.

SON'S VOICE: But you haven't been listening.

MOTHER'S VOICE: My life was cut short when your sister was put in the grave. You place something on an upper shelf and cannot find it again.

SON'S VOICE: You haven't listened, but I have never read to you before. Shall I tomorrow—perhaps?

MOTHER'S VOICE: *(continues the poem which opened the scene)*
    "—let them sleep"—"Mourn a space"

SON'S VOICE: What did you say? It is in the poem which you have never heard.

MOTHER'S VOICE: I have been to your sister's grave under the trees, with the
     birds, the ivy is growing over the slab of her tomb.

SON'S VOICE: Mother, come—

(The Dream Curtain rustles, swings from side to side, and finally lifts. The stage is quite dark, but for an indefinite moonlight—the moon itself unseen—penetrating the darkness. MOTHER and SON are walking up a country road which the scene need barely indicate. Where they are does not matter, nor what they look like, except that the light outlines their heads and bodies continually attracting each other. Their walk is an unbroken circuit on the stage. The house subsequently referred to in their speech, the audience never sees, but for the dim handle of the door at the end of the scene.)

MOTHER: I knew you would be here today—your birthday.

SON: I have been wanting to every day now, busy all year, afraid the fog
     streaming in the window of the compartment had hurt you. You insisted
     on keeping it open. I was worried.

MOTHER: It was better I was not on the train now.

SON: I came in the coach this time. So many people.

MOTHER: How are you?

SON: You, mother? You are not cold in this night air? Let me wrap the scarf
     around you. *(He does so.)*

MOTHER: It is not cold tonight. I have been able to breathe better for a long
     time. Your father was here with our grandson today.

SON: You do not weep, mother, as you used to. That's better. We think of our
     dead so long, we only do over in our minds what they did living.

MOTHER: The living regret the dead not having what the living have.—It's this
     house.

SON: We have walked fast. You're not tired?

MOTHER: Listen, your father is inside amusing your nephew, we can try to
     overhear him.

(SON and MOTHER stand still listening, their backs to the audience.)

FATHER'S VOICE: They do not return, child. There is a legend that they would speak from their graves outside a village before morning. Someone came to listen, stretched out, put his ear to the ground, and they whispered: "Sisters, brothers, we are being overheard, we must not speak." My son dreams often about your grandma, he tells me that he knows she is dead in the dream and she knows but does not mention it. They say nothing about it for love of each other, so that there will be no difference between them or a fear that he will wake.

MOTHER: One moment. (*She hurries in.*)

SON: (*calling her*) Mother, the door—leave the keys with me! (*Nervously tries the door knob which rattles.*)

(*Dream Curtain lowers and rises immediately.*)

Scene 2

(*Sunlight, end of day.* DOCTOR's *outer office, a hospital. Entrance left. Window center background, uncurtained, shows a square of blue sky. Door to inner office right.* NURSE's *desk left.* NURSE *busy in chair faces audience.* THE GIRL, *back to* NURSE, *works at small garden table cattycorner left. Garden bench center foreground, small green rug at the foot.*)

SON'S VOICE: (*off stage left*) You'll wait home for me, father? B-r-r-r, too cold for spring. Would be nice if the heat were on in the new rooms, when we bring ma home tomorrow. I think I gave you the keys?

(*The solitary note of a bird is heard.*)

NURSE: (*as* SON *appears*) Twit, twit, why not hire a hall with the canary, mister? Do you think your voice will soothe the patients?

SON: Excuse me, I'll bring a silencer the next time. Is the doctor in?

NURSE: One of these guys with an imagination, eh? He's busy. Please take a seat?

SON: Thank you. (*sits down on bench*)

DOCTOR: (*showing his face at the inner office door*) Mame, busy?

NURSE: (*hurries over*) Not rushing! What's on, Doctor?

DOCTOR: The ether clinging to me. What perfume is on you today, Mame?

NURSE: The birthday gift you bought me. Like it?

DOCTOR: I'll say, Cleopatra's Egyptians had the right idea. Myself feels so low I could share a pyramidon. Dated tonight?

NURSE: Not if you help me move first. Carry my trunk down two and up one flight of stairs? Easier going down than up. But not far to go!

DOCTOR: Okay, I have some dictation first. As soon as I'm thru. For me?

(*Points to* SON *who has been winding his watch. Shuts door of his office. Fidgeting,* THE SON *has caused his hat to slide off the bench. He stoops to pick it up, resting one knee on the floor. As* THE NURSE'S *skirt brushes past him, he looks up at her and recites gallantly:*)

SON: "here on this lowly ground, teach me how to repent." Do you know poetry?

NURSE: Don't mind me, make believe it's stage grass.

(THE SON *smiles up at her, caresses the rug approvingly, folds and smooths the hat like a pillow, and stretches full length on the rug.* THE DOCTOR, *his dictation in his hand, comes out of his office; unnoticing walks past the back of the bench center and over to* THE GIRL *at the small garden table cattycorner left.*)

DOCTOR: May 18/26, married, housewife, in U. S. since 1892. Diagnosis: active, favorable June 14/26. Referred here by herself. Complaint: cough wakes her with the cockcrow every morning.

GIRL: How many times did you say the patient coughs, please Doctor?

DOCTOR: Always.

SON: (*still stretched out on the rug. To himself*—) All ways: coughs. Sleepy.

DOCTOR: (*continues to dictate, unnoticing*) reexamined the 16th, month of February, brumous. Lives with her son, Duven Anew, probably a widower, admittedly ungraded, desk neutral, green doors, cream walls, 10th floor, elevator never runs above the fifth, riveters have invaded the ninth, tank seen from the window and the verdigris turret of a semi-religious lodge, rental paid December 20/26, $60. Therefore so much—blank—could be paid in support of her upkeep. Her sister-in-law, widow, testified before four armchairs, two on each side of the table that—. These facts must do. No column left for No Information? Put her down as inactive, the totals will check. (*bends over* THE GIRL'S *table to review his dictation.*)

SON: (*rises impulsively and steps over to* THE NURSE'S *desk*) How long will this take, Thirsty?

NURSE: Do you think I know? The Doctor's still busy, can't you see?

SON: I see that. Is there anything else you see? May I speak to him? Are you the new Doctor, sir?

DOCTOR: (*without turning*) Sorry to disappoint you, I'm passed my internship. I think I know the case. A thin soul. We can do nothing about it. You can leave her here or take her home. There isn't much hope either way.

SON: She's been here 5 months, and you've been here how long and haven't seen her! Don't you ever take a look at people?

NURSE: Did *you* hear what the Doctor said?

SON: I wasn't talking to you. If you want me to talk at you, it's a quiet office you've lots of patience here. I want the Doctor to *look* and speak to *me*.

NURSE: (*condescending, speaking emphatically to him*) We have many patients here. (*to the* DOCTOR *loftily*)

> There was once a Strictly Anonymous
> Who wanted to shoot Doctor Goitre Pus
> But senses confused
> Impatient he mused
> Till his gun took fire from the shape he was.

Ready, Doctor?

DOCTOR: *I'll* call it a day!

SON: (*half to himself, half to* THE NURSE *turned away from him*) Sorry . . . my temper . . . is there water here?

NURSE: And lily cups in the corridor.

SON: (*whispers*) Thanks. (*exits left*)

(THE NURSE *and* DOCTOR *walk to the garden bench center and stand on the rug for a moment in an embrace, but do not kiss.* THE GIRL *at the table cattycorner left continues to work, her back turned to them. They separate and return to* THE NURSE'S *desk,* THE NURSE *fixing her hair,* THE DOCTOR *standing near her, as the* SON *returns.* THE DOCTOR *then walks into his office right.*)

NURSE: Name, please?

SON: I—I have been here before. (*returns listlessly to the garden bench, sits down, gazes at the green rug, his hat hanging from his hands held between his knees.*)

(*Enter two Negro* ATTENDANTS *in white jackets, one with a duster, the other with a flannel rag. They go about cleaning up as at the end of a day.*)

NURSE: (*to herself as she walks into* THE DOCTOR'S *office*) I wonder if this bench could be moved and the rug hung over the window ledge to air.

(*As she shuts the door behind her, the* ATTENDANTS *move her desk and chair out left, then return.*)

ATTENDANT R.: (*sighing abstractedly, after a while*) I don't ask questions, I do. I give her everything.

ATTENDANT D.: When a bird hops on a window while I do stevedore work in the morning and play the music box and listens to the tune as long as it lasts and chirps its own tune, and stops chirping just as the music box stops—what kind o' bird would you say that was? Would you say dat bird flares up. That dat flare's a bird? Just because it's the same thing, does the same thing every morning because a man plays de music box or de gramphone and it's a bird all the same, would you give it a man's recognition, or a woman's? I know dat bird. I know it's just a bird. A Common ordinary sparrow. (*harpsichord plays "Wolsey's Wilde" in* THE DOCTOR'S *room*) (*with affected mystery*) Maybe it's on dere window, right now.

SON: (*to himself, hitting his left temple with one hand as if to remember*) It can't be. No, darling. (*The music stops.*)

(*The* ATTENDANTS *walk to the garden bench, take places at each end. They bend slightly at their hips, as tho they were reflected in each other, and as if to say "let's move this." THE* SON *rises and walks to the window, stands there for a while, his head against the sash. By this time the* ATTENDANTS *have moved the bench parallel to the table of* THE GIRL *still working cattycorner left. The back of her chair now faces the garden bench.*)

ATTENDANT D.: (*leaving left*) Good evening. It will soon be a very pleasant
    evening.

(THE SON *now walks over to the rug,* THE ATTENDANT *with rag in his back pantspocket trailing him, and stoops to pick it up. He flings one end out to* THE ATTENDANT, *who catches it. They walk to the window holding the rug between them.* THE SON *lets go his end of the rug, and* THE ATTENDANT *hangs it over the ledge so that most of it is out to air. As* THE SON *watches,* THE ATTENDANT *takes the rag out of his pocket and cleans the window, singing to the tune of "Le Pauvre Laboureur":*)

> The poor wage laborer
> Has two small sons all gold,
> They drive the plough to help him,
> They're not fifteen years old!
>
> There is no wealthy planter,
> Nor landlord I call sir,
> Not thriving on the pittance
> Of the poor laborer.

(*waves to* SON) Thanks, boss. (*out left*)
GIRL: (*rises from her work, places the seat of her chair under the table*) What have
    you brought here?
SON: (*knowing her*) Sweet. You? (*holds a finger to her cheek*) You. (*They embrace,*
    very much like THE NURSE *and* DOCTOR *earlier in the scene.*)
GIRL: What did you do this afternoon?

SON: The afternoon moon's out, let's open the window and look at it. (*He opens it.*)

GIRL: You know, it's your birthday.

SON: I never had a birthday till my mother died.

(*Dream Curtain lowers as the music of Byrd's "Wolseys Wilde" is heard again. It stops as the curtain rises after a short pause.*)

Scene 3

(*The court of a hospital—indicated by a sign rear left. The three walls of the stage meet a cerulean vault of sky at their crests. A wrought iron garden gate, entrance, shaded by a huge tree left. Against its trunk a ladder on which* THE ATTENDANT *with rag (in his backpocket) is busy pruning etc., in the branches. Right, a complementary gate, tree, and ladder on which* THE ATTENDANT *with duster (also in his backpocket) is similarly engaged. Both gates are closed, as is a wicket of wooden stakes center background. Cattycorner, left, garden bench and table, as at the end of Scene 2. A small rectangular bed of flowers, mostly tea roses and marigold, center foreground.* THE SON *and* THE GIRL *are tending it diagonally from the left forecorner,* THE GIRL *nearer the proscenium.*)

SON: (*sings, syncopating*)   Here lies a cousin
Here lie two
What my dead ones
Can I do for you?

Sit down and weep
And dig my grave deep?
Why talk, relations—
I'll take a walk.

GIRL: Very thoughtful of you. You should on your birthday. You've been working too hard.

(ATTENDANT R. *and* ATTENDANT D. *now comment in antiphon.*)

ATTENDANT R.:   One need not say the stars
                   Across the suns by which they see
                   View our earth
                   Disinterestedly.

ATTENDANT D.:   One has but need to sight
                   When bodies pass between
                   One heart for another heart
                   Does not always rest serene.

ATTENDANT R.:   The Trojan elders on the wall
                   Chattering like many crickets
                   Rued that there was ever war
                   Grieved it ailed their rickets.

                   Helen passed and rested
                   Her eyes on every one
                   The Trojan elders straightened
                   On thin legs in the sun.

(*The* SON *and* GIRL *have continued as they were, oblivious to the* ATTENDANTS. *She breaks off a marigold with its stem and presents it to him.*)

SON: Living sunlight. For me? For my birthday?

GIRL: When I look at it, I begin to wonder if my body is my own.

SON: (*kisses her*) What was I saying?

GIRL: When?

SON: Just now. Was I sleeping?

GIRL: Just a little maybe. (*kisses him*) You're always a little crazy (*said affectionately*). I dreamt last night. Interested?

SON: Yes, please.

GIRL: We were traveling in a car—

SON: Which I hired but didn't own, of course.

GIRL: We were traveling away from a town, and you were saying: "Hear it purr, this whir of motor? It is to our good, hubbub at the feet of any small traveler."

SON: And we reached a town?

GIRL: Yes, how do you know?

SON: How do I *know*? How do I know! I look at maps.

GIRL: Almost chilled, we reached another town, yes. And you said as five internes passed us in white jackets: "Poor thoughts, you have been with cigarette between two fingers. Come out of smoke."

SON: Do you want me to unfold your dream?

GIRL: Not yet. Let's work a little more first.

(The SON *and* GIRL *continue as tho nothing had been said. The* ATTENDANTS *resume in antiphon. Music, backstage,—"Bach's Fugue in E minor"—is heard on an organ muffled by distance for the duration of their passage.)*

ATTENDANT D.:

Being what you are, lady,
Is not a vain romance.
In love, lady, you don't see
The minute ants.

ATTENDANT R.:

Ants are everywhere
Showing an obsession
Like young suitors climbing stairs
For a life's progression.

ATTENDANT D.:

They bruise wood, graze on stone,
Fall, passing, in a jutting place:
But a loved countenance
And body show one face.

ATTENDANT R.:

They run tearing up a wood,
Where the sun is scant,
To meet the wise plumiped
Ululant.

ATTENDANT D.:   Better than dingles in the moon
                  Is a crater in the sun
                  My premise is not
                  To be argued with anyone.

(*Music stops.*)

Once every year this tree needs shining.

ATTENDANT R.: Once every year these leaves need dusting.

(*They come down from their ladders and busy themselves collecting the sprigs, pods, etc., which have fallen off the trees to the ground.*)

(THE SON *and* GIRL *having stopped tending the garden are now seated on the ground, overlooking the garden from its left forecorner.*)

SON: We came to the garden in flower for the gathering. Not all dreams should be spoken, sweetheart.

GIRL: What were you saying?

SON: Beautiful, do you know how many tea roses, fling flower-pale, with love, as towards your head in a ring, petals after the spring? Their stems bend to the great wind which rises. The petals of rose are a ruin in the way. O beautiful, gather them—flowering of surmises fades after today. Put them in a cup—when each gate closes—zest lost and cruel, reflect what days consume—we will see the amorous agony, the roses' fences of perfume.

GIRL: That hardly helps, does it?

SON: Did I ever speak to you about my dead sister? When she was a little girl, she was very ill for a spell, and when they nursed her back to health my father renamed her "Lost and Found." He could be funny. She wanted to marry like you. She did. She died when her son was a month old. She was beautiful. I remember her the center of a lighted room at her engagement dance. The other day I touched the hem of the blue opera cloak she wore that night—for the first time in eighteen years. I was only seven then. Dead, the young remain young in the mind.

ATTENDANT D.: It happens every first of the fifth month of every year—

ATTENDANT R.: That there comes a time when twenty years are but one day and when may come days which are like twenty years—to be precise each first of the May.

SON: I have a photograph of her. The dead in a photograph reveal a forward look like a face among cloud and wind such as a rock grows to express. Look here. (*Rises,* THE GIRL *with him, moves his hand into his inside coat pocket*) Do you want to see?

GIRL: Now? I couldn't look at her face now. Please. Forgive me. (*Breaks into tears, and rushes out right, her face hidden in her hands.*)

SON: (*Making no move to follow, stands center foreground, his eyes dwelling on a photograph which he has taken from his pocket. The two* ATTENDANTS *have come up behind him and are also looking over his shoulder. He returns the photograph listlessly to his inside pocket and faces about to greet them naturally.*) Tell me, is this the Lutterworth Hospital?

ATTENDANT R.: Yes—

ATTENDANT D.: sir.

SON: What a day I've had finding it. Thanks. Will you permit me, for your kindness. (*He takes the right hand of each* ATTENDANT *and joins them, so that they now face each other hands clasped.*) I've come to take my sister home, attendants of the—, workers of the—, what shall I say? Thanks.

(*The* ATTENDANTS *wave their hands as if to include the entire hospital court.*)

ATTENDANT R.: —Of the Lutterworth world.

SON: (*Shakes both their hands*) Thanks. There? (*points to entrance left towards which he moves.*)

(*The* ATTENDANTS *go off right to the gate, where they stop, face each other and continue in antiphon.*)

ATTENDANT R.:   He came also still
                                 Where his mother lay

ATTENDANT D.:   As dew in April

                                  That falleth on the spray

(They go out right, shutting the gate.)

*(*THE MOTHER *and* FATHER *enter left.* THE FATHER *leads her to the garden bench in front of which they remain standing, lost in grief.* THE SON *hurries over to meet her. From now on the scene is a lament taken up as in canon.)*

SON: Mother, we do not always want burdens. I know, mother. To be what we are now will never be sufficient.

MOTHER: The whole earth lies dead.

FATHER: She has been so much myself, how can I ever lose her, how can I pretend to? I seem to be looking everywhere into darkness in the sunlight. In a dream last night she was carrying her black kid gloves in her hand. With her usual smile she asked me to keep them for her. When I asked, why keep, she answered you will know me by my step, father. I can never forget her step.

MOTHER: My son, your sister is dead. Alive and speaking to me just now, she asked for water and when I brought it, not for me, she said, drink it, look how parched *your* lips are. How long ago is it that I looked into her eyes?

SON: Her eyes are stopped with earth, mother, how can we look into her eyes?

FATHER: We will not need to come here anymore, to escape or strive with anyone. Young I escaped the hounds of several nations; with others fleeing for each other, and I shall never wish to be young again. Why have I lived? For this? The boat I steered once split on a rock. Why didn't I drown. It would have been a lark.

MOTHER: Sunlight is in my daughter's room the first hour of her death.

FATHER: The shades must not be drawn if she is to be where the sun is.

SON: Her lips must be white, mother.

MOTHER: O head, her head, my—both scattered—I must go now to her grave,
pick all the sharp stones under which her heart might lie. Where the dust
is broken, I will lie on heaped dust.

SON: You must not go alone to her room, mother.

MOTHER: She is more alone than we, my son. We mourn only ourselves, our
own earth selves.

(THE SON *moves to stop her but he is held back by* THE FATHER.)

FATHER: Let her. She will not be happy elsewhere.

(THE MOTHER *opens the wicket and walks out lost to sight. Against the blue sky a slab of
tombstone over a strip of turf the size of the green rug of Scene 2 is seen. The door remains open.*
THE FATHER *sits down on the garden bench, his face buried in his hands.* THE SON *sits down
beside him.* THE GIRL, *tear-stained face, returns right, falls to the garden-bed, her body shaken
with quiet sobbing.* THE SON *walks diagonally across the stage to her and kneels beside her.*)

SON: (*caressing her head*) An expansive garden is nipped, my egotist. The
flowers are doomed for the room. Our roses each by each strip of their
grief. Sob . . . Each pale corolla is love's brief.

(*The Dream Curtain falls as the music stopped earlier in the scene continues.*)

Scene 4

(*The music ending Scene 3 stops as the Dream Curtain rises. A dim foreground of stage which
might be the hall of an apartment lighted by a high, vague shaft of sunlight over a spiral stairway
right.* THE SON *seated on the lowest step glances at his watch. The other actors enter left and
walk towards the foot of the stairway where the main action takes place.*)

DOCTOR: "Sentimentally I am disposed to harmony, but organically I am
incapable of a tune."

NURSE: Excuse me, are the Attendants following?

DOCTOR: I guess so. Attendants!

ATTENDANTS: (*off stage*) Coming!

SON: Father!

FATHER: Coming! (*He is soon seen descending the staircase.*)

(*Enter* ATTENDANT D., ATTENDANT R. *and* THE MOTHER *grey with illness supported between them on their arms.* THE FATHER *and* SON *hurry over to her.* THE DOCTOR *and* NURSE *follow them.*)

ATTENDANT D.: Sound ground, again!

ATTENDANT R.: Hail sail! Hale sailing!

SON: Kisses!

FATHER: All the streets were hushed while you were gone.

MOTHER: My silence was with you.

FATHER: Everything that you are was with me.

MOTHER: I've been watching the leaves on the trees, growing—how shall I
     say—into ebb-gold; it's hard to explain what happens when you're away,
     waiting for just this.

SON: We won't have to eat ourselves and gradually be eaten away, in any case,
     now.

FATHER: (*to everybody*) She'll improve every day, wait and see.

MOTHER: I *will* feel better home.

NURSE: (*solicitously to* THE FATHER) Her homecoming must not be made too
     exciting: there's the danger of relapse.

DOCTOR: (*to* THE FATHER) There's only tension in the power of a spring.
     Suppose we take her upstairs.

SON: Can you make it, mother?

MOTHER: If I can't, will I frighten you? (*She tries one step and exhausted,
     supports herself on* THE SON.)

SON: Never mind! We'll carry you up.

DOCTOR: (*to* ATTENDANT D.) Can you get us a chair, please.

FATHER: A chair's an idea!

ATTENDANT D.: Everywhere with energy—yes, sir! (*Out left, where off stage a
     harpsichord begins playing "Wolseys Wilde" as in Scene 2.*)

MOTHER: Why do you trouble these others about me?

SON: Why?

(A muffled shot left. The music stops. The shaft of sunlight is dimmed suddenly.)

ATTENDANT R.: He's taking time. Shall I go join him?

NURSE: Yes. (ATTENDANT R. *out left*) (*to* DOCTOR) How about *us*?

DOCTOR: We may be needed. Come. (*Both out left*)

SON: (*Looks with absorbing anxiety at* THE MOTHER, *as if trying to distract her from the others.*) Where did we hear that music?

(THE MOTHER eyes him anxiously for a long while, but does not answer. ATTENDANT R. returns listlessly, his head drooping in grief. A chair hangs held by one hand against the side of his body.)

FATHER: What's happened?

ATTENDANT R.: They explained nothing. Said he shot himself. A girl there said a bird was chirping caught in a harpsichord and he was curious about it. *Then*, they shot him. But he is dead either way and they've explained nothing.

FATHER: Shooting isn't explained much these days.

SON: Wasn't it the same in your time? (THE MOTHER'S *eyes are now a plea to whatever force in him will keep her from fainting.*) Mother!

ATTENDANT R.: May I help? (*They sit her down on the chair, lift it and begin to carry her upstairs as the light fades rapidly. They speak as they climb.*)

FATHER: In the time of the Indian war the wife of Van Tienhoven testifying her joy in a merciless slaughter danced thru the city, kicked an Indian's head before her as a football.

ATTENDANT R.: Step!

(The voices of NURSE *and* DOCTOR *returning)*

NURSE: In the sunset his skin appeared burnished.

DOCTOR: In their crime you mean the rays of the sun's passing lasted longer than delight. (*They reach the bottom of the stairway.*) May we help?!

FATHER: Yes! Join us. (NURSE *and* DOCTOR *are heard going up the stairs.*) They
wired from Strasbourg that a man there was found guilty, condemned to
be beheaded and afterwards burnt, and was executed: for transforming
himself into a wolf and carrying away and devouring a great number
of sheep. They did not mention on what evidence he was convicted,
but it should seem the court of justice which passed the sentence were
transformed into another sort of animal.

ATTENDANT R.: Step! (*A knock as of a shoe stubbing a stair is heard.*)

FATHER: Careful, was anything underfoot?—Minuchihr would treat as worse
than evil those who treated people contemptuously.

ATTENDANT R.: Step!

FATHER: All one's friends—quotes!—all one's best citizens, reformers,
educated classes, had joined the banks to force submission.

ATTENDANT R.: Step!

MOTHER: How many more turns? Where are you all?

SON: The last, and you weigh nothing.

(*The Dream Curtain falls and rises immediately.*)

Scene 5

(*Night. Musical accompaniment underneath stage thruout this scene as at considerable distance, but clear. In the foreground, off center,* THE MOTHER *and* SON *seated with their backs against a knoll partly face away from the audience, and towards a prospect extending to an unlighted arc of footlights of an oblong platform, occupying about 3/4 of the length of the stage, against a high drop rear. At the center of this platform three low steps lead to the main stage. Between these steps and the knoll, several paper lanterns suspended at random in mid-air, tho emitting little light, seem to render the air fluorescent with a light of greater intensity than the moonlight of Scene 1. In the center of the main stage, the green rug of Scene 2 has been laid lengthwise parallel to the wings. The music is the second movement of Bach's "Sixth Brandenburg Concerto."*)

SON: I am no longer myself. I am the fifteenth after the eleventh.

MOTHER: It is lovely here.

SON: We were all there today, all whom the flood did, and fire, all whom war, death, age, agues, tyrannies, despair, law, chance had slain.

MOTHER: I like the wind best in my eyes. (*She takes both his hands and holds them. He bends his head so that his eyes rest on the knuckles of her hands.*) Do you think of me, as I think of flowers, like eyes shut, lashes like white flowers fringing—(*The arc of footlights of the oblong platform, rear, lights with a suddenness almost the effect of sound. From a fold in the high drop,* ATTENDANT R. *appears, walks down the steps of the platform to the main stage and across the green rug to* THE MOTHER *and* SON *who rise to meet him.*)

ATTENDANT R.: (*bowing slightly*) I am in your dreams, my confidants.

SON: And so you are, our confidence in yours. My mother—(THE MOTHER *nods*)

ATTENDANT R.: I am proud to meet one of whom it has been said

> "we understood
> Her by her sight; her pure, and eloquent blood
> Spoke in her cheeks, and so distinctly wrought,
> That one might almost say, her body thought."

SON:

> The old store of the air is pleasant here
> Where it seems the Old World and the New
> unite.

ATTENDANT R.: (*continuing* The Son's *discourse*)

> On a commodity like bread, for example,
> That remains food even under the moon,
> You'll see if you watch our maskers. Will you
> stay?

MOTHER: We're late but would regret to go away.

SON: Are all the actors masked?

ATTENDANT R.: (*bowing slightly*) One who is not thanks you for staying. (*He retraces his way back to the platform rear where he now stands at the entrance fold in the back drop.*)

MOTHER: To think—it is all that I would imagine a stage to be.

SON: You have never seen a play. Aren't you happy you will see a play! (*They sit down as at the opening of the scene, and he holds her hands.*) Your hands are cold.

MOTHER: Give me yours.

ATTENDANT R.: (*as Prologue*) The play is simple:

> He came also still
>> Where his *sister* was
> As dew in April
>> That falleth on the grass.

> He came also still
>> To his *sister's* bower
> As dew in April
>> That falleth on the flower.

> He stroked his girl's hand,
>> Whom he had led
> In grief with him
>> To his sister dead.

> In his girl's eyes
>> A hospital
> Looked into him—
>> Before, her eyes had been all.

> Forgive their sorrow, then,—
>> In this stage of grief
> While the state makes war
>> Their act is brief.

Another word:

The day she died
Was his birthday,
He could remember it
As her day.

(*He opens the fold in the drop to let in* THE DOCTOR, *followed by* THE GIRL *dressed in mourning, her face thickly veiled.*)

GIRL: Have we heart, we find no mind to which we can let go our love; you
    with a mind can find no heart to come to you and know. It's like verse:
    cold gilt sun, wind, dawn itself glazes our eyes.
DOCTOR: Then what are you in mourning for.
GIRL: So you won't see me today. The dead in whom your past is—do their
    loves keep you more than the leaves of spring?
DOCTOR: Damn it, go!
GIRL: Passing me on the street today Sam MacVea
                  Was sorry that I looked so much blacker than he

(*She goes out weeping quietly.*)

DOCTOR: (*Appearing suddenly at a loss, impulsively approaches* ATTENDANT R.)
    I'm acting understudy. Please, my cue!

(ATTENDANT *merely lowers his head in response.* THE DOCTOR *does the same.*)

SON: (*rising impulsively*) I'll take your part for you! (*Leaps across the path* THE
    ATTENDANT *had previously taken to the platform.* THE DOCTOR *goes out,*
    as THE SON *takes his place.* THE ATTENDANT *now fully draws open the fold*
    in the back drop. On a simple bier of wood lies the dead body of ATTENDANT
    D., THE NURSE *standing at its head.*)
ATTENDANT R.: (*speaking as Chorus*)
                  Machines—luxury and beauty are only their spray
                  You should have had bread easier in your day.

(THE FATHER *appears behind* THE NURSE. *With the unseeing eyes of a person recognizing another in a dream, yet unable to speak,* THE SON *walks very slowly towards him, finally holds him at arm's length and gazes at him.* THE FATHER *returns his* SON'S *stare without a sign of recognition and lets his eyes roam. Meanwhile, main stage,* THE MOTHER'S *head has fallen back on the knoll. Her mouth is slightly open. The fingers of one hand rigidly outstretched touch the floor of the stage.*)

> NURSE: Poor fellow, to be dead, his shack without a roof, while the wind
> strives with the sun on a bit of window pane.

(THE FATHER *now listlessly walks to the foot of the bier,* THE SON'S *stare following him, takes some crumbs from a side pocket in his coat and lets them fall to the ground.*)

> FATHER: For the birds whom no one has been feeding lately.
> ATTENDANT R.: (*announces with the effect of climax*) Said like a draught of
> water! Time out!

(*The footlights of the platform are extinguished as suddenly as they were illuminated early in the scene. The lights of the paper lanterns also go out, permitting all the actors, except* THE SON *and* THE MOTHER, *to leave in the darkness. A blue light now opens a path from the knoll, where* THE MOTHER *lies, across the rug and to the steps of the platform, on the top stair of which* THE SON *is standing. His hand is splayed across his face, which he strokes as if to feel it in every part. Continuing to stroke his face, he retraces his way to the knoll. Without raising his hand he falls slowly as in a spiral full length on his face to the stage, stretching out his other hand till it covers* THE MOTHER'S.)

> SON: Mother, do you hear?

(*The Dream Curtain falls; then, the Theatre Curtain.*)

Act II

Scene 1

(A living room. Midday. Settled around the garden table of Scene 2, foreground, left, DOCTOR, NURSE, FATHER *and* ATTENDANT R. *sort various papers, and occasionally stir and pour themselves drinks from a white jug. Right,* THE MOTHER *and* THE GIRL *seated at each end of the garden bench seem unaware of each other as they face the footlights thruout the scene.* THE GIRL *is nearer the right door. Another door left. Over the window ledge center background, the green rug as in Scene 2. In front of it,* THE AUNT *stands arms akimbo and glares at* THE SON. THE COUSIN—*her own son—stands awkwardly between them. The action of* AUNT, COUSIN *and* SON *goes on apart from the conversation at the garden table and obviously concerns* THE MOTHER *and* GIRL.)

AUNT: Nephew, you're a witness. You can't deny I have talked to my niece (*points to* GIRL) for fifty minutes and that she has not peeped a word to answer your aunt. You've an impious, stubborn hussy of a sister. You're behaving just as selfishly as she. If you don't persuade her to go back to work, nephew, you're a gnat!

SON: Calm yourself, she may speak to you yet, aunt. If you insist, cousin, on always bringing your mother in, like a storm thru the window, the strike must go on.

COUSIN: I came thru there! (*points finger downward, at right door. As* AUNT *paces back and forth in anger,* SON *with both hands on the floor pretends looking at crack between floor and door. Rises, shakes his head skeptically, pretends nonplus to* COUSIN *who in quick exasperation moves his head negatively from side to side. Meanwhile—*)

FATHER: (*curiously to* NURSE) What year is it?

ATTENDANT R.: (*impatiently to* DOCTOR) It's purely a question of advertising.

DOCTOR: (*matter of fact, to* ATTENDANT) It is plain, moreover, that work now brutal under suitable conditions—and in ten years who'll need to work?

NURSE: (*to* FATHER) 1910, I believe. Beside age, embonpoint. (*Touches* THE FATHER'S *vest with the tip of her right index finger and smiles patiently.*) Bright cheeks, yes, are a beautiful asset, but when lips color blue, an actress' experienced appearance contracts the camera desperately.

FATHER: (*laughs socially, to* NURSE) Fight beauty, conspicuous Empire and England.

ATTENDANT R.: (*impatient, to* DOCTOR) Revolution, not all around a table!

DOCTOR: (*decisively, to* ATTENDANT) We'll speak from their gravestones, yet.

AUNT: Niece, your mind is made up, I take it! You will let our machines rust, because strangers are striking. You'll do that to our living?

MOTHER: Our?

AUNT: Ours. If not ours, whose! Didn't we bring you to Manchester and here so we could all live peaceably together. O my heart, my head, my head, one would think you're not my sister. Where would you be now if we hadn't brought you over this side the ocean?

ATTENDANT R.: (*lifts his face to the air, sniffs*) Scent?

SON: If you weren't on the other side in the first place, aunt, she'd have had potatoes for her meals without quarrels, and you no mother to hit.

COUSIN: My mother hit her mother? (*points to* THE MOTHER *who almost cringes, places her hands over her ears in pain.*)

SON: (*after nodding repeatedly with mettlesome glee in his eye, assumes an explanatory tone.*) You see that's not as impossible as it seems. (*Eyes fixed on* COUSIN, *approaches him and speaks with increasing emphasis rising to fierce logic. Once or twice* COUSIN *makes startled sounds of fear.*) If sisters-in-law own one percolator together, and one is inclined to brew what can the percolator do! If the percolator—!

(COUSIN *apparently more frightened by his own imagination and* SON'S *play than anything else falls to floor of the stage in a fit. Pantomime of* COUSIN, *as* AUNT *and* SON *look on, approach and retreat alternately, in separate horror. At the same time,* ATTENDANT *who has taken a small oboe from his inside coat-pocket executes the familiar tune played by criers in front of burlesque music halls—"O the beans are great, a million on a plate"—.* FATHER *and* NURSE *clap hands in unison.* DOCTOR'S *handclapping syncopates theirs. Music stops. As the last stages of* COUSIN'S *fit continue—*)

ATTENDANT R.: (*to* FATHER) I need hardly say—

FATHER: (*to* ATTENDANT) It is just as stupid to regard the Christo-Teutonic form of the family as absolute, as it is to take the same view of the Roman form or of the classical Greek form, or of the Oriental form.

NURSE: (*to* FATHER) Which, by the bye?

DOCTOR: (*to* NURSE) All of them really constitute an historically interconnected—shall I say developed—series.

COUSIN: (*Rises, limp, arranges his clothes.* AUNT *helps him.*) Steak, mother, steak, steak, I could eat three pounds of steak all by myself.

SON: (*walks off, in disgust, towards window*) Rabid thieves—pah! (*opens window, breathes visibly excited.*)

AUNT: (*to* MOTHER) Fiends! Look at my son—. What you've done to him! Your stubbornness is driving him out of his mind. It will take all our savings to restore him.

COUSIN: (*tugs her by a sleeve, pantomimes, warning her to keep a secret*) Mmm . . . m . . m . . m. Whose saving? What savings?! (*She pantomimes, shoos him off.*)

AUNT: If you're not stones, you'll not connive with strangers to split our factory on the rocks. Think only of yourselves—not us—why should you strike and starve with hoodlums who are nothing to you. Take into account, if we're lost, you're lost.

MOTHER: If a morsel cannot be swallowed, sister, is it food to eat? My daughter can't eat while her friends starve. Our lives are consumed in wrangles, tears, hurts. Perhaps she is wise to think we can from now on continue separate lives. (*coughs violently*) It is hard for me to speak. The stove—the draught is still bad—smoked again when I made it today. The soot stays in my throat. She has worked seven years, and we're still not able to check the draught. What else can I say.

GIRL: (*speaks now as* MOTHER's *daughter and* SON's *sister*) I don't wish to go back and make window curtains in your chimneys, Aunt! Do I make myself clear to you?

AUNT: Clear! You'll be dead and in hell, before you've cleared yourself with your aunt! (*to* COUSIN) Come! (*Exits right, followed by* COUSIN *who stops at the door and faces* SON.)

COUSIN: Steak—steak—steak—(*sings the words to notes of do, re, mi. Giggles maniacally. Exit.*)

(MOTHER *and* GIRL *are still where they were on garden bench.* THE MOTHER *tries to hide her tears, as she wipes an eye with a small handkerchief.*)

DOCTOR: (*rises*) Democracy—bleachery! (*begins to move to door left. The others around garden table—their session obviously ended—file after him as he goes out.* NURSE *follows.*)

FATHER: A spectre is haunting Europe. (*out*)

ATTENDANT R.: (*sings casually*)

> Debout les damnés de la terre
>
> Debout! les forçats de la faim! (*saunters out*)

(THE MOTHER *rises, tragic, head high, eyes fixed on distance, follows him.*)

SON: (*casually sings as he translates*) Arise you damned of—. Sister. Sis. (*Places his hands on the shoulders of* GIRL *who is still sitting on garden bench with her back to him.*)

GIRL: (*looks at him for the first time in the scene*) Sister?

SON: (*Passage of time felt in his look, as the previous action of the scene fades into what he senses now.*) No.—She is dead and gone. (*He walks around the bench, sits near her. They face forward, her hands are in her lap, her head rests on his shoulder, but he does not seem conscious of it.*) No man sick with ever such sickness, but shall, if he hear this, recover his happiness.—So sweet it is! Aucassins looked the long way and saw a man. (*pause*) But why are you crying, said the man. By right, only I have something to cry about. (*pause*) I was hired out to a rich farmer, given four oxen to drive his plough. Three days ago, I lost the best of the team. (*pause*) As you see, I've not the worth of anything but what is on my body. (THE MOTHER *who has appeared from right now stands silently behind them, expressionless look of the dead, places a jacket around him. He opens it and reveals a torn lining.*) I've a poor old mother who owned nothing but a feather mattress, and they've dragged it from under her back, so she lies on the bare straw.

GIRL: Shall we go to her?

(*He turns his head to* THE GIRL'S *and kisses her eyes, mouth and forehead as the Dream Curtain falls.*)

Scene 2

(Instrumental music from the final chorus of Bach's "Matthew Passion"—subdued, underneath stage—opens on the set of Act I, Scene 3, minus ladders, garden table and sign near left, and continues thruout the scene as suits the needs of the action. A headstone—new property—is at the right end of the bed of flowers. At its left end the green rug (instead of turf) extends its length parallel to the proscenium. THE COUSIN, his back to audience, is seated at the unseen narrow end of the headstone.)

ATTENDANT R.: *(stands at right gate, whittles a point on a stake evidently missing from wicket rear, and sings so that the melody of Bach's "Around thy tomb" conforms to his whittling.)*

> On your grave we raise our rag
> Red with the staunched blood of your chest—
> Rest you safely, safely rest.

(continues to hum and whittle)

GIRL'S VOICE: *(behind gate, right)* I'll say there is no sign keep off the grass on the other side and that the bird who sings has a friendly voice.

SON'S VOICE: A man's voice, darling, which tombstones transmute into a bird's.

GIRL'S VOICE: Is it late to ask much of its grace, when we are here—I am sure, dear, this is the place.

SON'S VOICE: Death's woe, shall we assume the gate's to knock on when the breach is already in us.

GIRL'S VOICE: Should you pass her door and not stop for love of her, Aucassins—

SON'S VOICE: And his—my—mother not look on us together now, than I he and you she—he should be her love no more, nor she his.

GIRL'S VOICE: I wish I had known your sister and your mother, Aucassins.

(They knock. ATTENDANT R. opens the gate for them.)

ATTENDANT R.: Your birthday greetings, friend.

SON: You're right, friend. He remembers me from last year, dear!

ATTENDANT R.: *(bows slightly)* The lady is new.

SON: The lady is mine. (ATTENDANT *bows acknowledgingly.*) She decided to come with me, being unknown to me before.

GIRL: (*eyes half-closed, her lashes trying to keep out the sun, extends a hand to* ATTENDANT *which he holds a moment*) What brilliant sunlight; it spots the reflections of the leaves' green on my hands. Does spring keep you here despite itself?

ATTENDANT R.: Like a negative picture, the lights and shades reversed, the dispensation of the lives passed of those who lie here becomes my waiting on them.

GIRL: I'm in love, and in love, too, a portrait recalls its negative: as people when they say "I didn't see nobody," and the nobody, really a body, shines,— How else do you spend the time?

ATTENDANT R.: Northward is land. To the south, land. To the east, sun. If there were a deformity in an oriole which flies here in the spring, I could pick it.

SON: Do you conserve birds here?

ATTENDANT R.: It would be presumptuous to say one directs what appears to direct itself to us? The black and orange of the bird attracts me with its hanging nest. It may distract others' attentions otherwise. (*A bird is heard and is silent.*)

COUSIN: How do you catch such a bird?

SON: We're not alone. Your assistant?

ATTENDANT R.: Well. He is here.

SON: (*looks toward* COUSIN) If the sun were not in my eyes, I'd say a face familiar like a relative's which had somehow crossed my sight before. His words made queer thought, like a filching poet's which play on two deaths.

GIRL: And a third perhaps who was of consequence to the other two. (*to* ATTENDANT) Do others come here? Do they weep?

ATTENDANT R.: A hand hurts and the body hurts. There are no separate ills. Some weep. We expect several anniversaries today. (*to* SON) And this is yours.

GIRL: His birthday.

SON: But is he sitting at my mother's grave?

ATTENDANT R.: So many years removed from her.—Should he trouble you?

(FATHER *and* AUNT *enter thru wicket gate rear.*)

SON: My father and my aunt! I expected we'd be by ourselves. Forgive me,
    darling, for having spoiled your day.

GIRL: I'll not let your disappointment trouble me. Why should she? (*caresses*
    his hand—agitated, clenched)

SON: I know, death has good standing. But not the self-plagiarism of my aunt's
    tears.

GIRL: Try and be good to her. She's mad.

SON: (*approaches* FATHER) Our aunt met you? Others are expected here.

FATHER: Please. The right to mourn is not appropriated.

SON: You were my mother's good sister, aunt. Words are pebbles in our sorrow.
    (*to* FATHER, *after embracing him*) Times when we are here, the use of
    grief so separate we do not know each other. We may have met, done and
    known the same things somewhere and not known each other.

FATHER: As you say it, it seems possible. I almost feel it happened. Haven't
    you forgotten something?

SON: My sister's grave. Where is the knoll and aisle? (*He looks around a*
    moment as GIRL *joins them.*)

FATHER: (*to* GIRL) She was about as young as you. (*to* SON) Somehow her
    thought brings up little things—a dream I had of feeding bread crumbs
    to the birds.—Or was it a dream you had in which you said that I, too,
    dreamt.—An actor in an old costume spoke: "We have just landed in
    New Netherland!" then, he read a verse. The words were:

> 'The land where milk and honey flow
> Where healing plants as thick as thistles grow
> Where flowers on Adam's Rod blow:
> The land—Eden.'

Sails blew and people landed to the words. The turf I mourned was not
your sister's. Another's body had taken her shape. How can I confine
my thoughts so I can remember her step? I am so poor forgetting it, my
memory makes me feel like an old actor.

SON: We should—shall—have more than crumbs, father. (*holds* GIRL'S *hand*)

FATHER: (*to* SON, *and looks at* GIRL) Your sweetheart? Wear her well.

SON: Thanks. (*Places hands on* FATHER'S *shoulders, then slowly drops them.*)

AUNT: (*rummages in pocketbook*) I have something for you. For you both!

SON: The moneyed relation that tore from our family its sentimental veil.

AUNT: No. Your mother's earrings. They're yours. Take them. (*He does.*) I have
   nestled everywhere till now, but now I go. (*unnoticed, leaves rear*)

SON: (*to* GIRL, *and looks at earrings*) They're of glass, dear, and looked—look—
   like jewel chips. My young mother wore them at my sister's marriage, and
   the dancers—some of them—did not know her from the bride.—Will
   you try them on? (*she does*)

ATTENDANT R.: (*who has been whittling, takes a red rag from his pocket, ties it to
   stake which he places point down in garden bed, sings as before to the music of
   "Around thy tomb"*)

> Dead in your grave but alive in us
> In the strength you had, in your strength we
>   have—

SON: Wear them well, sweet friend, sister.

ATTENDANT R.: (*joins others, and to* GIRL) Permit me, but I must say to you
   they are beautiful. (*then offers hand to* SON *who takes it*) Sorrow both
   fades and glistens because of them.—And do you know who lies here?
   (*points to green rug*)

SON: It is not hard to guess: one who on a first of May could have said as
   much as you have said to me, wishing me well on my birthday.

ATTENDANT R.: He was my friend, and the very one you say—shot in the
   working world. So a bird is brought down thru the attendant air.

FATHER: The grave is a new grave. He might very well have been one who was
   shot in a strike. (*looks down, around him*) And I see the ground on which
   your aunt stood has been drawn from under her feet. In place of old
   wants, new.

(DOCTOR *and* NURSE *enter right.* ATTENDANT R. *drops* SON'S *hand to welcome them.*)

ATTENDANT R.: Greetings! Arise damned of earth!

DOCTOR: Greetings!

NURSE: Greetings! (*Her voice echoes the* DOCTOR'S *and she seems taken aback by it, becomes the* NURSE *in the ward.*) My voice echoes yours. The place, Doctor, makes me think of patients who are asleep.

DOCTOR: (*having approached green rug, faces red rag on stake in garden bed and the others who have gathered round him.*) All present: because they do not breathe beneath us and breathe only in us.

SON: (*stubs heels on garden plot as he accidentally steps backward; sways somewhat vertiginously, clasps* GIRL'S *hand and balances.*) In us.

DOCTOR: Watch yourself. The ground's onesidedness becomes more and more impossible. From many lands local tunes travel thru the world. You see these local flowers are from all lands for all lands.

SON: (*to* GIRL) Wire to May to wire.

DOCTOR: Those who pretend not to notice, and those merely with their backs to us, who exist to accumulate but do not accumulate so we may exist— (*the notes of the bird are heard for a second and are silenced.*)

NURSE: The bird—sounds like an oriole.

ATTENDANT R.: I had a friend in Baltimore who—

COUSIN: (*who has got up very slowly—a camera is strapped across his chest*) How do you catch such a bird?

GIRL: Would you?

FATHER: Of what use would he be to you?

COUSIN: (*distractedly*) I'll have a cage. How do you catch such a bird?

ATTENDANT R.: (*smiles sadly*) My assistant, our assistant! I mean he happens to be here. (*to* SON, *as he gaily taps* SON'S *temple with a finger*) Where in your capital? (THE COUSIN *shrugs his shoulders and starts to move off*) Why, then, there can no longer be wage labor.

SON: (*moves toward* COUSIN *and taps camera sharply*) Does your lens?—Does it sound? (COUSIN *again shrugs his shoulders, and resumes his sitting position at the unseen end of the tombstone*)

SON: (*reassured*) Why, then, proceed!

DOCTOR: I was going to say: the accumulators have produced their own gravediggers.

NURSE: (*to* DOCTOR) But tell him.

DOCTOR: (*to* SON) Do you know me? (SON *shakes his head negatively.*)

FATHER: (*regretfully, to* SON) Don't you? (SON *tries to remember, but shakes his head as before.*)

DOCTOR: (*to* SON *and* GIRL) O, well, our marriage is at dawn. You're both invited.

NURSE: Remember, we invite you both.

SON: Thanks.

DOCTOR: (*to* FATHER *and* NURSE) Shall we go now, since those who sleep here are ours. (*They leave left, quietly.*)

SON: (*Watches them go, then turns to* GIRL, *walks with her toward gate, right.*) A wedding—did he say where?

ATTENDANT R.: (*Picks a marigold with its stem from the garden bed, speaks to it.*) Those who sleep under you, comrade flower,—the intellect has become common property.

(SON *and* GIRL *leave right as the Dream Curtain falls.*)

Scene 3

(*Night: the stage empty or the scene barely indicated as in Act I, scene 1. Musical accompaniment, distant, underneath stage, begins with the second movement of Bach's "Sixth Brandenburg Concerto."* SON *enters right, helping* GIRL *to step over an obstacle.*)

SON: Watch out for the third rail.

GIRL: Now that I have taken your advice, I must say there is no third rail. This is open country and the steel tracks beneath are not electrified.

SON: I see: and in last night's paper I saw that the Mesquakies, their reservation lowlands under water this spring, are too late to tap the maple trees for sugar, their principal medium of exchange.

GIRL: What will they use now?

SON: Corn maybe: to get the persimmons, porcupine quills, cranberries, wild rice and soft buckskins not produced by the Mesquakies.

GIRL: What is money?

SON: Clockwork in the dark. See, look around you: the universal equivalent that prevents the farmer from bringing his pig to market, that hides the ties between peoples—the time they put in on the things they make for themselves and for others. Did you work today? Did I? Our work is congealed in money, which grinds out the night-worker's shift until he touches at least a crumb.

GIRL: I wish I had more of it, tho.—What do you regret most?

SON: Nothing now. Let me see, what did I do before we were in love? I think I regretted most to be alive when those who had meant most to me were dead.

GIRL: You're speaking of your sister and your mother. Tell me, if you could see them now would they terrify you? Would it be like standing at the edge of a falls and suddenly not finding yourself alone, someone hurrying over while you were watching?

SON: I can only see them as I see them. I would be frightened more by being short-changed, especially if our breakfast depended on it.

GIRL: Silly. I would regret most not being able to outlive any death. Except yours. (*She leads as they begin waltzing very slowly—or perhaps they are dancing a sarabande—first up stage, then gradually turning right,—to the musical accompaniment no louder than before. They speak: occasionally somewhat out of breath as they dance.*) I'm thirsty.

SON: I have been for hours. Kiss me.

GIRL: I wonder how long it'll take to that doctor's wedding at this rate.

SON: If we dream, we are there. (*Their dance quickens and slows down again.*)

GIRL: I wish I knew something about the beginnings of these suburbs.

SON: A certain surgeon had a beautiful garden here. Here in New York, the grain sowed in the middle of May was harvested in the middle of August. They had a fruit called *forerunners*. The buildings have become morning glories of overnight. (*He arches over her in the dance which now adds to the quiet of sleep about them.*)

GIRL: Tell me more. (*Again, their pace speeds a little.*)

SON: One wrote of an east river: a narrow passage where runneth a violent
stream both upon Flood and Ebb called Hell-gate. The river's still here.

GIRL: I meant you to say what other flowers grew here. (*The dance slows
down again.*)

SON: Morning stars, maritoffles—a very sweet flower—, maid-in-the-mist.

GIRL: Dripping in the rain waters.

SON: Divers birds chirping harmonious discord; (*dancing very slowly*) in every
pond and brook green silken frogs warbling untuned tunes strove to
bear a part in the music. Strawberries so plentiful that in June when the
fields and woods were dyed red with them, the country people armed
with bottles of wine, cream and sugar, instead of coat of mail, and
everyone's sweetheart upon his horse behind him, disrobe the fields of
their red colors, and turn them into their old habit.

GIRL: Who's dancing me back to Old New York?

SON: Not me, tho its trees one time were so laden with peaches travelers
doubted there were more leaves than fruit on them.

(COUSIN *pursued by* ATTENDANT R. *scampers in right, collides with the dancers.*)

COUSIN: Poor me! I was always so frugal, too.

SON: Hey!

GIRL: Watch out!

ATTENDANT R.: (*to* SON *and* GIRL) I beg your pardon. (*tries to catch* COUSIN
as he addresses him) That fortune you scraped together from the dead
and living, you've sat long enough (*tosses head towards* SON) behind his
mother's gravestone without a thought of refunding. (*traps* COUSIN)
Give it up!

COUSIN: The fortune's bonded. Why ferret me?

ATTENDANT R.: (*very skeptically*) Well—

SON: (*seconding* ATTENDANT'S *skepticism*) That's right, too.

ATTENDANT R.: (*prods* COUSIN) Small fish are fried best whole with the
backbone severed to prevent curling up.

COUSIN: You can't fry me! Besides where can I curl up!

ATTENDANT R.: Waste oxygen on you? No!—Attention! Your eyes! Look!
Before you is the future. Behind you the past! (*turns* COUSIN *about face like a pivot*) Behind you is the future. Before you the past! (*hurls him into the wing left*) Off is out!

SON: (*calls after him*) Remember, cousin, if you appear at any wedding you're still a relation—fortunately or unfortunately!—What a night to have to stumble on dumbness!

ATTENDANT R.: We may have to wash hands of relations who fry themselves! What does the hour say about dumbness?

GIRL: Shame! But the field's really darker since he broke into our dance.

(*A pause in the music.* ATTENDANT R. *who has followed* COUSIN *part of the way is heard stumbling near the wing left. Again, a harpsichord plays "Wolseys Wilde." A red lantern, till now unseen, on the floor of the stage rear left lights suddenly and shows* THE ATTENDANT *standing over a man stretched full length on the green rug of the previous scenes.*)

SON: (*holds* GIRL *by a hand as they face each other in a pause of their dance, center of stage*) Get that clatter? We're really starting to move now. Stand still, the tracks are beginning to drive under us.

ATTENDANT R.: Man, what's the idea sleeping on the tracks. The turf's cropping up thru the ties.

(*The man yawns, stretches, rises slowly:* ATTENDANT D.)

ATTENDANT D.: Propped on the earth, and from where, what sleep (*stands tall*) awake. (*yawns*) Have I escaped from death of sleep? (*Scratches his head*) A creeping thought says: now like a lamp that don't matter, short-circuited, on the road, before blue morning go out. What's up, Rag, in whose memory am I?

(*The lamp goes out, but the darkness of the scene is soon compensated by a light as of dawn beginning high at the right, where a marble facade appears, its flight of stairs and balustrade leading to an entrance. The sun is now red in a top corner window, at which* ATTENDANT D. *looks up. A Bird chirps and stops. The music stops.*)

ATTENDANT D.: (*to* R.) Speak up, mummy, I enjoy taking in that flame up there like torchlight on a swan's breast. (*gets down for a moment on one knee to tie a shoelace*)

ATTENDANT R.: (*as both now saunter slowly, right, past* SON *and* GIRL) I thought you weren't with us any more—not dusting as you used to.

ATTENDANT D.: Oh, I see what's troubling you! I've been at Valenciennes, man, sleeping on the railroad tracks, striking that is to stop the movement of coal cars to the wrong people.

ATTENDANT R.: Aren't you dead—dead-tired, I mean.

ATTENDANT D.: Fresh as a daisy. I'll stake your face I could push up all the daisies—only I don't care to. Why should I!

SON: (*to* GIRL) Listen! They've—We've traveled with them. We must be as far as Valenciennes. I know him. too. We might have guessed, we were going somewhere with that fast sun coming up. I know him, tho. Where *have* I seen him? (*They move as if stepping off something, in the direction of the* ATTENDANTS.)

GIRL: Don't run so. (*catches up with him, feels around his shirt pocket near his chest*) Darling, may I look at your dead sister's picture. (*Train whistle sounds as in Act I, scene 1.*)

SON: (*his head bent down to hers, straining to listen; shouts*) Wait till the train pulls out, the gravel is grating under us!

GIRL: (*continues above the prolonged whistle of the train*) You said your mother's face, darling, was oval. A woman's on the train reminded me. You remember you were telling me over her gravestone. (*He makes a gesture of not being able to hear thru the noise. The whistling stops.*)

ATTENDANT R.: (*to* D., *casually*) I vaticinate a revolution.

SON: (*to* GIRL) Remember? (*to himself*) Yes, the surgeon's knife from another world. (*to* GIRL) He was the attendant at the hospital where my mother—

ATTENDANT R.: (*who has overhead, turns round and greets the* SON *with a long look of sad recognition, grips the* SON's *arm*) Sorry,—she died? (SON *nods. In turn, grips* ATTENDANT R.'s *arm with right hand.*)

SON: (*after a very brief pause*) We're going to a wedding.

(ATTENDANTS *consulting each other, pleased, accept the invitation in pantomime. It is now morning, sunlit and blue. From behind the facade right, very clearly, comes the melody of the first movement of Mozart's G minor symphony, as the four go up the stairs discretely together, and continues to play after the Dream Curtain falls.*)

Scene 4

(*The music of Mozart continues thruout. The properties are substantially as at the end of Act II, scene 3. But the action now takes place on three levels. On the stairhead, the garden table of previous scenes, dressed with bottle of white wine, glasses and a dish of cakes, has been added.* ATTENDANT R., *red rag evident in his upper jacket pocket stands by drinking. The greatest part of the stage is filled with waltzing wedding guests—strangers—except for the characters already familiar who occasionally waltz into view and disappear among the newcomers. Left foreground, on the green rug once more laid parallel to the length of the proscenium,* THE SON *and* GIRL *are seated facing the footlights.*)

SON: (*tapping a finger to rhythm*) Graced, graced, the eyes grow black with dancing. What a city New York is: live as you live. It always projects thoughts so little forgotten, everything worth remembering insists on now.—How many dead are among how many live?

GIRL: (*strokes his face and eyes with a finger*) Some dead. Some alive. What tears strike you among what thoughts?

SON: None. Except that as one who works, you have a right to rest, and I keep you awake with an old repertoire. Why do you listen?

GIRL: It's up to me in a way, yet not entirely.

SON: You mean it's up to our time to quicken the pace, make of all time a kind of phoenix we hear before we sleep again. Like the calm of more than enough work going round, and everybody free to do a little.

ATTENDANT D.: (*Simultaneously with* SON's *last speech has made his way thru the waltzers and up the stairway to* R., *now brushes the latter's red rag briskly, lays duster aside on the stairhead, pours himself a drink and toasts*) To May First! To May! (R. *returns toast silently, as they are joined by*)

FATHER: Everybody happy and taken care of? Is there no one gliding from footrest to footrest at my daughter's wedding? No jail nearby? No troops mustered? Then congratulate me. It's high time I have lived to see it.

(ATTENDANT R. *pours drinks for three, and* FATHER *drinks to their health.*)

On the other hand, we have this hand.

GIRL: We should be on the stairhead, or you will maybe say we're there.

SON: Do you mind—

GIRL: If we sit here while you talk to me? I don't mind.

SON: I remember when I was small we lived in a walk-up. When I looked
down long enough, my nose against one of the windows facing the
airshaft, the window would become frameless. In the dancehall on the
first floor of the house opposite I could see only the heads of people dark
under the lights, dancing. I dreaded and loved it. My sister's wedding
took place in another hall, with probably too many relatives around to
take care of, because I sat against a pillar and felt very lonely.

GIRL: Almost tearful when one of them became fussy over you? I suppose you
were very small.

SON: (*laughs slightly*) Yes, I remember now, the more my aunt fussed, trying to
make me look pleasant, the more tearful I became.

GIRL: (*smiles, again strokes his face and eyes with a finger*) I'm not trying.

(THE AUNT *has come thru the crowd and is now on the stairhead.* THE COUSIN *who has followed
her remains half way up the stairs, undecided. She greets everybody, bustles, pantomimes to*
COUSIN *to come up. He does. She holds out the tray of cakes to him. He takes one diffidently,
goes down the steps again and is lost among the dancers. She follows him, carrying her train.*
ATTENDANT R. *waves his rag in* D.'S *face goodnaturedly.*)

SON: (*moves forehead to* GIRL'S, *looking into her eyes*) Why not try? (*pause*)
What do you see?

GIRL: Your eyes are softer than mine. Did your sister have your eyes?

SON: When I look at yours I can't say. Whose voice shall I use now that I am
near yours?

(NURSE *and* DOCTOR—*bride and groom—ascend the stairway—to be greeted by* FATHER
on the stairhead.)

ATTENDANT R.: (*now pours drinks for all and drinks to them*) One thing we
   pray of Diana. Let whoever never loved, love tomorrow, let whoever has
   loved love tomorrow.—One world!

(ATTENDANTS, FATHER, DOCTOR *and* NURSE, *as a little procession, now go down the stairway.
As they join the dancers, the* ATTENDANTS' *voices are heard in antiphon.*)

ATTENDANT D.: She sings.

ATTENDANT R.: We are voiceless.

ATTENDANT D.: How shall our silence find its end?

MOTHER: (*appears at the fringe of the crowd, stands behind* SON *and* GIRL *who
   get up after her first sentence.*) Today the floor is polished and you're not
   dancing. I am sorry if I startled you.

SON: (*to* GIRL) Darling, meet my mother.

MOTHER: But we know each other.

(*The music continues as* THE MOTHER *precedes* SON *and* GIRL *waltzing together now, among
the dancers.*)

SON'S VOICE: (*as he stoops to pick up something lost in the crowd*) New gloves,
   mother?

MOTHER'S VOICE: (*as she is lost among the dancers*) I am wearing them for the
   first time.

GIRL: (*not seen in the crowd*) They are beautiful.

(*The Dream Curtain falls.*)

The End

FIRST I

(1940)

PART II

HALF OF "A"-9

FIRST HALF of "A" - 9

by

Louis Zukofsky

New York

1940

CONTENTS

Guido Cavalcanti's *Donna Mi Prega*, its music and emotion of intellect; Marx's *Capital*, extracts from Chapters 1-13 and *Value, Price and Profit*; some concepts in modern physics; the translations; and the mathematical analogy to the form of the poem; as printed here,—all entered into the writing of the first 75 lines of *"A"-9*.

These aids are presented in the foregoing order, the poem last, so that if the intention to have it fluoresce as it were in the light of seven centuries of interrelated thought has at all been realized the poem will explain itself. In any case, the aids may forestall exegesis. The *Restatement* at the end of the volume is intended merely as restatement.

If the venturesome boldness of the vernacular translations be considered a form of relief imposed upon the poet by the difficulty of an exacting task, they may not appear so bold after all. Mr. Reisman's slang may even illuminate some things about the use of words and prove that a living poem can retain its essential emotion in whatever language.

As for the ultimate value of the first half of *"A"-9*, aside from what has already been said—a Briton pronounces *capitalism* with the accent on the second syllable: ca-pit'-al-ism. *"A"-9* may mean more if it be taken also as a sign that ca**pit**alism will capitulate.

Louis Zukofsky

Nov. 24/39

Guido Cavalcanti, Canzone

Donne mi priegha perch'i volglio dire
D'un accidente che sovente é fero
Ed é sí altero ch'é chiamato amore
Sicche chi l negha possa il ver sentire
Ond a'l presente chonoscente chero
Perch' i no spero ch om di basso chore
Atal ragione portj chonoscenza
Ché senza natural dimostramento
Non o talento di voler provare
Laove nascie e chì lo fá criare
E qual è sua virtu e sua potenza
L'essenza e poi ciaschun suo movimento
E' l piacimento che'l fá dire amare
E se hom per veder lo puó mostrare:—

In quella parte dove sta memoria
Prende suo stato sí formato chome
Diafan dal lume d' una schuritade
La qual da Marte viene e fá dimora
Elgli é creato e a sensato nome
D' alma chostume di chor volontade
Vien da veduta forma ches s'intende
Che 'l prende nel possibile intelletto
Chome in subgetto locho e dimoranza
E in quella parte mai non a possanza

Perchè da qualitatde non disciende
Risplende in sé perpetuale effecto
Non a diletto mà consideranza
Perche non pote laire simiglglianza:—

Non é virtute mà da questa vene
Perfezione ches si pone tale
Non razionale mà che si sente dicho
Fuor di salute giudichar mantene
E l antenzione per ragione vale
Discerne male in chui é vizio amicho
Di sua virtu seghue ispesso morte
Se forte la virtú fosse impedita
La quale aita la contrara via
Nonche opposito natural sia
Mà quanto che da ben perfett e torte
Per sorte non po dir om ch abbi vita
Che stabilita non a singnioria
A simil puó valer quant uom l obblia:—

Lesser é quando lo volere a tanto
Ch oltre misura di natura torna
Poi non si addorna di riposo maj
Move changiando cholr riso in pianto
E lla fighura con paura storna
Pocho soggiorna anchor di lui vedraj
Che n gente di valore il piu si trova
La nova qualità move a sospirj
E vol ch om mirj in un formato locho
Destandos'ira la qual manda focho
Inmaginar nol puo hom che nol prova
E non si mova perch' a llui si tirj
E non si aggirj per trovarvi giocho
E certamente gran saver nè pocho:—

Da ssimil tragge complessione e sghuardj
Che fá parere lo piacere piu certo
Non puó choverto star quand é si giunto
Non giá selvagge la biltá son dardj
Ch a tal volere per temere sperto
Hom seghue merto spirito che punto
E non si puó chonosciere per lo viso
Chompriso biancho in tale obbietto chade
E chi ben aude forma non si vede
Perchè lo mena chi dallui procede
Fuor di cholore essere diviso
Asciso mezzo schuro luce rade
Fuor d'ongni fraude dice dengno in fede
Chè solo da chostui nasce merzede:—

Tu puoj sichuramente gir chanzone
Dove ti piace ch i t o sí ornata
Ch assa lodata sará tua ragione
Dalle persone ch anno intendimento
Di star con l' altre tu non aj talento:

Karl Marx, Capital

Translated by Eden Paul and Cedar Paul (Everyman Edition, E. P. Dutton & Co., N. Y., 1932)

PART ONE. Commodities and Money

Chapter I. Commodities

p. 8   As values, commodities are nothing but particular masses of congealed labour time.

9   . . not the outcome of labour . . air, virgin soil, prairie, primeval forest, . . A thing can be useful and the product of human labor without being a commodity. One who satisfies his wants with the product of his own labour, makes a use-value but does not make a commodity . . he must produce . . use-values for others—social use-values . .

17   . . thus resembles Mistress Quickly, of whom Falstaff said: "A man knows not where to have her." . . not an atom of matter enters into the reality of value. We may twist and turn a commodity this way and that—as a thing of value it still remains unappreciable by our bodily senses. . . follow this up from its inconspicuous configuration to the glaringly obvious money form. Then the enigma of money will cease to be an enigma.

30   Aristotle tells us . . "5 beds = 1 house" . . "cannot be distinguished from" . . "5 beds = so much money".

31   .. "It is really impossible that things so different should be commensurable" .. it can only be "a make-shift for practical purposes." .. Why impossible? The house is something of the same kind as the bed .. one and the same. This one and the same thing is—human labour.

35   .. value comes for the first time to show itself in its true light as a jelly of undifferentiated human labour. . . As a commodity .. a citizen of that world. . . no preferences as to the particular form of use-value in which it secures expression.

44   .. a very queer thing indeed, full of metaphysical subtleties and theological whimsies. In so far as it is a use-value, there is nothing mysterious about it—whether we regard it as something whose natural properties enable it to satisfy human wants, or as something which only acquires such properties as the outcome of human labour. . . the table .. wood, an ordinary palpable thing. . . stands with the feet on the floor: . . over against all other commodities, it stands on its head; and in that wooden head it forms crotchets far stranger than table-turning ever was.

44   Thus the enigma of commodities does not arise out of their use-value. . . physiological fact .. expenditure of human brain, nerve, muscle, sense organ .. magnitude of value .. duration of this expenditure, or the quantity of labour, our senses distinguish between the quantity and the quality of labour.

45–
46   .. the mystery of the commodity form .. that it mirrors for men the social character of their own labour, mirrors it as an objective character attaching to the labour products themselves, mirrors it as a social natural property of things. . . the social relation of the producers to the sum .. of their own labour, presents itself as .. not between themselves, but between the products of .. labour. . . commodities .. social things .. at the same time perceptible by our senses. . . in vision, light actually passes from one thing, the external object, to another thing, the eye. . . On the other hand .. the value relation between the labour products which finds expression in the commodity form, have nothing whatever to do with the physical properties of the commodities or

with the material relations that arise out of these physical properties. We are concerned only with a definite social relation between human beings, which, in their eyes, has here assumed the semblance of a relation between things... enter the nebulous world of religion. In that world, the products of the human mind become independent shapes, endowed with lives of their own .. The products of the human hand do the same thing in the world of commodities. I speak of this as the *fetishistic character* which attaches to the products of labour .. in virtue of the relations which the process of exchange establishes between the labour products .. material relations between persons and social relations between things... useful thing, on the one hand, and thing of value, on the other .. useful things .. produced expressly for exchange ..

47   .. different kinds of labour .. ignoring their actual unlikeness .. reducing them to terms of that which they all share as expenditures of human labour power—abstract human labour... They do not know that they are doing this, but they do it. Value does not wear an explanatory label. Far from it, value changes all labour products into social hieroglyphs... for the specification of a useful object as a value is just as much a social product as language is... When .. Galiani wrote, "wealth (value) is a relation between two persons," he should have added, "but the relation is hidden away within material wrappings."

48   Physical and chemical science have analysed air into its elements, but the familiar bodily impressions produced on our senses by the atmosphere persist unchanged.

48–   .. in the chance and ever-varying exchange relations between products the
49   labour time socially necessary for their productions exerts its coercive influence like an over-riding law of nature. The law of gravity exerts an over-riding influence in like fashion when a house tumbles about our ears.

49   "What are we to think of a law which can only assert itself by periodical revolutions? It is nothing but a law of nature resting on the unconsciousness of the persons concerned."—Engels.

56 Economists are strange creatures. For them there are but two kinds of institution; works of art, and works of nature. Feudal institutions are artificial, bourgeois institutions are natural. . . the Greeks and Romans must have had a process of production, an economy that is to say, which must have constituted the material foundation of their world, just as the bourgeois economy constitutes the material foundation of the modern world.

57–
58 The commodity form is the most general and the least developed form of bourgeois production. For this reason, it makes its appearance early, though in a less dominant and typical manner than to-day. For this reason, likewise, the fetishistic character of commodities is comparatively easy to discern. But when we come to more developed forms, even this semblance of simplicity vanishes. Whence did the illusions of the monetary system arise? The mercantilists (the champions of the monetary system) regarded gold and silver, not simply as substances which, when functioning as money, represented a social relation of production, but as substances which were endowed by nature with peculiar social properties. Later economists, who look back on the mercantilists with contempt, are manifestly subject to the very same fetishistic illusion as soon as they come to contemplate capital. It is not so very long since the dispelling of the physiocratic illusion that land-rents are a growth of the soil, instead of being a product of social activity!

58 . . one more example relating to the commodity form itself. If commodities could speak, they would say: "Our use-value may interest human beings; but it is not an attribute of ours, as things. What is our attribute, as things, is our value. Our own interrelations as commodities proves it. We are related to one another only as exchange-values." Now let us hear how the economist interprets the mind of the commodity. He says: "Value (exchange-value) is a property of things; riches (use-value), of man. Value, in this sense, necessarily implies exchanges; riches do not."

58 What substantiates this view is the remarkable fact that the use-value of things is realised without exchange, by means of a direct relation between

things and men, whereas their value is realised only in exchange, only in a social process. Surely, in this connexion, every one will recall the excellent Dogberry's instruction to neighbour Seacoal: "To be a well-favoured man is the gift of fortune, but to write and read comes by nature."

Chapter II. Exchange

59 Commodities are things, and are therefore passive in man's hands. If they are refractory, their owner can use force, can, .. take them withersoever he will. . . "women of easy virtue." If thousands are to enter in relation one with another as commodities, the guardians of the commodities must enter into relation one with another as persons whose wills reside in these objects, and must behave in such a way that neither appropriates the commodity of the other, nor parts with his own, except by means of an act performed with mutual consent. . . must reciprocally recognise one another as private owners. . . legal relation . . contract .. voluntary relation, in which the economic relation is reflected.

59 Do we really know anything more about the "usurer," when we say that his actions conflict with "eternal justice," . .

60 ".. twofold .. the use of every object. . . . The one is peculiar to the object as such, the other is not, as a sandal which may be worn, and is also exchangeable. Both are uses of the sandal, for even he who exchanges the sandal for the money or food he is in want of, makes use of the sandal as a sandal. But not in its natural way. For it has not been made for the sake of being exchanged."
Aristotle, *De republica*, I, i, cap. 9.

62 ".. And no man might buy or sell, save he that had the mark, or the name of the Beast, or the number of his name."

68 The difficulty that faces us is, not the understanding that money is a commodity, but the understanding how, why, and by what means, a commodity can be money.

68   What happens is, not that a commodity assumes the aspect of money because all other commodities universally express their values in it; but the converse of this, that they universally appear to express their values in it because it is money.

69   .. Without any cooperation on their part, commodities find their own form of value ready-made in the shape of another commodity that exists outside and beside them. These things, gold and silver, as they come out of the bowels of the earth, are simultaneously the direct incarnation of all human labour. Hence the magic of money. That human beings are behaving atomistically in the extant social process of production, and that therefore the material form of their productive relations is independent of their own control and of their conscious individual activities—these things are disclosed first of all by this, that the products of their labour, generally speaking, assume the commodity form. The enigma of the fetishistic character of money is, therefore, nothing more than the enigma of the fetishistic character of commodities, which dazzled us at first, but has now grown manifest in money.

Chapter III. Money, or the Circulation of Commodities

81   We have seen that the exchange of commodities implies contradictory and mutually exclusive relations. The differentiation of commodities into commodities and money does not sweep away these inconsistencies, but it develops a form in which they can exist side by side. This is generally the way in which real contradictions are reconciled. For instance, it is a contradiction to say that a body is continually falling towards another and is at the same time continually flying away from it. The ellipse is a trajectory which, while allowing this contradiction to subsist, at the same time solves it. . . As soon as (a commodity) has reached the spot where it can serve as a use-value, the commodity falls out of the sphere of exchange into the sphere of consumption. Our only present interest is in the sphere of exchange. . . a study of the change of form, the metamorphosis, of commodities which effectuates the social circulation of matter.

82 . . commodities as use-values are contraposed to money as exchange-value. On the other hand, both the opposites are commodities, . . units composed of use-value and value. But this unity of differences manifests itself at two opposite poles, and at each pole in an opposite way. Being poles, they are necessarily opposite and necessarily connected. The commodity is really a use-value; the essentiality of its value appears only ideally in its price . . contraposed gold . . Conversely, the bodily substance of the gold counts only as the embodiment of value . . money. In its reality . . it is exchange-value. Its use-value manifests itself solely in the ideal form, in the series of expressions of relative value, in which it enters into relation with the contraposing commodities as the complex of its real use forms. These antagonistic forms of commodities are the real forms in which the process of their exchange has its movement and its being.

83 The exchange of commodities, therefore, is effected by means of the following changes of form:

$$\text{Commodity—Money—Commodity}$$
$$\text{C--------M--------C}$$

The result of the whole process is, so far as concerns the objects themselves, C—C, the exchange of one commodity for another, the circulation of materialised social labour. When the result is achieved, the process is at an end. . . The jump taken by the value of the commodity out of the body of the commodity into the body of the gold is . . the "salto morale" (desperate leap) of the commodity. If it should fall short, then, though the commodity itself is not harmed, the owner of the commodity certainly is. Thanks to the social division of labour, his labour is as one-sided as his wants are many-sided.

84 But only as money can (his product) acquire a general socially valid equivalent form—and the money is in some one else's pocket.

91 . . Money does not disappear because it ultimately drops out of the series of metamorphoses undergone by a particular commodity. It is constantly

being precipitated into new places . . vacated by other commodities. . . in the complete metamorphosis of the linen (linen—money—bible), the linen drops out of circulation, and money steps into its place; then the bible drops out of circulation, and money steps into its place.

92 . . If the interval in time between the two complementary phases of the entire metamorphosis of a commodity becomes too great, if the cleavage between the sale and the purchase becomes too pronounced, the essential unity between sale and purchase asserts itself convulsively by producing a crisis. The antithesis . . inherent in a commodity, the antithesis between use-value and value; the contradiction . . that particular concrete labour only counts as abstract general labour; the antithesis between the personification of objects and the representation of persons by things—these . . contradictions, all of them immanent in the commodities, acquire fully developed and mobile forms in the oppositions manifest in the metamorphosis of commodities. These forms, therefore, entail the possibility . . of crises.

95 . . Money is continually withdrawing commodities from circulation and stepping into their places, and is thus perpetually moving farther and farther away from its starting-point. Although, therefore, the movement of the money is merely an expression of the circulation of commodities, it seems as if, conversely, the circulation of commodities were only the outcome of the movement of the money.

99 "It is products which set money in motion and make it pass from hand to hand. . . . The speed of its motion can make good a deficiency in its quantity. In case of need it passes from hand to hand without a moment's pause." Le Trosne

100–
101 . . in a slackening of the currency of money, we see mirrored the disintegration of these processes, (sale and purchase), their movement towards reciprocal independence, a stagnation in the changes of form and therefore in the social interchange of commodities. Of course, we cannot ascertain, merely from a study of circulation, whence this stagnation arises. From a study of

circulation we simply learn that stagnation exists. But the general public, seeing that, as the currency of money slackens, money appears and disappears less frequently at all the nodal points in the course of circulation, is naturally inclined to think that the retardation is due to a quantitative deficiency in the circulating medium.

101   "Money being . . . the common measure of buying and selling, every body who hath anything to sell, and cannot procure chapmen for it, is presently apt to think, that want of money in the kingdom, or country, is the cause why his goods do not go off; and so, want of money is the common cry; which is a great mistake. . . . What do these people want, who cry out for money? . . . The farmer complains; . . . he thinks that were more money in the country, he should have a price for his goods. Then it seems money is not his want, but a price for his corn and cattle, which he would sell, but cannot. . . . Why cannot he get a price? . . . (1) Either there is too much corn and cattle in the country, so that most who come to market have need of selling, as he hath, and few of buying; or (2) there wants the usual vent abroad by transportation . . .; or (3) the consumption fails, as when men, by reason of poverty, do not spend so much in their houses as formerly they did: wherefore it is not the increase of specific money, which would at all advance the farmer's goods, but the removal of any of these three causes, which do truly keep down the market. . . . The merchant and shopkeeper want money in the same manner, that is, they want a vent for the goods they deal in, by reason that the markets fail. . . ." (A nation) "never thrives better, than when riches are tost from hand to hand." Sir Dudley North, *Discourses upon Trade*, London, 1691.

101   . . But if, on the one hand, it be a popular delusion to regard stagnation in production and circulation as due to insufficiency of the circulating medium, it by no means follows, on the other hand, that an actual scarcity of the medium (due, perhaps, to bungling legislative attempts to regulate the currency) may not give rise to such stagnation.

105   "Silver and gold, like other commodities, have their ebbings and flowings. Upon the arrival of quantities from Spain, . . . it is carried into the Tower and

coined. Not long after there will come a demand for bullion to be exported again. If there is none, but all happens to be in coin, what then? Melt it down again; there's no loss in it, for the coining costs the owner nothing. Thus the nation has been abused and made to pay to the twisting of straw for asses to eat. If the merchant were made to pay the price of coinage he would not have sent his silver to the Tower without consideration; and coined money would always a keep a value above uncoined silver."—North

109   Finally we have to ask how it is that gold can be replaced by worthless symbols of itself.

110   . . Its functional existence absorbs . . its material existence. Being a transient and objective reflex of the prices of commodities, it functions only as a symbol of itself, and can therefore itself be replaced by symbols. One thing, however, is essential. This token which functions as money, must have an objective social validity of its own; and the paper symbol acquires such a validity by its enforced currency. State compulsion of the kind can take effect only within that domestic sphere of circulation which is restricted by the frontiers of the community; but it is only within that sphere that money fully assumes its function as circulating medium, or coin.

117   . . plebeian debtors, who became slaves . . feudal debtors, who lost their political power when they lost the economic basis on which it had been upbuilt. . . the money form (and the relation between creditor and debtor has the form of a money relation) . . mirrors only the antagonism between economic conditions of existence that lie at a deeper level.

120   . . a crisis can only occur when the lengthening chain of payments and an artificial system of balancing them one against the other have been fully developed. Whenever there is a general disturbance of this mechanism, and no matter what its cause may be, money suddenly quits the ideal form of money of account and materialises as hard cash. Profane commodities can no longer replace it. The use-value of commodities becomes valueless, and their value is routed by their own form of value. . . During the crisis, the contrast

between the commodity and money, its form of value, becomes accentuated into an absolute contradiction. It does not matter, now, what the phenomenal form of money may be. The money famine is just as urgent whether payment has to be made in gold or in credit money, such as banknotes.

120 "The poor stand still because the rich have no money to employ them, though they have the same land and hands to provide victuals and clothes as ever they had; which is the true riches of a nation, and not the money." John Bellers, *Proposals for Raising a College of Industry*, London, 1696.

122 . . how small are the amounts of hard cash requisite for the carrying on of large-scale commercial operations . .

PART TWO

Chapter IV. Transformation of Money into Capital

131 The simplest form of the circulation of commodities is C—M—C, the transformation of a commodity into money, and the retransformation of money into a commodity; selling in order to buy. However, side by side with this form, we find another, which is specifically different. We find the form M—C—M, the transformation of money into commodities, and the retransformation of commodities into money, buying in order to sell. Money that circulates in the latter way is thereby transformed into capital, is already potential capital.

137– . . the circulation of capital has no limits. It is as the conscious representative
38 of this movement that the owner of money becomes a capitalist. His person, or rather his pocket, is the point from which money sets out and the point to which it returns. . . use-value is never to be regarded as the direct aim of the capitalist. Nor is the profit on any single transaction his aim, for what he aims at is the never-ending process of profit making.

139   "That infinity which things do not possess when they are moving directly forwards, they possess when they turn round." Galiani.

140   Value thus become processional value, processional money, and as such capital. It falls out of circulation, and then returns to circulation, maintains itself and multiplies itself in circulation, comes back out of circulation enlarged, and is always beginning the same circuit over and over again. M—M, money which begets money, such is the description of capital given by its first interpreters, the mercantilists. . . in the case of interest-bearing capital, the circulation M—C—M is abbreviated, for it presents itself to us as a result achieved without the services of any intermediary, presents itself so to say in the lapidary style as M—M, money which is equal to more money, value which is greater than itself.

144   Whereas . . both parties to an exchange can gain as regards use-value, it is impossible that they should both gain as regards exchange-value. Here we must rather say: "Where equality exists, there can be no gain." (Galiani, *Della moneta*)

150   The capitalist class of a country cannot, as a whole, overreach itself.

Turn and twist as we may, the sum total remains the same. If equivalents are exchanged, then no surplus value is created; and if non-equivalents are exchanged, still no surplus value is created. Circulation, the exchange of commodities, does not create value.

154   I use the term *labour power* or *capacity for labour*, to denote the aggregate of those bodily and mental capabilities existing in a human being, which he exercises whenever he produces a use-value of any kind.

156   Owners of money or owners of commodities . . and persons who own nothing but their labour power . . are not natural products. . . nor . . met with in all historical epochs.

157–
58   The capitalist period is . . characterised by this, that in the worker's eyes labour power assumes the form of a commodity which is his own property, and for this reason his labour takes on the form of wage labour. Moreover, it is only from that moment that the products of labour universally assume the form of commodities.

159   . . the seller of labour power must perpetuate himself "in the way that every living individual perpetuates himself, by procreation." . . withdrawn from the market by wear and tear and by death . . continually replaced by at least an equal quantity of new labour power. . . the means of subsistence of those who will replace labour power . . the worker's children.

162   "All labour is paid after it has ceased." . . everywhere the worker gives credit to the capitalist. . . "lends his industry . . risks nothing, beyond the loss of his wages. . . . The worker does not hand over anything material."

164   The process whereby labour power is consumed is, at the same time, the process whereby commodities and surplus value are produced. The consumption of labour power, like the consumption of every other commodity, takes place outside the market, outside the sphere of circulation. Let us, therefore, leave this noisy region of the market, where all that goes on is done in full view of every one's eyes, where everything seems open and above board. We will follow the owner of money and the owner of labour power into the hidden foci of production, crossing the threshhold of the portal above which is written: "No admittance except on business." Here we shall discover, not only how capital produces, but also how it is itself produced. We shall at last discover the secret of the making of surplus value.

PART THREE. Production of Absolute Surplus Value

Chapter V. The Labour Process

169   . . labour power in action, a *worker*. . . He confronts nature as one of her own forces, setting in motion arms and legs, head and hands, in order to appropriate nature's productions in a form suitable to his own wants.

173   There are various things which do not enter directly into the labour process; and yet, without them, that process cannot go on . . the earth, since it provides the worker with the platform for all his operations . . Among . . instruments . . the product of previous labour . . workshops, canals, roads . .

In the labour process . . man's activity, with the help of the instruments of labour, brings about changes in the subject matter of labour, changes intentionally effected. The process disappears in the product.

175   . . defects apart, in the finished product the labour by means of which it has acquired its useful qualities has apparently vanished.

189   By transforming money into commodities which form the material elements of a new product or serve as factors in the labour process, and by incorporating living labour power with their dead substance, the capitalist transforms value (past labour, objectified labour, dead labour) into capital, into self-expanding value, into a monster quick with life, which begins to "work" as if love were breeding in its body.

If we now compare the process of creating value and the process of creating surplus value, we see that the process of creating surplus value is merely the process of creating value prolonged beyond a certain point.

190   It does not matter . . whether . . labour is already embodied in the means of production, or . . superadded by labour power; the labour counts only in accordance with its duration. It consists of so many hours, days, or what not.

191 . . the slave is merely a vocal instrument, distinguished only as vocal from the beast as semivocal instrument, and from the inanimate tool as dumb instrument.

Chapter VI. Constant Capital and Variable Capital

199 The lifetime of a given instrument of labour is . . spent in the incessant repetition of a larger or smaller number of the labour processes in which it is used. Its life may be compared with that of a human being. At the end of each day, every one of us is twenty-four hours nearer death. But we cannot tell from looking at any one how many days he has already died. In spite of this difficulty, life-insurance societies can draw trustworthy conclusions as to the average expectation of life, and can make a good profit out of their inferences. So . . with the instruments of labour.

. . perfectly clear . . an instrument of production can never transfer more value to a product than the value which it itself loses in the labour process through the destruction of its own use-value. If it had no value to lose, if it were not itself a product of human labour, it could not transfer any value to the product. It would help to create use-value without creating exchange-value. Of such a kind are all the means of production . . supplied by nature without human aid; the earth, wind, water, unextracted iron ores, timber in the primeval forest, and so on.

Chapter VII. Rate of Surplus Value

211–
12

The nature of this material is .. a matter of indifference: it may be cotton, it may be iron, or what not. The value of the material is likewise indifferent. The only important thing is that there should be a sufficiency of it to absorb whatever amount of labour has to be expended during the process of production.

"Out of nothing, nothing can be created" (Lucretius) .. we mean the transformation of labour power into labour... the worker produces nothing more than the value of his labour power ..

213–
14

.. *necessary labour* .. necessary for the worker, because it is independent of the social form of his labour... necessary for capital, and for the world of capital, because the continued existence of the worker forms their foundation.

214

The second period of the labour process .. in which the worker has overstepped the limits of necessary labour time .. calls upon him for the expenditure of labour power, but it does not serve to create any value for him. It serves to create surplus value, which smiles upon the capitalist with all the charms of an entity created out of nothing. This part of the working day I term, *surplus labour time*; and all the labour expended in it I term, *surplus labour*. If we are to understand value in general, it is of supreme importance that we should learn to regard it as a mere congelation of labour time, as nothing more than materialised labour; and for the understanding of surplus value, it is just as important that we should learn to regard this as a mere congelation of surplus labour time, as nothing more than materialised surplus labour. What distinguishes the various economic types of society one from another (distinguishes, for instance, a society based upon slavery from a society based upon wage labour), is nothing other than the way in which surplus labour is extorted from the actual producer, from the worker.

Chapter VIII. The Working Day

231 . . on the basis of the capitalist method of production, necessary labour time cannot possibly constitute the whole of the working day. The working day cannot possibly be restricted to this minimum. At the other end of the scale, the maximum . . It cannot possibly be prolonged beyond a certain duration. . . a horse that is worked day after day can only work for 8 hours out of the 24.

235 Surplus labour was not a new discovery made by capital. Wherever a part of society has a monopoly of the means of production, the worker, whether free or bond, must supplement the labour time necessary for his own maintenance by surplus labour time in which he produces the means of subsistence for the owner of the means of production . . when a society is so constructed that . . the use-value of products predominates over their exchange-value . . an unquenchable thirst for surplus value cannot arise as the direct outcome of the very nature of the method of production.

". . such works as those of ancient Etruria, which amaze us even in their ruins" . . '*Brussels lace* presuppose(s) wage lords and wage slaves.'

244 "Moments are the elements of profit."

246 (1863) . . "William Wood, 9 years . . 7 years and 10 months when he began to work . . 'ran moulds' . . work every day . . at 6 a.m. . . 'I work till 9 o'clock at night six days in the week. I have done so seven or eight weeks.' . . J. Murray, 12 . . 'I have not been in bed since the night before last. There were eight or nine other boys working last night. All but one have come this morning. I get three shillings and sixpence. I do not get any more for working at night. I worked two nights last week.' . ."

256– . . workers of all occupations, ages, and sexes, that press on us more insistently
57 than did the souls of the slain on Ulysses . . milliner, Mary Anne Walkley . . exploited . . by a lady with the fine-sounding name of Elise. . . where the

allowance of airspace was only one-third of the number of cubic feet regarded by hygienists as the necessary minimum. At night they slept two by two in stifling cubicles into which a bedroom was divided by wooden partitions.

259   In Marylebone, blacksmiths die at the rate of 31 per thousand per annum . .

260   ". . boys who work at night cannot sleep . . by day . . will be running about." . . "Light . . acts upon the tissues of the body directly in hardening them and supporting their elasticity. . ."

262   (such "labour power" [speaks]) — "George Allinsworth, age 9, came here as cellar-boy . . next morning we had to begin at 3, so I stopped here all night. Live five miles off. Slept on the floor of the furnace, over head, with an apron under me, and a bit of jacket over me. . . Aye! It is hot in here. Before I came here I was nearly a year at the same work at some works in the country. Began there, too, at 3 on Saturday morning—always did, but was very gain [near] home, and could sleep at home. Other days I began at 6 in the morning, and gi'en over at 6 or 7 in the evening." . . Jeremiah Haynes, age 12 . . "A king is him that has all the money and gold. We have a king [told it is a queen], they call her the Princess Alexandria. Told that she married the queen's son. The queen's son is the Princess Alexandria. A princess is a man." William Turner, age 12: "Don't live in England. Think it is a country, but didn't know before." John Morris, age 14: "Have heard say that God made the world, and that all the people was drowned but one; heard say that one was a little bird." William Smith, age 15: "God made man, man made woman." Edward Taylor, age 15: "Do not know of London." . .—"This girl spelt God as dog, and did not know the name of the queen." *Children's Employment Commission, Fifth Report,* 1866.

266   ". . so fond of reflecting and reasoning, a man is not worth much who cannot give a good reason for everything—however bad and however absurd the reason may be. . ." Hegel

274   .. no more moved by the prospect of the .. final disappearance of the human race than they are disturbed by the prospect that the earth may one day fall into the sun. When there is a boom on the stock exchange, every one who takes part in the swindle knows that sooner or later the crash will come, but each man hopes that the disaster will involve his neighbours ..

276   "No minor .. 12 .. and under .. 15 .., shall be employed in any manufacturing establishment more than 11 hours in any one day .." *Revised Statutes of the State of Rhode Island*, cap. 39, #23, July 1, 1857.

279   "We hear to-day only of retrogression, and see only progress." (Macaulay) What eyes, and especially what ears!

283   All the boundaries set by custom and by nature, by age and by sex, by day and by night, were effaced.

300   .. children so small that they had to be placed on stools in order to do their work.

305   .. though capital, in its memorials to parliament, had depicted them with a Rubens' brush as floridly healthy.

307   The establishment of a normal working day .. the outcome of a protracted civil war, more or less veiled ..

311   .. which shall at length make it clear when the time "which the worker sells is ended, and when his own begins."

Chapter IX. Rate and Amount of Surplus Value

313 *The amount of surplus value produced .. is determined by the compound ratio between the number of labour powers exploited simultaneously by the same capitalist and the degree of exploitation of each individual labour power.*

314 .. a reduction in the number of workers employed may be compensated by a proportional increase in the length of the working day. Within certain limits .. the supply of labour exploitable by capital is independent of the supply of workers... When they tell us that the market price of labour is determined by supply and demand, they believe that they have found a fulcrum thanks to which they will be able, not like Archimedes to move the world, but to stop its motion!

315 An absolute limit is imposed upon the average working day, for by nature's decree it must always be less than 24 hours. Consequently *there is an absolute limit upon the extent to which a reduction .. in the number of the workers exploited can be made good by increasing the degree of exploitation of labour power.*

316 .. the value of .. additional means of production may vary as much as you like, may increase or diminish or remain unchanged, may be large or small—still, all this has no influence upon the process of creating value by the labour powers that set the means of production in motion.

317 .. a great many intermediate terms are needed before the student can understand that 0/0 can represent a real magnitude... The vulgar economists, incapable of learning, are content, in this case as in others, to stake their money on appearances, and to ignore the law which regulates and explains them. They believe (in contrast with Spinoza) that "ignorance is a sufficient reason."

319 At a certain stage of capitalist production it becomes necessary that the capitalist shall be able to devote all the time during which he functions as capitalist .. to the appropriation and therefore to the control of others' labour, and to the sale of the products of this labour... The owner of money or owner

of commodities does not become metamorphosed into a real capitalist until the minimum amount advanced for production greatly exceeds the medieval maximum... at a certain point, what have been purely quantitative changes become qualitative.

PART FOUR. Production of Relative Surplus Value

Chapter X. Concept of Relative Surplus Value

333   The value of commodities is inversely proportional to the productivity of labour. So is the value of labour power, since this is determined by the value of commodities. Relative surplus value, on the other hand, is directly proportional to the productivity of labour, increasing when productivity rises, and decreasing when productivity falls... It is, therefore, the persistent tendency of capital, .. to increase the productivity of labour, in order to cheapen commodities, and thus cheapen the worker.

Chapter XI. Cooperation

344–   .. cooperation enables the execution of a particular undertaking to be extended
45   spatially .. On the other hand .. bringing .. the workers into closer proximity, by the aggregation of various labour processes, and by the concentration of the means of production. .. the combined working day .. impresses on individual labour the characteristics of average social labour ..

346   .. the capitalist process of production is .. of a two-fold nature .. a social labour process intended to produce use-values, .. a process for making surplus value.

349   .. workers .. in the labour process .. have already ceased to belong to themselves. .. As cooperators, as members of a working organism, they are themselves only a particular mode of existence of capital. Consequently, the productivity of the worker as an associated worker is the productivity of capital.

Chapter XII. Division of Labour and Manufacture

355   .. manufacture introduces the division of labour into a productive process, or develops that division further; on the other hand, .. it combines handicrafts which were formerly separate. Whatever the starting-point, the final result is the same, namely a productive mechanism whose instruments are human beings.

359   The manufacturing period simplifies, improves, and multiplies the implements of labour by adapting them to the exclusive and peculiar functions of the detail worker. . . it simultaneously creates one of the material conditions for the existence of machinery, which arises out of a combination of simple instruments.

368   What is narrowness, and even imperfection, in the detail worker, becomes perfection when he is regarded as no more than a limb of the collective worker. . . "when they once begin, they must go on; they are just the same as parts of a machine."

377   .. authority in the workshop and authority in the society, as far as the division of labour is concerned, are in inverse ratio one to the other.

382   .. large-scale industry .. detaches science from labour, making of science an independent force of production, and pressing it into the service of capital.

384   ".. thinking itself, in this age of separations, may become a peculiar craft."

387   .. Homer's *Odyssey*, XIV, 228: "Different men take delight in different works."

Chapter XIII. Machinery and Large-Scale Industry

395 Moses says: "Thou shalt not muzzle the ox when he treadeth out the corn." But the Christian philanthropists of Germany, when using their serfs to drive mills, fastened a large circular piece of wood round the necks of these human cattle, to prevent them from putting meal into their mouths.

.. the Dutch .. got the windmill .. from Germany, where the discovery had led to a pretty quarrel between nobleman, priest, and emperor as to which of the three the wind "belonged." "Air makes bondage," ran the word in Germany, whereas in Holland the wind brought freedom... windmills .. to prevent two-thirds of the country from becoming waterlogged marshes ..

397 Of all the great motive forces handed down from the manufacturing period, horse-power was the worst; partly because a horse has a head of his own .. Nevertheless .. the term "horse-power" has survived to this day as the traditional measure for the quantity of mechanical force.

403 An organised system of working machines .. one and all get in motion by the transmitting mechanism from a central automaton, constitutes the fully developed form of machinofacture. In place of the individual machine, we now have a mechanical monster whose body fills the whole factory ..

405 The first attempts at the invention of a locomotive were in the direction of trying to construct a machine with two feet which were to be raised from the ground alternately like a horse's feet. Only after a considerable development of the science of mechanics, and after the accumulation of practical experience, does the form of a machine come to be decided in full accordance with mechanical principles, and only then is that form emancipated from the traditional form of the tool that gave birth to the machine.

407 Large-scale industry, .. had to gain control of its own characteristic means of production, the machine itself; had to produce machines by machines.

408   In manufacture, the organisation of the social labour process is purely subjective, is a combination of detail workers; in machinofacture, large-scale industry has a purely objective productive organism, in which the worker is nothing more than an appendage to the extant material conditions of production.

409   But just as man needs lungs before he can breathe, so does he need something that is the work of human hands before he can consume the forces of nature for productive processes.

411   Not until large-scale industry becomes established, do men succeed in making the products of their past labour, their embodied labour, work gratuitously on a vast scale like the forces of nature.

413   . . machinery . . The less labour it contains, the less value does it impart to the product. The less of its own value it gives up, the more productive is it, and the more, therefore, does it approximate to the forces of nature in its services.

. . it is easy enough to see that the machine, which is no more able to create new value than is any other constituent of constant capital, cannot create any value under the name of "interest."

413   It is likewise clear that here, where we are concerned with the production of surplus value, we cannot assume apriori the existence of any part of that value under the name of "interest."

416   Since capital pays, not the labour that is applied, but the value of the labour power that is applied, the use of machinery to capital is limited by the difference between the value of the machine and the value of the labour power replaced by it. Inasmuch as the division of the working day into necessary labour and surplus labour is a different one in different countries, and in the same country differs in different periods, or, during the same period,

in different branches of industry; and inasmuch as .. the real wages of the worker sometimes fall below the value of his labour power and sometimes rise above that value—the difference between the price of the machinery and the price of the labour power it replaces may vary to a considerable extent, although the difference between the quantity of labour requisite to produce the machine and the total quantity of labour replaced by it remain constant.

417 Hence in a communist society the scope for the use of machinery would be very different from what it is in bourgeois society.

418 Nowhere else .. do we find so shameless a squandering of the energy of human muscles as we find in England, the land of machines.

419 An American revolution and a universal crisis were needed, that working-class girls, who spin for the whole world, might learn to sew!

422 .. capital .. by nature a leveller .. demands as an inborn right that there shall be equality in the conditions of the exploitation of labour ..

431 The development of machinofacture fixes a constantly increasing portion of the capital in a form in which, on the one hand, its value is capable of continual self-expansion, and in which, on the other hand, it loses both use-value and exchange-value whenever it loses contact with living labour.

434– This explains the economic paradox, that the most powerful instrument for
35   shortening labour time, proved to be the most unfailing means of placing every moment of the worker's time and that of his family at the disposal of the capitalist, for the purpose of bringing about the accumulation of capital. Aristotle .. letting his fancy run, said: ".. —if the weavers' shuttles were to weave of themselves—then there would be no need either of apprentices for the master craftsmen or of slaves for the lords." .. Antipater of Thessalonica .. acclaimed the invention of the water-wheel for grinding corn (an invention that is the elementary form of all productive machinery) .. "Cease from grinding, ye women who toil at the mill; sleep late, even if the crowing cocks

announce the dawn. For Demeter has ordered the Nymphs to perform the work of your hands, and they, leaping down on the top of the wheel, turn its axle, which, with its revolving spokes, turns the heavy concave Nisyrian mill-stones. We taste again the joys of the primitive life, learning to feast on the products of Demeter without labour."

473 .. machinery considered in, and by itself, shortens the working day .. machinery, by itself, lightens labour, whereas its capitalist use intensifies labour; by itself, it is a victory of man over the forces of nature, but, in the capitalist use .. it impoverishes him; ..

505 The straw cuts their fingers, and also their mouths, with which they constantly moisten it.

517 .. the regulation of the working day has been the first thing to impose a reasonable restraint upon the murderous and meaningless caprices of fashion, caprices that are so much out of harmony with the system of large-scale industry; .. John Bellers remarked as long ago as 1699: "The uncertainty of fashions does increase necessitous poor. It has two great mischiefs in it. First, the journeymen are miserable in winter for want of work, the mercers and master weavers not daring to lay out their stocks to keep the journeymen employed before the spring comes, and they know what the fashion will then be: secondly, in the spring the journeymen are not sufficient, but the master weavers must draw in many apprentices, that they may supply the trade of the kingdom in a quarter or half a year, which robs the plough of hands, drains the country of labourers, and in a great part stocks the city with beggars, and starves some in winter that are ashamed to beg." *Essays about the Poor, Manufactures, etc.*, p. 9.

525 Large-scale industry has torn away the veil which used to hide from human beings their own social process of production .. Technology .. discovered the few basic forms of motion, which, despite the diversity of the implements used, are necessarily assumed by every productive activity of the human body; just as the science of mechanics discerns in the utmost complications

of machinery, nothing more than the perpetual repetition of the simple mechanical powers.

All stable and stereotyped relations .. venerable prejudices and opinions, are swept away, and the newly formed becomes obsolete before it can petrify. All that has been regarded as solid, crumbles into fragments .. at long last people are compelled to gaze open-eyed at their position in life and their social relations.

527   As early as the end of the seventeenth century, John Bellers (a phenomenal figure in the history of political economy) clearly realised the necessity for abolishing the present system of education and the present mode of the division of labour, which create hypertrophy and atrophy at the opposite poles of society. *Proposals for Raising a College of Industry of all Useful Trades and Husbandry*, London, 1696, pp. 12, 14, and 18.

546–   In .. agriculture, the most revolutionary effect of large-scale industry is that
48   it destroys .. the peasant, who is replaced by a wage worker. . . . The capitalist method of production completely severs the old bond of union between agriculture and manufacture, which were held together when both were in their infancy. At the same time, it creates the material requisites for a new and higher synthesis, a union of agriculture and industry, upon the basis of their antithetically elaborated forms. With the constantly increasing preponderance of urban population aggregated in the great centres, capitalist production increases, on the one hand, the mobility of society, while destroying, on the other, the interchange of material between man and the soil, that is to say the return to the soil of its constituents that are used by human beings in the form of food and clothing—a return which is the permanent natural essential for the maintenance of the fertility of the soil. Thus it simultaneously destroys the physical health of the urban worker and the mental welfare of the rural worker. But, while thus destroying the natural and spontaneously developed system for the circulation of matter from the soil to human beings, and from human beings back to the soil, it necessitates the systematic restoration of such a circulation as a regulative law of social production, and its restoration

in a form adequate to the full development of mankind... The dispersion of the rural workers over large areas breaks down their powers of resistance, at the very time when concentration is increasing the powers of the urban operatives in this respect. In modern agriculture, as in urban industry, the increased productivity and the greater mobility of labour, are purchased at the cost of devastating labour power and making it a prey to disease. Moreover, every advance in capitalist agriculture is an advance in the art, not only of robbing the worker, but also of robbing the soil; every advance in the fertility of the soil for a given period of time, is simultaneously an advance towards the ruin of the permanent sources of this fertility. The greater the extent to which a country tends to start its development upon the foundation of large-scale industry (as does the United States, for instance), the more rapid is this process of destruction. Capitalist production, therefore, is only able to develop the technique and the combination of the social process of production by simultaneously undermining the foundations of all wealth—the land and the workers.

Karl Marx,
Value, Price and Profit

Edited by Eleanor Marx Aveling
(International Pubs., N. Y., 1935)

43 On the basis of the wages system even the *unpaid* labour seems to be *paid* labour. With the *slave*, on the contrary, even that part of his labour which is paid appears to be unpaid.

44 Part of the labour contained in the commodity is *paid* labour; part is *unpaid* labour.

45 *Rent, Interest, and Industrial Profit* are only *different names for the different parts* of the *surplus value* of the commodity, or the *unpaid labour realised in it*, and they are *equally derived from this source, and from this source alone.* They are not derived from *land* as such nor from *capital* as such, but land and capital enable their owners to get their respective shares out of the surplus value extracted by the employing capitalist from the labourer.

52 . . paid with names, instead of with things.

H. Stanley Allen, *Electrons and Waves: An Introduction to Atomic Physics*

By permission of the Macmillan Company, publishers (London, 1932)

44 When the temperature of a solid body is gradually raised, the body first becomes visible in the dark as a dull red and then passes through a series of stages till it reaches a state of incandescence. Below 400°C. the radiation emitted does not affect the eye, and the waves which have a wave-length greater than 0.00008cm. are called infra-red waves. As the temperature is increased above 400°C. red waves are added which excite the sensation of vision, and with rising temperature shorter waves are added, the colour changing from dull red to cherry red, then to orange, and finally the body appears white-hot. In the last stage the spectrum of the light extends from the extreme red to the violet, wave-length about 0.000033cm., and will include ultra-violet waves of still shorter wave-length that do not affect the eye. In the case of the ideal radiator—the so-called "black body," which is at once a perfect absorber and a perfect radiator—there is a certain wave-length corresponding to maximum emission of energy. As the temperature is raised this wave-length becomes shorter and shorter. . .

In 1900 Planck published a description of his attempt to account for the distribution of energy in the spectrum of full or "cavity" radiation. In the interior of a completely enclosed space, maintained at uniform and constant temperature, there will be a stream of radiation resembling that from the ideal "black body," the quality and intensity of the stream depending on the temperature of the enclosure. Radiation of a definite kind is, as we know, associated with a certain wave-length λ or a certain frequency of vibration v. These two quantities λ and v are connected by the relation $c = v\lambda$, where c is the velocity of light.

The problem of finding the relation between the energy of a particular kind of radiation and the frequency, for an assigned temperature of the enclosure, can be solved experimentally.

To secure agreement with the experimental results Planck assumed the existence of vibrators of frequency v, which could only possess energies represented by hv, $2hv$, $3hv$, .. and none other. That is, if we take n to stand for any integer the energy of a vibrator is given by the expression $E = nhv$. This is equivalent to assuming the existence of a unit of energy hv, where h is a constant known as Planck's constant. A better way of stating Planck's hypothesis is to say that radiation of any assigned frequency v can be emitted and absorbed only as an integral multiple of an element of energy hv. We cannot strictly call hv an "atom" of energy since the amount is not a universal constant, but depends on the frequency.

In Applied Mathematics a quantity called "Action" is employed, which is defined as the product of energy and time, and if we consider the action during one complete period of vibration we find it equal to h, so that we may regard h as an atom of action.

Another way of interpreting h, which is sometimes convenient, is to regard it as a natural unit of angular momentum, the physical dimensions of angular momentum being the same as those of action.

Arising out of the work of Planck on the quantum theory an important suggestion was made by Einstein in 1905. This was the hypothesis of the existence of "light quanta," according to which the energy of radiation, instead of spreading out from the source in all directions, as the wave theory would indicate, is concentrated or localised in certain .. bundles or units. On this view propagation of light takes place in a way resembling in many respects that met with in the corpuscular or emission theory of Newton. It is as though the energy of the radiation were concentrated in space, being always confined to a very small volume. Further, the energy of a "light quantum" or "photon" is definite in amount for light of a given colour, being equal to the product of Planck's constant and the frequency of vibration. . .

This hypothesis of Einstein is consistent with the experimental facts observed in the domain of photo-electricity (the separation of electrons from atoms by light). It is, however, inconsistent with the phenomena of interference and diffraction, which require some form of wave theory for their explanation.

48 "Physical Science, like common sense, takes for granted that there is a reality behind the phenomena, which is independent of the person by whom, and the particular methods by which it is observed, and which is also there when it is not observed. Strictly speaking all talk about *what is not observed is metaphysics*." W. DeSitter

50 "In experience we encounter nothing like the physicist's point in space. I speak of here, at this point, and put my finger on the spot. But where my finger touches the table is not a point; it is a patch of more or less indefinite outline .. Were I to point with a needle instead of my finger I should still get a patch of some extension which could be seen and measured under a microscope.

Even so it is with time. We know of no instant as such .. We are conscious of time only through the occurrence of events, and we can know of no events that are instantaneous .. Not only is the instant of the physicist unrevealed to us in sense-perception, but even our actual present 'now' is blurred and indistinct .. Our places are never points; our times are never instants; there is always more or less indefinite extension or duration." Dr. J. P. Dalton, *Rudiments of Relativity*, 1921.

64   The theory of relativity introduces the idea of a certain velocity which cannot be exceeded. We cannot be quite sure whether the velocity of light is actually equal to this limiting velocity or differs from it by an amount too small to be determined by our experiments. The latter alternative is that favored by Whitehead. The idea of a maximum velocity is a purely kinematical conception, but it has a dynamical equivalent. The greater the velocity of a body the more difficult is it to bring about an increase in the velocity. When the velocity approaches that of light the increase in the velocity due to an assigned impulse becomes very small. This is equivalent to saying that the inertia or mass of a body increases with its speed. (*Experiments and Theory*, J. J. Thomson, Lorentz and Kaufman).

65   The theory of relativity leads to an expression of the kinetic energy of a moving particle which reduces to the familiar ½mv² of ordinary mechanics for small velocities, but as the velocity increases the kinetic energy increases more rapidly than this expression would indicate, and tends to become indefinitely great as the velocity approaches that of light. It can be shown that the increase in the mass of a body due to its speed is equal to the energy due to the motion divided by the square of the velocity of light. If the units are chosen so as to make the velocity of light unity the increase in the mass becomes numerically equal to the energy, which is some justification for the expression "the inertia of energy" employed by some writers on relativity.

Translations of Guido Cavalcanti's Canzone

Donna mi Prega

(Dedicace—To Thomas Campion his ghost, and to the
ghost of Henry Lawes, as prayer for the revival of music)

Because a lady asks me, I would tell
Of an affect that comes often and is fell
And is so overweening: Love by name.
E'en its deniers can now hear the truth,
I for the nonce to them that know it call,
Having no hope at all
          that man who is base in heart
Can bear his part of wit
          into the light of it,
And save they know't aright from nature's source
I have no will to prove Love's course
          or say
Where he takes rest; who maketh him to be;
Or what his active *virtu* is, or what his force;
Nay, nor his very essence or his mode;
What his placation; why he is in verb,
Or if a man have might
          To show him visible to men's sight.

In memory's locus taketh he his state
Formed there in manner as a mist of light
Upon a dusk that is come from Mars and stays.
Love is created, hath a sensate name,
His modus takes from soul, from heart his will;
From form seen doth he start, that, understood,
Taketh in latent intellect—
As in a subject ready—
    place and abode,
Yet in that place it ever is unstill,
Spreading its rays, it tendeth never down
By quality, but is its own effect unendingly
Not to delight, but in an ardour of thought
That the base likeness of it kindleth not.

It is not *virtu*, but perfection's source
Lying within perfection postulate
Not by the reason, but 'tis felt, I say.
Beyond salvation, holdeth its judging force,
Maintains intention reason's peer and mate;
Poor in discernment, being thus weakness' friend,
Often his power meeteth with death in the end
Be he withstayed
    or from true course
        bewrayed
E'en though he meet not with hate
        or villeiny
Save that perfection fails, be it but a little;
Nor can man say he hath his life by chance
Or that he hath not stablished seigniory
Or loseth power, e'en lost to memory.

He comes to be and is when will's so great
It twists itself from out all natural measure;

Leisure's adornment puts he then never on,
Never thereafter, but moves changing state,
Moves changing colour, or to laugh or weep
Or wries the face with fear and little stays,
Yea, resteth little
                    yet is found the most
Where folk of worth be host.
And his strange property sets sighs to move
And wills man look into unformèd space
Rousing there thirst
                    that breaketh into flame.
None can imagine love
                    that knows not love;
Love doth not move, but draweth all to him;
Nor doth he turn
                    for a whim
                              to find delight
Nor to seek out, surely,
                    great knowledge or slight.

Look drawn from like,
                    delight maketh certain in seeming
Nor can in covert cower,
                    beauty so near,
Not yet wild-cruel as darts,
So hath man craft from fear
                    in such his desire
To follow a noble spirit,
                    edge, that is, and point to the dart,
Though from her face indiscernible;
He, caught, falleth
                    plumb on to the spike of the targe.
Who well proceedeth, form not seeth,
                    following his own emanation.

There, beyond colour, essence set apart,
In midst of darkness light light giveth forth
Beyond all falsity, worthy of faith, alone
That in him solely is compassion born.

Safe may'st thou go my canzon whither thee pleaseth
Thou art so fair attired that every man and each
Shall praise thy speech
So he have sense or glow with reason's fire,
To stand with other
     hast thou no desire.

Ezra Pound
(from *Guido Cavalcanti, Rime,* 1931)

A Lady Asks Me

A lady asks me
    I speak in season
She seeks reason for an affect, wild often
That is so proud he hath Love for a name

Who denys it can hear the truth now
Wherefore I speak to the present knowers
Having no hope that low-hearted

    Can bring sight to such reason
Be there not natural demonstration
    I have no will to try proof-bringing
Or say where it hath birth

What is its virtu and power
Its being and every moving
Or delight whereby 'tis called "to love"
Or if man can show it to sight.

Where memory liveth,
    it takes its state
Formed like a diafan from light on shade

Which shadow cometh of Mars and remaineth
Created, having a name sensate,
Custom of the soul,
    will from the heart;

Cometh from a seen form which being understood
Taketh locus and remaining in the intellect possible
Wherein hath he neither weight nor still-standing,

Descendeth not by quality but shineth out
Himself his own effect unendingly
Not in delight but in the being aware
Nor can he leave his true likeness otherwhere.

He is not vertù but cometh of that perfection
Which is so postulate not by the reason
But 'tis felt, I say.

Beyond salvation, holdeth his judging force
Deeming intention to be reason's peer and mate,
Poor in discernment, being thus weakness' friend

Often his power cometh on death in the end,
Be it withstayed
  and so swinging counterweight
Not that it were natural opposite, but only

Wry'd a bit from the perfect,
Let no man say love cometh from chance
Or hath not established lordship
Holding his power even though
  Memory hath him no more.

Cometh he to be
  when the will
From overplus
Twisteth out of natural measure,

Never adorned with rest Moveth he changing colour
Either to laugh or weep
Contorting the face with fear
    resteth but a little

Yet shall ye see of him That he is most often
With folk who deserve him
And his strange quality sets sighs to move
Willing man look into that forméd trace in his mind
And with such uneasiness as rouseth the flame.

Unskilled can not form his image,
He himself moveth not, drawing all to his stillness,
Neither turneth about to seek his delight
Nor yet to seek out proving
Be it so great or so small.

He draweth likeness and hue from like nature
So making pleasure more certain in seeming
Nor can stand hid in such nearness,

Beautys be darts tho' not savage
Skilled from such fear a man follows
Deserving spirit, that pierceth.
Nor is he known from his face
But taken in the white light that is allness
Toucheth his aim

Who heareth, seeth not form
But is led by its emanation.
Being divided, set out from colour,

Disjunct in mid darkness
Grazeth the light, one moving by other,
Being divided, divided from all falsity
Worthy of trust
From him alone mercy proceedeth.

Go, song, surely thou mayest
Whither it please thee
For so art thou ornate that thy reasons
Shall be praised from thy understanders,
With others hast thou no will to make company.

Ezra Pound
(**XXXVI**, *A Draft of Cantos XXXI-XLI*)
1935

A Dame Ast Me

(First and second strophes of
Donna mi Prega)

It's so hot an' proud comin' so often, dough
A natural freak, I'm itchin' t'speak becuz
A dame ast what wuz love. Wut is it? I t'ink
A heel in a crowd is not too dumb to know—
It may be all greek, a lot of cheek or fuzz
To wise guys—it does no good to teach a gink
Who'll never ever be high's a Georgia pie
Yet git by fine widout no experiments.
I don't wanna, gents, nor am I apt 'a prove
Where it wuz born, how it begun to move,
What its good points are an' how it gits in high
An' how by an' large it is its own movements
An' de pleasin' sense of what it feels "to love"
An' if guys see it clear's a t'ing in a groove.

It sets up 'n dat part memory hails from
An' pulls a quick change into a range of light
Very like at night when Mars' shadow comes down
An' remains. De heart gives it de flair to come
T'rough; d' soul—oomph. Its name's a feelin', same's "a sight
T'sore eyes." It's made: 'n'right den an' dere goes to town
After takin' shape from a form which is seen
In de bean only if ya foist get de drift;
In dat case it'll shift yet for a right guy'll stay
In place, dough it can't rest because it don't weigh
Down but spreads out like electric light, so clean
Is its sheen everywhere, 'cause it's got lift.
A swell gift; but 'tain't all fun, y' figger out de lay.
It can't show true color any udder way.

Jerry Reisman

A foin lass bodders

A foin lass bodders me I gotta tell her
Of a fact surely, so unrurly, often'
'r 't comes 'tcan't soften its proud neck's called love mm. . .
Even me brudders dead drunk in dare cellar
Feel it dough poorly 'n yrs. trurly rough 'n
His way ain't so tough 'n he can't speak from above mm. . .
'n' wid proper rational understandin'
Shtill standin' up on simple demonstration,
My inclination ain't all ways so hearty
Provin' its boith or the responsible parrty
Or what its vertus are to be commandin'
The landin' coincidin' with each gyration
Or if prostration makes it feel less tarty
Or 't' sumthin' to be seen by any smarty.

In that extenshun where memory's set up
Loove takes position, in condition right, till
It's light's diffusion from a penumbra
Of Mars' contention makes it stay het up
Wid such ignition, recognition, title,
The soul goes choosin' clothes, the heart longs sombre—
Once in that likeness it is cumprehended
Commended possible to the intellective
Faculties, subject ov place, and dhare abidin'
In such dimension whatev'r force betidin',
For so its quality has not descended
So splendid, perpetually effective,
Not so elective, but to thought subsidin'
Because othrewise it can't go presidin'.

No, it ain't vertue tho it is that comin'
Out as perfection, in connection righted
Not az benighted mind, you feel 't I tell you,
Beyond desert, you know it's justice—hummin'
Wid predilection worth correction blighted,
Somewut poor-sighted—its weakness, friends tell you—
Often it is such vertue 'ts death approaches
If 't poaches so its pow'rr plods and iz halted
In no wise vaulted but wid contr'ry weight you're
Surprised, not that it were opposite nature
Only a slight lack of perfection encroaches,
And such as no man can say 't's chance defaulted
Or that loove's bolted from its lordly stature
Worth the same, forgotten all nomenclature.

Living it ranges when its will is flaunted
Far beyond measure, from born treasure turnin',
Then not adornin' itself with rest ever
Moves so it changes colour, laughs till 't weeps—haunted
Its image's seizure 'n' fear, an' leisure yearnin',
Scarcely sojournin' in one place tho ever
You'll see that he was where worthy folk throve; the
New love, the quality 't has, moves to such sighing
So that descrying the thing's place man causes
Such clamour to rise, fired his passion pauses;
No one can know its likeness who don't prove the
Fact, love won't move tho it draws t' himself, aye 'n'
It don't go flying off to beds ov roses
Nor cerrtainly to pick large or small posies.

Like his own sweetheart's is love's disposition
So that his pleasure it seems has her assurance,
Breaking with durance to stand where he surges,
Not that the fleet darts of beauty lack vision,
Rather tried measure of fear is your pure ans-
wer to man's prurience when high spirit urges:—
And no one's able to know love by its features,
Complete ewers of whiteness aim to contain it,
Whose ears retain it the same don't see 'ts figure,
Coming from it man's led eye on love's trigger
Away from colour and apart from all creatures
Where sutures in darkness take the light, plane it,
Fraud can't sustain it, say faith is love's rigour
So that kindness comes forth but from his vigour.

You may go now assuredly, my ballad,
Where you please, you are indeed so embellished
That those who've relished you more than their salad
Days 'll hold you hallowed and away from shoddy—
You can't stand making friends with everybody.

Louis Zukofsky

The "Form"

E. Pound has explained Guido's *Donne mi Prega* as follows: "The canzone was to the poets of this period what the fugue was to musicians in Bach's time. It is a highly specialized form, having its own self-imposed limits... The strophe ... consist(s) of four parts, the second lobe equal to the first as required by the rules of the canzone; and the fourth happening to equal the third, which is not required by the rules as Dante explains them.

"Each strophe is articulated by 14 terminal and 12 inner rhyme sounds, which means that 52 out of every 154 syllables are bound into pattern. The strophe reverses the proportions of the sonnet, as the short lobes precede the longer. This reversal is obviously of advantage to the strophe *as part of* a longer composition."

(Each strophe uses 8 rhyme sounds: 5 occur 4 times, and 3 twice.)

The first half of "A"-9 follows this pattern exactly.

In addition, the first 70 lines are the poetic analog of a conic section—i.e. the ratio of the accelerations of two sounds (r, n) has been made equal to the ratio of the accelerations of the coordinates (x, y) of a particle moving in a circular path with uniform angular velocity. I.e. values of

$$\frac{\frac{d^2y}{dt^2}}{\frac{d^2x}{dt^2}} = \tan\theta \text{ where } \theta = \arctan\frac{y}{x}$$

are noted for five symmetrically located points. The time unit in the poetry is defined by 7 eleven-syllable lines. Each point is represented by a strophe. Mr. Jerry Reisman is responsible for this part of the "form." The coda is free.

The following table explains all this more fully:

point	θ	$\tan\theta$	lines	n's & r's used
1	0°	0	1-7	13n, 13r
			8-14	13n, 14r
2	90°	∞	15-21	13n, 13r
			22-28	14n, 13r
3	180°	0	29-35	13n, 13r
			36-42	13n, 14r
4	270°	∞	43-49	13n, 13r
			50-56	14n, 13r
5	360°	0	57-63	13n, 13r
			64-70	13n, 14r
Coda (free)			71-75	11n, 11r

"A"-9

(First half)

An impulse to action sings of a semblance
Of things related as equated values,
The measure all use is time congealed labor
In which abstraction things keep no resemblance
To goods created; integrated all hues
Hide their natural use to one or one's neighbor.
So that were the things words they could say: Light is
Like night is like us when we meet our mentors
Use hardly enters into their exchanges,
Bought to be sold things, our value arranges;
We flee people who made us as a right is
Whose sight is quick to choose us as frequenters,
But see our centers do not show the changes
Of human labor our value estranges.

Values in series taking on as real
We affect ready gold a steady token
Flows in unbroken circuit and induces
Our being, wearies of us as ideal
Equals that heady crises eddy. Broken
Mentors, unspoken wealth labor produces,
Now loom as causes disposing our loci,
The foci of production: things reflected
As wills subjected; formed in the division
Of labor, labor takes on our imprecision—
Bought, induced by gold at no gain, tho close eye

And gross sigh fixed upon gain have effected
Value erected on labor, prevision
Of surplus value, disparate decision.

Hands, heart, not value made us, and of any
Desired perfection the projection solely,
Lives worked us slowly to delight the senses,
Of their fire shall you find us, of the many
Acts of direction not defection—wholly
Dead labor, lowlier with time's offenses,
Assumed things of labor powers extorted
So thwarted we are together impeded—
The labor speeded while our worth decreases—
Naturally surplus value increases
Being incident to the pace exhorted:
Unsorted, indrawn, but things that time ceded
To life exceeded—not change, the mind pieces
The expanse of labor in us when it ceases.

Light acts beyond the phase day wills us into
Call a maturer day, the poor are torn—a
Pawl to adorn a ratchet—hope dim—eyeing
Move cangues, conjoined the coils of things they thin to,
While allayed furor the obscurer bourne, a
Stopped hope unworn, a voiced look, mask espying
That, as things, men want in us yet behoove us,
Disprove us least as things of light appearing
To the will gearing to light's infinite locus:
Not today but tomorrow is their focus.
No one really knows us who does not prove us,
None or times move us but that we wake searing
The labor veering from guises which cloak us,
As animate instruments men invoke us.

Dissemble—pledging complexions so guarded—
Cast of plied error leaves such error asserted
But stand obverted, men sight us things joined to
Change itself edging the full light discarded—
In machines' terror a use there averted—
Times have subverted the plenty they point to:
Things, we have not always known this division—
Misprision of interest, profit, rent—coded
Surplus, decoded as labor—evaded
As gain the source of all wealth so degraded
The land and the worker elude the vision—
A scission of surplus and use corroded
And still, things goaded by labor, nor faded,
But like light in which its action was aided.

We are things, say, like a quantum of action
Defined product of energy and time, now
In these words which rhyme now how song's exaction
Forces abstraction to turn from equated
Values to labor we have approximated.

First Half of "A"-9

Restatement

I

The poem sings about things embodying a common denominator of past work, tho this abstract evaluation of them hides the fact that things are goods made to be used by people. If things could speak, they would point out that those who buy to sell them in the exchanges withdraw them from their proper owners who work in order to enjoy them.

II

Things would say that the exchanges hide the labor embodied in things when the exchanges equate them to gold. Furthermore, things would say that only in times of crises—when gold is not powerful enough to substitute for scarcity (that is, things that can be only imagined)—does it become clear how all this confusion is caused by the state under which things are produced. For, subject to the forces governing production, things take on the quality of so many subjected human wills, while the labor engaged in making them, part by part, itself takes on the quality of a divided thing subject to the same forces. Under this scheme, things are produced to be exchanged for gold at a profit, but the profit does not come out of the fact that things are exchanged for gold, or that work is bought by gold. Those with intent eyes on the exchanges have so hidden what really takes place when they hire people to produce things for them to exchange at a profit, that it is no longer clear that profit (surplus value) comes out of work, and that the foresight exacting profit is irreconcilable with work.

III

Yes, things would say that the different organs of the human body are engaged to make them, and that they are the embodied images of perfection people have in mind, and that they are for the enjoyment of people, who give their lives making them, rather than just so much work forgotten after a time. Could they speak, things would say that under a scheme producing for profit, they become of little worth like the lives of the people hurried away in making them,—and that only the mind can penetrate the worth of human labor hidden under the many ruins of things forgotten after a time.

IV

As duration, things would cite their physical existence in light, an energy the action of which ultimately explains them. For now appearing in the working day, they are together with the poor nothing but mysterious, worn springs, appendages to the extant material conditions of production. They would call out against the exploitation of the poor, who have had and still have fastened (as in China) large circular pieces of wood round their necks, as human cattle. And they would sense the poor's hope that the unpaid labor in things will voice its right desire to be completely paid to the poor in things: since the poor know them intimately, having animated them in the labor process the end of which is their embodiment.

V

Extricating themselves from the enigmas of obsolete social relations, things would confront people clearly as the purposive applications of labor thru time. In this light, tho discarded now, they would point to abundance, as against the misuse of machinery impoverishing the worker today when it can enrich him. Finally, things would speak of their use neglected behind names such as interest, rent and industrial profit, now hiding the unpaid labor realized in them—a use which obviously should consummate the conditions of all wealth: the earth and its workers in the light moving their activity.

CODA

Applied mathematics employs a quantity called "Action" defined as the product of energy and time. Perhaps things are such quanta of "Action" when they are defined as time congealed labor. But now the poem first brought into being by this abstract evaluation has been forced to turn from it to the labor present in the words of the song itself, the form of which the things speaking have assumed.

UN
POEMS
LATIONS

COLLECTED
AND TRANS-

UNCOLLEC-
TED POEMS,
1923-1977

A Parable of Time

Where time has been
Men see
Things past
Phenomenally:—

Even in my time
A great house stood
With a face
Of painted wood.

An old man came, and went,
And a lady of position;
Both spoke low, and bowed,
Befitting their condition.

People of high feeling—
They dwelt reserved;
Yet when they moved away
Some tattlers were perturbed.

The great house lost its roof
And is now a timber yard;
The man who owns the walls
Presents a shabby card.—

Yet why worry who he is
As time goes on men see
Most things
Phenomenally.

*

No sound.   But sun.
Lie under.   Overhead
the last peace is perfected.
In a kind of steady weather
graves marl the fallow dead.

*

The people change and the birds in the air,
And the air itself. In the town
None stirs till real summer is there;
We pass it, we feel a way down
Broken asphalt to cold floods on the sand.

*

All the stars have filled the heavens,
And a few I recognize
Tremble over the ocean—

Come, we might as well be walking
With the shadows on the land—
Nothing—you heard nothing
But your feet upon the sand.

*

"It is well on this June night
To lie naked by our fire
And watch a queer boat cruising—
A will-o-the-wisp by its light—
For smugglers whose calling is their choosing.
But really, Wickson, my desire
For water may grow stronger
If we lie here any longer.

God knows, Wickson, there's a chance
If you care to go for water
And walk the mile of marsh
That you'll meet the coast-guard's daughter.
But since chances may not keep,
Wickson, I had rather go to sleep."

*

Always the May-day sun
sought out night's bed when love
coursing thru Athens' trees
the diurnal odysseys

love came and by the night was led,
Marathon ran on to wed:

    Hymenee!

against the temple torch
hymned the boyish head—

    Hymenee!

to its mouth the double-pipe,
cheeks blown, apple ripe,
eyes bright from out the dark!

    *   *   *

    "Hey!—hey!"

still lighted after Athens,
still May, still reveller's each gaze,
night's constant—not his choice,
Love firing his voice—

"It's great to be a Mormon,
they've so many wives!—"
the corner boys serve Aphrodite,
sub aeternitatis specie

*

September among the headstones
Dispersed along the footways.
Clear and fair weather.
The mourners wander here.

Grow tall, grass of the gravestones.
Dark, twined green, the headstones over.
Draw aside where we have wandered
With the clouds that wander over.

See a mother, small:
Time has aged,
But has not assuaged.

See a brother, tall,
Comfort her:
She, and daughter, will not stir.

Time has been
And time has altered
But her grief
Has never faltered.

Time has been,
And he has grown,
Shows but little of the boy,
Save what his grief has shown.

Time has been, but has not changed
What has lain and lain below,
What was young is ever young,
In the mind, as years ago.

But be lost behind the headstones
Dispersed along the footways.
Cerulean skies, fair weather.
Observers wander here.

Grow tall, grass of the gravestones,
Bend, green trees, the headstones over,
For those who were and those who are
As the clouds that wander over.

*

Comes a day when the round tracts of sky
Emit such light
From their own sun and blue
As seems not meant for ordinary sight.

For he whose sight by chance might wander high
Walks heedlessly,
As never in his life he has,
Or may not ever in all life to be.

And he might feel like sun itself, could sun
But feel its might
When, passing through the pristine sky,
The immersed gold of its passing lasts longer than delight.

*

And they rest: the manifold light rays—

Misty my elbows press in the shore grass:
In dew, in thru blades risen before me,
My eyes look into night:

And they take in breakers in moonlight—
Moonlight white in the breakers—

The same which is said to deflect to the source of its coming—
(after an age it is found the light of our sphere travels finite,
The boundaries of our dawn are finite)—

And they glance far out, down the shore line,
The changing furrows;—

Purling, as from wells near
    households mornings—

        Bird not only for me I feel
        Beginning to fly speckling the ocean—

The sea near, falling, crickets single.

*

Play lost, banjos! Across the areas of ocean's flowing
The red phosphor fades! Autumn! Your tunes
Strummed far, must lose—Oh, the noise of the ocean, the
    evening flooding,
Drowns them out with the dunes!

Banjos on the beach! Autumn! Strum, for I follow you
Even to those sea-heavens you seem to drive
Like the voice the naked human voice before the waste
    dark ocean,
Singing   to remain alive.

The Sadness After

We were thy great lovers, Poseidon,
We thy great lovers are dead;
Hail us farewell—the pine-tree
To thee sacred, the shut sleeping face.

Hail us farewell, as you only,
Powerful always, Poseidon, must hail,
Your winds on the feet of us, blown ones,
Pale ghosts seeking our verge.

*

    The sun—
Sign on the wave
On the shoulder: dun

Flesh grows darker even
Before the eye.
Sand: the foot
Sinks in it.

Cannot
Be hurt:

Each bone single
When, if ever,
Did it crush to mingle,

Tortured? Stand
Naked by the wave, in the sun,
Burn,
Burn dun.

*

Across the smoke, over all past living,
I drink tonight, I am yours again, am one;
Across this table where you drink to everyone
But me, five candles overrun.

You have left me alone to myself, a sixth
Candle overrunning, you have singled me out
Alone, have made me yours, not one along with
            the others, and my flame leaps,
Rouses bright in the fond darkness folding it
                about.

*

And about these lights, they are the lights
Within the waters, liquid, springing up in me;
And about these waters that are me
They flow to shore, again, again, flow back
In the blue night, and from the leaves in autumn rollick,
Voyaging; I, too, go voyaging.

And about these inn-walls under trees, reflections
Of their gables, frame and windowed lights within the waters,
They are the lit deck of the world-ship gleaming,
Illumined, in the night, the cut waves leaping to the deck.
Yea, and about these trees their barks goosefooting
At the base, on each little rise of earth above the waters;
About the clouds swayed over them—the trees, hoarse,
Straining; about the leaves falling through them,
              upon me, upon the waters;—
They are one by one the tall masts and the smoke-tops

and the blown free birds of the world-ship,
Lifting, tree-populated, mist-swollen, skimming on the heavens.

And about this me of writhing nerve,
I have said I would not rack the brain to make it clear,
I have said the heart should shrivel being nerve,
And eyes and face die a cat's that wrinkles
Green and gray, tortured, dreading touch;
But not the brain's racked, but racks the body;

The heart
Clockwork happy working in the dark;

About this brain that racks this me,
The fine skull shelters it—the brain, controlling,
Balancing the feet to stand,—the lights brimming under,
The harbor air over, two trees two extended hands touching them.

E. Rockway, L.I.

*

"And the strong men shall bow themselves, and the grinders
Cease
Because they are few,
And those that look out of the windows be darkened."

Hear it?
The old burden,—forget it, you're not to bow.
Darkened windows—

Haven't we laughed,
You alone, I alone, walking, smoking, together,
Spurning what was putrid?

Know.

> Like the budding of fruit in your garden,
> Home, when the time comes for the budding of fruit—
> For you, too, a time!

(I wait for the train)

So I let myself, thrown single, waiting, body sleepless, pace now singing,
Invisible night rolls, and my eyes roll boreal aloneness!
Whiteness sings like silver balanced satellite aloft high-swinging
To the Night, the Night, the Night Now Primary.

And it follows that my body's singing walking
Unparalleled swinging times the night's aloneness,
And such modes of night as trees dark-planted,
Trunks, and no sorrow above sleepers' human houses.

For a Thing by Bach

Our God, immortal, such Life as is Our God,
Our God, apportion us thy rest,
So those of ours we live to love
                vaunt not against us,
But are merged, together our blood. Our wish:
For their selves, for our selves!

Our God, immortal, such Life as is Our God,
Our God, share with us under thy vault of strength,
So it lies on all thy beloved that they pass
                underneath like the stars
On further pilgrimage. Hope nor force wasted, our wish:
For their selves, for our selves!

Our God, immortal, such Life as is Our God,
Our God, if this cannot be,
We accept your lives, thy will, give us at least
                such portion of rest
As allows us to pass under lone, but not futile, stars. Our wish:
Impeding none, our selves alone!

Our God, immortal, such Life as is Our God,
Our God, if like to errant stars we flutter
In our passage ever, of thy source—
                (as to the immortelle,
Form, color, long after the gathering, is given)—give. Our wish:
Give measureless your urge that is our strength still increase.

A PREFACE
AND
18 POEMS
TO THE
FUTURE

A PREFACE

Mr. T. S. Eliot has told us that "Poets in our civilization, as it exists at present, must be difficult." But they must be more than that if they are to outlive their experience—a refined sensibility for appreciating love, war, death, El Greco, Krazy Kat, Negro Spirituals and relativity,—and mean anything to the future. Especially if the future will find it necessary to subordinate the cries and twists of our present to the creation of a singular sociological myth as great in its way, and as binding on peoples, as the solar myths of the ancients in their times.

Forgetting the ancients, however, and our present—a refined sensibility for appreciating love, war, death, El Greco, Krazy Kat, Negro Spirituals and relativity—it becomes clear why the quotations accompanying my 18 poems, indicative of such a singular sociological myth as mentioned above, are from *Pilgrim's Progress*.

Because, Bunyan, who had a conception of Deliverance by the right way, straight and narrow, was, if similitudes are employed, a Revolutionary pessimist with a metaphysics such as George Sorel wrote of in his *Reflections on Violence*: "C'est une métaphysique des moeurs bien plutôt qu'une théorie du monde, c'est une conception d'une marche vers la délivrance étroitement liée: . . . Le pessimiste regarde les conditions sociales comme formant un système enchaîné par une loi d'airain, dont il faut subir la nécessité, telle qu'elle est donnée en bloc, et qui ne saurait disparaître que par une catastrophe l'entraînant tout entier."

In these 18 poems, then, the pessimistic philosophy of proletarian violence, the only contemporary Deliverance to minds thinking in terms of destiny and necessity.

Bunyan wrote against the ameliorating Mr. Worldly Wiseman and for Evangelist: "'But how did it happen that you came out of your Country this way?' 'It was as God would have it; for when I was under the fears of destruction, I did not know whither to go; but by chance there came a man, even to me, as I was trembling and weeping, whose name is *Evangelist*, and he directed me to the Wicket-gate, which else I should never have found, and so set me into the way that hath led me directly to this house!'"

And Sorel: "dans la ruine totale des institutions et des moeurs, il reste quelque chose de puissant, de neuf et d'intact, c'est ce qui constitue, à proprement parler, l'âme du prolétariat révolutionnaire; et cela ne sera pas entraîné dans la déchéance générale des valeurs morales, si les travailleurs ont assez d'énergie pour barrer le chemin aux corrupteurs bourgeois, en répondant à leurs avances par la brutalité la plus intelligible."

New York,

Oct. 17, 1926

1.

Song of the Fateful Set Free

And why did you not bring them along with you? Then Christian
wept, and said, Oh how willingly would I have done it, but they were
all of them utterly averse to my going on Pilgrimage.

Pilgrim's Progress

No gang-plank and no rung of rope,
But we heave where the waters slope,
Darkness lengthens from the pier,
Masthead high the stars appear,
We have left the festive rockets
And the wealth of nations' pockets
And our fate is the one fate
The fate of constellations.

We have known as much while dancing
And we hid as much while glancing
With love that was not love,
For our desire was but for hands, to lift, to move
All boats from sand-bar; only
To leave the shallows shadowed to make us lonely,
For our shade was but the one shade
The shade of constellations.

O you upon the sand-dunes,
Your grasses swelling under, your tunes
That reach but to the shingle,
We fall from you, are single,

We fall from all the nations
Back to the sea of glowing constellations,
For we see now as the sea does—
The sea of burst waters.

Of what use to tread your lush field
When we knew it would not yield
Us in our time or on our way
The steadfastness that makes men gay;
When every branch of fruit that hung,
And every serenading voice, but rung
A furthered, nearing fear,
Our fear under the constellations.

Heave! now we are fear and the master,
Sea slopes gently, we hasten faster;
Heave! we know our path, its end
Where constellations blend
Showing clearly height has grown;—
On whom last a star has shone
His strength is but one thing,—
The strength of burst waters.

New York

2.

Greeting to the Fateful Returned

If you will go with us, you must go against Wind and Tide.

Pilgrim's Progress

And can they say,
Speaking after,
Merely a vain path
Wasted your years?

Me, to-day,
Greeting you,
Your eyes move to laughter,
Your lips to tears.

Drawn skin to bone
Your hollow cheeks
Control a smile
That meets me, level;

But distract in tone
Your voice flows harsh,
As flow on stones
Falling waters level.

And as you speak
I feel unblinking
Dust that gathered, came
And left you utter;

Feel how bleak
The sun was, chinking
All your human frame,
Like shutter.

New York

3.

I saw also that he looked this way and that way, as if he would run;
yet he stood still, because, as I perceived, he could not tell which
way to go.

Pilgrim's Progress

Snow-shovelers in the dark streets
Under a high sky where blue cloudlets glisten;
Red lanterns swinging; soft, the thud of a pick—
Stop for a time and listen.

Stop for a time. As if you choose, hear
Only till you grow one with the scrape under snow.
Nothing but bodies move and shovels hasten
While snow is piled to thud on thud and blow and blow;

While snow is raised to thud on thud,
Under a high sky where blue cloudlets glisten,
Under tenement windows void like seas
Where one might stop, walk on, but to listen.

Manhattan

4.

Proletarian Home

Poor hearts, I wonder in my mind what they do!
Pilgrim's Progress

Her four holy candles of the Friday night,
Heart! how they dwindle
In circles on the ceiling, sputter!
  Cannot she breathe, heart?

No, sitting there white—
His mother: she is certain she knows the spindle
Of life that carried them both goes; gutter,
  Candles! and dissolve, heart!

Ah, their hearts dissolve till they go up as two black,
  mourning smoke threads
From each of their candles to the circled ceiling;
And the others are not near them now; when the room darkens
  How she fears for them, Heart!

And she fears for him too, their heads
Already like mourners; against the windows, for all their feeling,
Blank, black luminousness of the dark that hearkens
  Not a word to her prayer for his prospects.

New York

5.

But the night was as troublesome to him as the day.

Pilgrim's Progress

This is no human earth: nothing
Is here but a dead figment and a gleam
Of stars toward the river and the sea
Solemn around this place of dock and beam.

The rails of cars end here: why they
Were laid where steps seem but the fall of water down
Alone, and one himself a shadow
Grown, is more than light and water say.—

Fifty years and this might be our day.
Our night has come to rot away.
Our sons who come to hold a sway
Should walk their night as in the day.—

Why one has lived a life in his own
House and light to find continuance
In storehouse grilles and soot and river
Stench and tank is more than these can say.

These tanks we built are so much mightier
Than loving hands we dropped; night air
So blue about them, so pure and high,
One questions almost what it's doing there.—

Eclipse, and this might be our day,
Our night has come to rot away,
But ours who come to hold a sway
May walk at night as in the day.—

East River Streets

6.

East River Wharves, Jackson Street

(In New York of 1926 the Police were called New York's Finest)

Ye cannot be justified by the Works of the Law; for by the deeds
of the Law no man living can be rid of his Burden: therefore, Mr.
Worldly Wiseman is an alien, and Mr. Legality a cheat; and for his son
Civility, notwithstanding his simpering looks, he is but a hypocrite
and cannot help thee.

Pilgrim's Progress

Come, wish him plumb to hell!—
Man-trick in a machine, which we,
Annoying none,
Might drive to so much more advantage—
Rum-runner of New York's finest,
Sour taste of vigilance,
Afraid we are importing whiskey!

Look rather across the shore,
See, there are other men,
See the light of their furnace, scald of the night,
Bath of these waters.
You have brought me who cannot see the ground, to the river,
To this river of their labors,
Your arm gripping mine
To see I do not make a misstep.

I do not see: yet I could not make that misstep.
I do not see the ground, but the light of the furnace leaps
        and it is all
Like splashes of rain diffuse.
Be loyal to us.

For, see,
The Dipper swerves to sea,
The heavenly skippers swerve to sea,
Out of their void, swerve,
Be loyal to us,
One with their Night,
Be loyal to us
To the laborers of benighted shores.

Ah even in our Night the man of the police has motored off,
Never to know, we take and then are taken of a hand
To touch and keep,
That the sense of our nearness, feeling the waters
Plash, as from our pulse, a bond between us
And a strength that is ours,
Carries us on to All Men Benighted,
Their hate as of the Timeless Forces.

7.

There is an endless Kingdom to be inhabited, and everlasting Life to be given us, that we may inhabit that Kingdom forever.

Pilgrim's Progress

In their high courses now the constellations,
The largest trembling over port and wave,
Range fair above the piers to swerve with night—
The mist is passing out with light.

On shore where flames of furnaces sped flaring
All night into the sky and stream like rockets,
The flames stop suddenly as doomed with silence,
The lights grow golden on their sockets.

And even now like forms of bowed flame paling,
Their heads all lowered while the sun keeps state,
The night-gangs shift after their turn of burning
And earth looms vaster with their fate.

Brooklyn

8.

I was once a fair and flourishing Professor, both in mine own eyes,
and also in the eyes of others.
Well, but what art thou now?

Pilgrim's Progress

The moon is full to-night, lounging across the sky,
Over the garish entrance of the bridge, the traffic—
Triumphal arch—, and the night is autumn,
Blue night and fair and mild with mist. And white
It passes as I have passed white into its sight.

As I stand here I remember walking this late hour
After midnight down streets where there are lamps
All like the moon. A child might find perhaps in a penny arcade
Such lights and such a moon. After my grief making me
Walk to-night, the streets are one grand festival,
So many penny arcades happy being shut;
And, to the left, the servant-of-the-law
Suspecting me, one joke still grander. Does he not
Hear the dynamos in the very cellars under his feet?

The motors whiz by us like drunken men,
And there is nothing left of us
But one walker turning in himself to the moon.

Manhattan Bridge

9.

Come, neighbor Christian, since there are none but us two here, tell me now further what the things are, and how to be enjoyed, whither we are going?

Pilgrim's Progress

Nervure-sharp, O tipping tower,
Against the height
Your windows risen,
In the yellow winter light,
In the evening fog,
You might be a bell
Waiting
For the wind
To strike;—
A buoy
Tipping as the wind just falls.
And new seas.

Metropolitan Tower

10.

In the Era of Rays

—the reflection of the Sun upon the City (for the City was pure gold) was so extremely glorious, that they could not as yet with open face behold it, but through an Instrument made for that purpose.

Pilgrim's Progress

Once, and again it moves along the heavens!
Stubbing the cloud-fields—the searchlight, high
In the roseate twilight of rain-sky, green! green spring
In the heavens mild in the spring; or down suddenly
Earthwards, plunge deep suddenly earthwards,
Like escape, stampede of cattle horns, ghastly, ghastly,
Their giant heads invisible for joy, grief, cavalcade, plunge
        earthwards,
And into our hearts, O sacrifice,
But we emerge! (emerge upon a level roof that fronts the sky,
The skylight of your room to rear,)
So we can breathe, the rain air and the spring
Ours again, till once again it moves along the heavens,
Down or up, machine-rayed, powerful!

New York
R.W.

11.

The Pilgrim they laid in a large upper chamber, whose window
opened towards the Sun rising—

Pilgrim's Progress

I have slept and am passing Eastern Parkway;
I know by the station plant, and the many lights,
Like colored globules, round brittle trinkets in the night.
Red, green, yellow and blue, like steady ship lights—
And the engineers can be seen moving
Under them
The lights so close above them, they seem
To be pressing their heads with electric force.
Passing over ties in the dark, dim lamplight under bare posts,
Gaunt men like these posts, sometimes leaning on posts, the
     passion of creation
Evidently dead.

All night it will take before they are really gone,
Perhaps shaking their heads negatively in the dawn—
Going to bed.
And the lights gradually melt in the close, low upper dark,
Leaves on the air are seen in neighboring streets,
And the wind is felt above the worm-eaten posts
Nakeder, higher with dawn,
Asleep like lone trees, dead high trunks branchless among ties.
And those who go off to bed—
In sleep begins for them the sun.

Eastern Parkway Junction

12.

They also shewed him some of the Engines with which some of his
Servants had done wonderful things.

Pilgrim's Progress

How home-born the engines,
Like cattle in uneasy rest,
Stand loose and chafe
Or steam abreast.

Under dead night
Burning each their rations:
Like warmth of cattle near,
Good beasts of patience.

And where they steam
The shed of the station covers
Them. On its roof
Their warm light hovers.

So that a man might stand,
As under a cattle shed,
Dark and cozy-warm—
The outer night dead.

The outer night dead . . .
And a man's heart of caresses
For new sharers of burden with him
When he rests and no time presses.

Valley Stream

13.

"as fond of fine music and handsome buildings as Bunyan was." *B. S.*

Look it in the face, then, and it will smile as it always has on Caesar—
The moon, full, yellow, in the vast twilight over the railroad lost in
the silence.

So, once under the yellow disc, the dusk,
The one face under it perhaps Caesar's—crown cropped, nose medallioned,
contriving fated,
Hawked, fine in the twilight; or a lone step, motionless, perhaps even
before the time of Caesar, on the land he conquered,
Egyptian on a field of plinth, the head royal, the eyes souls, the
abdomen as the chest soul—
both suns—Egypt, ready to contrive, undying;

Granite thighs, granite man.
And again Caesarian man, Egyptian labor: iron trains, like glow worms
creep into Jamaica Station:
Indomitable seeking, man at work under the yellow moon,
Full, smiling,
Creeping out, far out, over the rail lines to ocean.

Note: The first line, not Shakespeare's but Shaw's, is from *Caesar and
Cleopatra*, Act IV.

Jamaica, L. Id. Railroad

14.

During the Passaic Strike of 1926, the Sexton of the rich parish of St. Mark's-on-the-Bouwerie, New York, imparted the news to my friend, S. T. H., that there was only room for two in his graveyard.

. . . .

I was born indeed in your dominions, but your service was hard, and your wages such as a man could not live on.

Pilgrim's Progress

There are two vaults left in St. Mark's-on-the-Bouwerie,
There are two vaults left to bury the dead,
O when the two vaults are filled in St. Mark's-on-the-Bouwerie,
How will the dead bury their dead.

For Justice they are shrewdly killing the proletarian,
For Justice they are shrewdly shooting him dead,
Good Heavens, when the vaults are filled in
     St. Mark's-on-the-Bouwerie,
How will the dead bury their dead!

15.

Rejoice not against me, O mine Enemy! when I fall I shall arise.

Pilgrim's Progress

What does it profit you
To meet us with politeness,
O you distant ones? So small
The brightness scattering out secret
It does not profit you at all.

When your nobility
Endures us but is critical
Cannot we, you distant ones,
Effectual our hate,
Smile, and scatter all your suns.

Do we not laugh at you,
You ant-folk in hot sands,
Thriving like unexplicable Desire—
Dark bands upon this Form of us—
Destroying, yet destroyed afire.

New York

16.

I was driven out of my Native Country, by a dreadful sound that was
in mine ears: to wit, that unavoidable destruction did attend me, if I
abode in that place where I was.

Pilgrim's Progress

They call and they call—foreign waters—
Somewhere, waters—the sirens call.
Plash, and they must flash across their night—
Foreign waters. Could I be there
Then I could be those waters of the moon perhaps,
No man-forsaken, half-light moon.

See! I am here afar you waters of the moon!
People, afar!
No stars appear, up here
Beyond my room—
Heavens' Innumerable
A little way and near.

They call and they call, Call foreign waters,
O stray lights on my windows,
Stray lights from our streets,
Fare you fair,
What is the city of freedom that your murk invokes
But grief unleashed to-night provokes!
Our air, our birthright, our familiar air,
Making my heart to tremble,
Why is it you dissemble
With my every intake-breath,
Light
In a somewhere, city of freedom and Immortal Night!

Manhattan

17.

Proletarian Sunday

—the River was very deep—
Pilgrim's Progress

The shore turns one large backyard
Of the world,
And as the waves, like gray mews of the twilight,
Are eddied

Inland one by one
Our children beam forth upon them
As on birds
And are laughter-riven.

Driven like pebbles from each wave
Their crystal play thru sunlight ends,
While on our waves they run from
Night extends,

Us older carrying on the sullen green.
So that we who deep the waters enter
Seem almost without offshoot or graft of green,
Seem night and the water's center.

Long Beach

N.
Y.
1927...

New York, my city,
Now song once
From the fluent single man
Finds not a voice for the new day's dawn,—
From Insufficiency more than one man together
Must, as in Egypt once,
Labor to give last littleness a norm if not a song,

Build them high walls, hugeness
Like Memnon
That sings an isolated note at dawn.

So may, two-footed
Find strength in common and reach where
Up—gullies of air
Each new day thrids
Tall companies
Of newly risen pyramids
(Structures in mass instead of song)—

Propitious the rays of sun,
Sand-color, on each new tower that prinks
You, city, as with a giantship of sphinx.

Then, what if before the single and once singing heart
A winter lies, a dispersed festival,
For the walkers, steel-shifters, thru canyons on parade,
The sun may yet be summery!

And you, New York,

Your buildings, morning-glories of over night,

For the mourner of past Song

    grace

        the adornment of a worn cravat—City! . . .

(Spinoza in a Winter Season)

Now sings the January wind
A winter lullaby
For all deep thoughts concerning God—

God's thought with other things dinned
Earthward by the wind, then towards the sky
Straight on the air with shout and prod.

And there is sun, much
Sun, even for the sickest in the other room—
"Infinite things in infinite modes

Must follow from the divine nature being such"—
And the sun dances on our yellow broom,
And where I nurse, or merely stare, corrodes.

*

What are these smoke-stacks
voices of ships by day

Bringing back night
for laborers

sleeping by day—

Walls of fog—dense
whiteness—breaking

as one with the wake

Blurred factory chimneys
from which the fog

never wakes?
New York, New York.

*

My watch!
Star-darkness wash over you—
Immediately you cannot enter them!

Unite your ticks with a siren's sound, a wash of wave,
A siren's sound set howling over waves!

But immediately to these star-darkened skies
You cannot go as wave to wave,
Tho' your hands cross eyes!

"He Came Also Still"

Small I come also still, that in the spring
May flower such blossoms of the earth, pall-
Florets I planted crying on your fall,
And meek buds you make worth remembering.
For you only is every growing thing,
Creepers across the earth and climbers tall,
And branches that bend over the carved wall
Of stone that commemorates time's reckoning.

And also small your earth is sealed; tomorrow
Earth lies no nearer to me for all sorrow;
No more removed, my loved one, than you dead

Whose form sunned in your last hours with me here
Slept, and your head. I place you on your brier
And feared, straightening you, to hurt your head.

*

The silence of the good that you were wrought of,
Do I find it transformed by some strange leaven
From you to earth only my earth knows aught of,
And know it silent mound outlined on heaven,
Till all the life of you in our still room
Returns to me—your presence past the wall
Of death, the confines of your dark? So fall
Death's guerdon to me neither sun nor gloom;

But quiet—your silence, when you would stir
With me—its being, what you are and were.
It cannot change though it must change the mode—
Not with you living, but with you dead to darkle—
Yet is no less obliged to corrode
In earth with you—earth, shadow of your sparkle.

*

O lowering belts
O ridged dead faces

Sad welts
Of earth

Turned faces
Of earth!

*

Someone said, "earth, bowed with her death, we mourn
Ourselves, our own earth selves,"—yet for me crept
Rattling a small wind bitter, and I wept
But your own little form that might be torn.
And suddenly I could see your face borne
Like the moon on my sight, it had not slept
But looked, as once, at rest through waking, stepped
To the grave peace of death and not yet worn.

"Look at the moon," you said: "Those are no tears
Falling, unclasped through space, for what appears
Dead crater sheds no tears." And your face from
Where it came vanished, so I was too soon
Oblivious among the wind, the moon
Clouding then, her high dissolution come.

*

During lunch hour I shall stretch opposite
The few great smoke-stakes of Bayonne, belong
To day-blue, to channel, to Staten Island.
I shall not eat, but stretch myself—the wit
Of gulls' sunned bellies blow my mind to song:
(And while I alone recall you dead), "Fly land
And water, no, nor stop at blue, among
Our skies, white birds, your flight be holy writ."

Futility of motion, and the love
Of sun will then be close to me.
And whether I shall grieve or not, sight then
Will be beyond all near felicity—
Being with blue sky-bubble over sea,
With gulls that near me are a thought thereof.

*

And human heart-beats; star-falling; engine-beats—
Iron behind iron; wall upon wall
Of night—and ranged—; where unhuman night is all.
Exposed to it one nears not nor retreats
From it; night alone, unified, completes
Nothing within one who being but small
Object to it is one always without. Star-fall
Thrills! how swift it is! but what force depletes

Its soundings, as it distances, dulls beat
Of thrill and beat of heart, so tho near, known,
The night almost as proffered bread to eat—
Stranger—the one can gaze but, feast alone,
And filled thus grow more empty, grow more numb,
Human heart-beats slowed, and never touched a crumb.

Critique of Antheil

(*Sunday Night, April 10, 1927, his Première in America*)

You come, George Antheil, to our America
Yours once—now?—no doubt you'll be sailing from it soon,
And because you said and music, after all, is written
    from the heart
I buy a ticket from a speculator,
Myself wracked seeking our living's perfect form,
    the bloom significant,
Myself to hear you.

I hear,
And if my nerves that work supposedly in perfect mechanisms
Would by fate turn outward, play a visible score,

That would be music,
Recessional dynamic—
A hymn sung by myself a solitary choir
Leaving my chancel of this world,
In laughter
For something like your time-space, your musical
    machines in fourth-dimensional blues.
      As you have it on your saxophone, perhaps,
              you joker!
        Time-space
        What is it?
        Is it?
        And space. We small, when space we time.
        Time, space, will have us all in time.
        Is it?
        Is it?
        Parallel meets parallel,
        Conceivable, no?
        I don't know—m-r-r-row—
        Or on your electric bells:
        And we dance on, dance on,
        For being relative in
            a steel factory, and space, blues,
            br-r-r-n, br-r-r-n

Ballet Mecanique—three parts—
    Allegro—Allegro—Allegro—
Young blood is the joke to them, your hearers.
They cannot see—these evening clothes—
    the sense of beginning forte, ending forte,
    of laughing, three times laughing, overturning,
    So one bloke says to a greasier one

As they quarrel, having disturbed each other,
Do I annoy you
Then let me annoy you—
Slap me on the bare wrist so to speak—
And they jeer when they dare,
                    but rarely dare.

And as for me, George Antheil,
I watch you, and what grafted your youth on jazz,
          rhythmically precise,
You recall a walking-stick, the body like the twig on
          which it lives,
Or whimsical sometimes, a boy's most playful cat in
          mythic mittens pounding a piano's keys
(i.e. when there is no mechanical piano to pump).
          Xylophones, xylophones, where are you going?
          We're gonna meet the negroes their saxophones blowing.

And it seems to me, George Antheil,
          You're, forgive me, a bit dilettante,
          Go-slumming, about niggers,
And that your trips to Africa bring back nothing but
          the usual wild-man Tom-tom
I heard 19 years ago—a kid—
          And this is 1927.
But when your wind machine ends, ends
          in a wail as I have heard the fires
          Wail at night—
          the riveters, acetylene torches
          in the scooped out squares of building
          sites, And stopped—

Music or no music
No wail can be too loud to drown this milksop audience,
No piano too many-teethed for their banality,
No percussion too strong to indent their brains.

Knock 'em on the head, George Antheil,
Run 'em over like an automobile,
For anyway they do not know their backsides from their elbows
And will only know them when backside and elbow both are broken.

Mockery of the vortex sucking them, leaving them
      more and more the drenched wet rags they are!
Horrible wail wrenching them when steel, and steam,
      and blast of new musical machines interpret
      them, wet rags anew—
Youth, you do not bow to them,
George Antheil, grasp in a jerk, only your conductor's
      hand, and leave.

And from where I sit
I can look down into the expensive pit
And spit.

(Awake!)

Propped on the earth
And from where, what sleep, awake! Your head—
And kissed the center of your forehead—
Knowing we have escaped from death
Of sleep; and as on aerial curtains wrought
Of morning with the wind and one more kissing thought
Death's words are naught:
"Now like two lamps irrelevant upon the road
Short-circuited before blue morning go out!"

Preface—1927

I look around at the economic appointors of my generation.
These pretend not to notice me,
Models of politeness and subterfuge they are;
And feeling myself of the natural forces to come, for
appointors, I suppose I have what displaces them,
Or at least being of the same quality as running
waters, for appointors, I have no pity.
I wish occasionally to tell them a thing or two, but the
occasional manner I have long known to be useless,
I must attack for the remaining sinned-against, if at all.
They—the appointors—have names and are guarded,
they have arrived, and seem well, being recognized.
Who, on the other hand is here to name me, who
guard my fellows when they are murdered?

Who am I, I laugh at the sink when I wash in the
morning, to write myself out against the cool
directive judgment of a whole world?
Who am I to starve in the face of well-being?

Who am I to snub my appointors when I must draw
    or die from among them?
Others sensitive are at least insulated by their common-
    sense, monied, thru fine ladies of rich husbands,
    the poets may work in a tower,
I must live with the whip of my being, it is necessary
    that the whip and I rub bodies,
To escape it would be laughable,
To escape it would mean I hide not only myself but
    betray others.
At night after the long labor and the day's hate for
    the bread, when the moon came with bitter
    reward in through my window
I arose to walk to the bath to attend the need of the body.
Who was I then but a while's brief engine burning up
    fuel, pouring out water,
Son of the boreal globed requiescat of moon, I had died
    and the grasses of winter were all lying over me.

Small me, me, always a courage returns to whisper the
    lines to the future, the dimness,
Turned though you be, myself, to a tumbler of dust
    that dust, let us hope, will reillume grasses—
In the moonlight—; in the sunlight, dead grass
    around, dust itself is alighted. Then. But now,

My fellows, living by the peculiar whip of our being,
    a while longer, and we must sting,
Or shine, being destroyed,
Blind the eyes of crude faces.
For this, these days, the fearful whip of our being is
    yet not enough,
The doors of the appointors are not shut enough in
    our faces,
We must hold our mouths firmer (perhaps we are dying),

Till what is back of the doors
Cries out for fierce valor:
"Who are they, these damned!

(These States 1927)

I

I look around
at the economic
appointers
of my generation.

For
appointers
I have
what
displaces
them.

II

of the quality
of running water—

blue marble
tile—

this bathroom—

the moon
comes
reward

in—
thru glazed window—

Who
am I
but a while's
brief engine
burning up fuel,
pouring out water

Son
of the boreal,
globed
requiescat of moon,
I have died,
and the grasses
of winter are all lying
over me.

III

turned tho' you be,
myself,
to a tumbler of dust,
that dust (Drink!),
will reillume grasses—

in the moonlight—;

in the sunlight
dead grass around
dust itself is alight!

IV

My fellows, each living, by the peculiar
Whip of our being—

A while longer—we must sting,
Or shine, being destroyed,
Blind the eyes of crude faces.
For this, these days, the fearful whip
     of our being is not enough,
The doors of the appointers are not
     shut enough in our faces.
Hold, our mouths, firmer.
(Perhaps we are dying).
Till what is back of the doors
Cry out for fierce valor:
"Who are they, these damned!"

    *

Autumn, then autumn—what of it?
A train's windage sucks up the country.
Funnels of air,
    it seems, resembling funnels of trees—

so one under them
is sucked up as up the funnel's small mouth—

    Hoa—hoa—and, across the earth's face
    with the train, sudden windfall—

Curse it, bro, yours is not a tree's soul
to be shaken in standing by the roadside—
you who were given of motion in durance.

*

Finer was the dead artist's hand
    which modeled a fountain-boy's
first cause so that its bronze gay
    orifice made water.

New York's not Nuremberg
    since even a fountain-boy
must hide his tiny with an Adam leaf
    astride a fish from whose false
      teeth the water gurgles.

*

O autumn fields, if we should break, beyond
Blue shutters, past boles of trees,
And reach wind-heaving
Launches of that lake

Who knows but that the
Evening blue mist ferrying
Would not perpetuate—perpetuate—our ferreting;
We shall not be spared, who does not know it,
The seasonal, who knows it as well as we—
My nostrils, O autumn fields,
    your high grass, contenting now
    the search of acrid smells?
A ferreting has torn the
Heart of us and
May tear always,
Even after desired objects which were ours,
Blue closed shutters, launch and water,

Ours, near, and they toppled as old paradise, and the lips
                              bite eagerly, blue
Because blue reaches mist—in the cold;
but eagerly!
O autumn fields, the boles are bruised!
As I break thru, thru, curse it! on crashing knees!

University: Old-Time

Dis in napa now trailing the sterilized.
                              Joyce Hopkins

Song 11

And the least see
your ministry

and the least sea
beside me

(Collaboration)

the water lifted me
in daylight

leaving my
ears

but your
breath

your fingers touch
an eyelash

even the water is dry now

> (lines 1-8 J. Reisman
> line 3 "leaving"—G. Oppen
> line 9—L. Z.)

mirror fugue on "The Gnat" by Carl Rakosi

THE GNAT—Carl Rakosi

Winter and wind,
the whole age

is an afternoon
around the house

a little snow
a sea blizzard

a yard clover
a lucky house

anabasis
for edelweiss

Six rivers
and six wenches

the twelve
victories.

Greetings.
Carl Rakosi

To which greetings, Mr. Zukofsky replied with:
Yeah bo'
it's a good gnat. Permit me, I will do a mirror fugue upon it.

The gnat
12 victories

6 rivers and
wenches six

edelweiss
for anabasis

a yard clover
a house lucky

a little blizzard
a sea snow

around the house
is an afternoon

wind and winter
the whole age.
Sink the pinna now and bring the tune out from the tympanum
and

you will have your original the best in a long time.

Greetings.

> *Louis Zukofsky*
> *Thanksgiving, 1932*

*

Of sleep where all your past goes on—
Who will say what dawn
Knows our loves more than sleep, or holds
Them clear as the leaves of spring

First loves no less for wintering
Greener while the summer takes
Our lives: with sleep gainsay the dawn,
In sleep where all our past goes on.

*

[for William Carlos Williams, *The First President:
An Opera in Three Acts* (1936)]

from scene two, Mrs. Arnold:

Sorrow! Sorrow little child
Weep, weep, sweet face.
There is no pity, pity for us
Alone in this wild place.

"March Comrades"

(Words for a workers' chorus, from "A"-8)

Workers and farmers unite
You have nothing to lose
    But your chains
    The world is to win
This is May Day! May!
Your armies are veining the earth!

Railways and highways have tied
Blood of farmland and town
    And the chains
    Speed wheat to machine
This is May Day! May!
The poor's armies veining the earth!

Hirers once fed by the harried
Cannot feed them their hire
    Nor can chains
    Hold the hungry in
This is May Day! May!
The poor are veining the earth!

Light lights in air blossoms red
Like nothing on earth
    Now the chains
    Drag graves to lie in
This is May Day! May!
The poor's armies veining the earth!

March comrades in revolution
From hirer unchained
    Till your gain
      Be the freedom of all
The World's May Day! May!
May of the Freed of All the Earth!

"Belly Lox Shnooks Oaky"

Belly Lox Shnooks Oaky
Went for a walk with a stokey
They were so doped
They could not have hoped
But to sink down to poke-pokey.

Cyclists

No road!
—No.
Idiot!
—What difference does it make!

   *

Eat the pie?
Not I
Said the eye.

Beef, pork, lamb?

*

Can a mote of sunlight defeat its purpose
When thought shows it to be deep or dark?

Sun, and think shadow.

Against the unjust,
Friends say,
You will do well
To point out a speaker's mistakes.

Promise them:
 how
   but implicitly.

Quiet,
Past an enemy in shadow
A mote of sunlight,
A beaded wave,
Rolls, the sun in small.

What Passion for a Baby?

Papa's out
Because
I'm off
Today.

—What's in
That zipper
Thing?

—The old juice!

—It's no
Government
Secret?

      Dinty sweetheart this is the age
      Of the zipper and the plane
      The Sun zips a cloud up
      And when the wind's right back
      It isn't going to rain!

         —Then?
      So zip, zip, zip
      And zoop, zoop, zoop
      And eat quick, eat quick, slo-o-ow
      Till the plane lands
      And we meet the bull-itical guard again!

Julia's Wild

Come shadow, come, and take this shadow up,
Come shadow shadow, come and take this up,
Come, shadow, come, and take this shadow up,
Come, come shadow, and take this shadow up,
Come, come and shadow, take this shadow up,
Come, up, come shadow and take this shadow,
And up, come, take shadow, come this shadow,
And up, come, come shadow, take this shadow,
And come shadow, come up, take this shadow,
Come up, come shadow this, and take shadow,
Up, shadow this, come and take shadow, come
Shadow this, take and come up shadow, come
Take and come, shadow, come up, shadow this,
Up, come and take shadow, come this shadow,
Come up, take shadow, and come this shadow,
Come and take shadow, come up this shadow,
Shadow, shadow come, come and take this up,
Come, shadow, take, and come this shadow, up,
Come shadow, come, and take this shadow up,
Come, shadow, come, and take this shadow up.

THE OVERWORLD

ceaseless artistries in Circumstance
Of curious stuff and braid
furthest hem and selvage flames
Of earth-invisible suns
magnitude without a shape
Who hurlest Dynasts from their thrones
(echo)
Καθεῖλε ΔΥΝΑΣΤΑΣ ἀπὸ θρόνων
O Loveless Hateless
till It fashion all things—fair

TRANS-LATIONS

930-1943

André Salmon

an arrangement from *Prikaz*

The Hermitage is on fire, the Museum of Alexander
Warms its grief in its cinders;
In an attic in the Kameny quarter
A coming honeymoon is blessed by a dying father.

The colonel and his five daughters
Go bathing each Tuesday . . . .
At the navel of Nadine
The cold of a carabine . . . .
Under the wheels of the telegas
Your breast of coral, Olga.
The youngest is Daïcha—
Drowned to be fished up again.

Perfection!
And sublime enormity!
The train without direction,
The train without schedule,
The train sped by a fool student pursuing his studies.

The navel of Nadine
Quavers like a cow-bell
At the pearl belly of Sophie
Gazes the love which she defied.
A Lett soldier
Tears her hair, crushes her under his boots, and cries
"All things are wrecked by women!"

A council of soldiers is held at the Opera.
A black and gray crow followed by rats
Crosses the Neva lined with tilted reflectors;
    for the downfall begins.

They hoist the black flags of danger on the tower of the Newsky,
The Kchessinska passes in her droshky.
Halt! a little sergeant
Infantile, glowing rose and blond,
Makes a sign to his men, peasants and workers in arms—
Allow me, the noble watch of the proletariat—

If they have shed blood, they have banished the lie!

Guillaume Apollinaire

The Gathering

We came to the garden aflower for the gathering.
Beautiful, do you know how many tea-roses, fling
Flowerpale, with love, as towards your head in a ring,
　　Petals after the spring?

Their stems bend to the great wind which rises.
The petals of rose are a ruin in the way.
O beautiful, gather them,—flowering of surmises
　　Fades after today.

Put them in a cup—when each gate closes—
Zest lost and cruel, reflect what days consume—
We will see the amorous agony, the roses'
　　Fences of perfume.

An expansive garden is nipped, my egotist,
Day's butterflies have fled to other flowers,
Henceforth remains only the garden's night-mist,
　　Butterflies of its hours.

The flowers are doomed for the room—unholy.
Our roses each by each strip of their grief.
Beautiful, sob. . . . Each pale corolla
　　Is love's brief.

Guillaume Apollinaire

Sequence from *The Writing of Guillaume Apollinaire*

I.

1890

X

All the women between 45 and 50 remember

having been in love with Capoul

M. Capus

And there are others

II.

The chef fleeces the geese

Fall snow

Fall and why haven't I

My love in my arms

III.

Mouth open on an harmonium

A voice made of eyes

Hauling the little people

An altogether very little old lady with pointed nose

I admire the blue enamelled kettle

But the rat enters the corpse and lives there

IV.

Passing me on the street the nigger Sam MacVea
Grieved that I was so much blacker than he

V.

I am no longer
Myself
I am the fifteenth
Of the eleventh

VI.

—Machines
Luxury and beauty which are only their spray

VII.

(Morgue)
And all together arms over arms under
Trilling military airs

VIII.

At last I have the right to greet beings I do not know

IX.

A Final Chapter

All the people will hurry to the square
Whites and blacks and yellow men and a few red
Workers from factories whose chimneys will
not be smoking because of the strike
Masons with plaster on their clothes
Butcher boys their hands still bloody from
the meat
Journeymen bakers pale with the flour sprinkling them
And the rank and file of clerks and the shopkeepers
who once employed them
Women terrible to look at carrying
children and some with others gripping their
skirts
Poor women without shame in make-up
and nodding strangely
The crippled the blind the maimed the
one-handed the limping
Even some priests and a few dressed with
elegance
And on the outskirts of the square the city
will seem dead even to its old trembling.

Alain Bosquet

The need to have you

It is midnight, hour that kills
great flesh and images,
bubbles show on our palms
to break open like flowers,
in us the groaning leper
attains the rain and the rainbow,
all things prepare for north winds:
our ranged eyelid,
our fingers that resemble obelisks
and our spinal columns
cartilage on cartilage
blooming with bites.
You are the sister of misfortunes,
you are the friend of distress
and at the bottom of your shoulders
are sparrows, caravans,
great faces become
marsh spiders,
but among your stars
you transfigure the sonata,
tall plumage, the water-color,
such a poem as moves,
an ocean for your birds,
a happy man like me,
too rich to express himself
and, under your curse
that lives to make me more mad,
a body, a criminal hide,
a body that will no more be fooled,
a body that will not live after itself.

Alain Bosquet

Pluck the Cascade

You are light, lace,
pure air, pith of elder-tree,
tint of bee, or music box,
and I, I am more soothing
than the look of the hippocampus,
more faultless than small grass,
than water, than your image.
Yet there is that cascade
to speak to us of our dullness
and of that evil which we call
"great love in despair."
Listen to wet silence,
and without waiting to be naked,
destroy our furious alabasters,
our skies, our villages which lie,
our guardian equivocal flowers,
and then also our habits,
false impersonations of life,
our bones jealous of our eyes,
and our heart always empty
for a gratuitous wreck.
But hold back, everything changes
in this too great a fall,
we will soon be despoiled
like sweet memory,
and the cascade will restore to us
our passion twisted with roses,
our poem of the Milky Way,
the plant with the wrinkled face
the town built of perfumes,

and then, some part in our being
still scarcely defined,
a fresh, warm rivulet
that will speak of a cascade
and that our astonished lips
knowing themselves so lively
will call: "our caprice."

Alain Bosquet

To Begin Again with Your Body

By degrees foundered seeing ourselves lonely
Like books too subtle and dusty,
We will grow thirsty for a magnanimous prayer,
And our sick forehead at last will own
Its harmony, that sidereal panther
On the point of recoil, and then, quite gently
Its equipoise, that other more rigorous cat
That scents music about our fever.
Then, in this new trail of eternity,
How merciful and how prophetic we shall become!
A shock will be enough to create our speech,
And the words "good morning" or "good night" will make us
Guilty of feeling or joyous being moved
Like rain transformed into a cathedral.
All will be clear to our fool's impenitence,
We shall go on to discover the starry scepter,
The crown of the birds, the purple of stinginess,
And, from appearance to appearance, we shall reach
The dazzling conquest of our grave sorrows.
Then I shall recall our frantic body
—That magician reduced to submissiveness—
So that the verb "see" be sweet under our eyelids,
So that our fingers touch our viny hands,
So that your breasts cause my warm lips to die,
So that your fear invent that unique pitching,
So that in the evening—our seeds soldering our shape—
We know how to find again, in a gesture more simple

Than decency or divine lassitude,
A daily promise of life
And so that at last, alas! despite our endowments
We cry in the dawn—yes, cry!—to be
So tenderly a bit of comprehensible flesh!

Alain Bosquet

To Go On

The south will be in our shoulders,
let us rejoin it so that it will dazzle us
and give us the world to find again.
There the earth is naturally warm,
with its believing hands, its patient ways,
and its uneasiness of old standing dew
that one names a height or a hanging.
Don't show your fear of the grand tour:
nothing is more sweet, more close
than the antelope that looks for a smile.
Blue will be the natural and calm
order to our bodies of the moment.
Some words, some miraculous phrases
will fill our laughing sails,
and to turn pale, dear insensible wound,
to turn pale will be a thing so fresh in its train
of flaming crystals and anemones!
Be still, don't speak to me before drinking
some mouthfuls of poisonous seasons,
meditate in those quiet shawls
that will unroll you under the tempest,
then seize me sweetly with your breath
like the friend who cannot conjure
false departures or uncertain love.

UN
EARLY PROS

PART IV

COLLECTED (1930–1936)

UNCOLLE-
CTED EARLY
PROSE (1930
-1936)

Charles Reznikoff: Sincerity and Objectification

I

Charles Reznikoff (born Brooklyn, N. Y. 1894) himself "set the type by hand and did the presswork" of 375 copies of his *Five Groups of Verse* in 1927. The collection of 67 pages included work published privately in 1918, '19, '20, '21. In 1927, also *Nine Plays*, 113 pages, 400 copies, representing work after 1921, appeared as a collection published by the author. A volume of 271 pages, 400 copies, *By the Waters of Manhattan, An Annual*, i.e. promising future annuals, appeared in 1929, again under the author's imprint, but this time, presumably because of the size of the volume involved, the task of printing and binding had been taken over by a company in Philadelphia.

That no influential American publisher or magazine editor has ever printed Reznikoff's work might supposedly be "explained away" by–"of regional interest." Yet even a cursory glance thru Reznikoff's volumes should affect one's awareness with the retention that this author has written not only of Genesis, Rashi, Uriel Acosta and Jehudah Halevi, but of Nat Turner, Meriwether Lewis, Chatterton, Farquhar and Aphrodite Urania. That notwithstanding these facts Reznikoff's works have received a minimum of public notice is probably salutary to the author's mind–which does "not wish to die, because the eyes can see, the ears hear, the fingers feel so much that is delightful"–as well as to his resignation which is content to do the manual work on his mental and emotional processes as they go on: the author at peace with everyone. That as an immediate result of this situation certain people interested in craftsmanship have missed access to this work is hardly salutary–at least to these people.

For example, concern with the materials and methods of writing has been deprived of the fact that, in 1918, Reznikoff published twelve lines (vide XII, *Five Groups of Verse*) containing in their elements the atmosphere of Eliot's "Waste Land" and "Hollow Men." The poem included the line

> Smooth and white with loss of leaves and bark

and since Eliot's *Poems* were first published in America in 1920, there can hardly be a question of the influence of method in a discussion of the line's value. Reznikoff reprinted this poem in the 1927 collection: one guesses, not for any care the author may have had for the particular dejection expressed, for since that state he has been concerned with other matters, but for the element of method then already apparent in the clarity of image and word-tone.

Simultaneously, Reznikoff excluded, from his 1927 collection, certain early work:

1)   Queen Esther said to herself What is there to fear? We move in our orbits like the stars.

But in the night looking at the black fields and river she could not help thinking of Vashti's white cheeks hollowed like shells.

2)   "Nightmares" containing the lines—
Seeing an ice-cream cart he called the girl away from
      the beggar.
She gorged on a bar of frozen rainbow
And he placed the pennies on the wet top of the cart,
      laughing.

By not re-printing the first example, the author definitely denied himself *symboliste* semi-allegorical gleam; by not re-printing the second example, he anticipated a conviction that surrealism in 1928 was not essentially novel, and that for him at least, ten years earlier, it was not worth doing.

The entire matter involves the process of active literary omission and a discussion of method finding its way in the acceptance of two criteria: sincerity and objectification.

II

Sincerity in writing is the representation of having heard, considered and seen and the certain avowal which follows that "this is so." To the interested, facts appear in such numbers they seem always to escape the attention, there is a constant need to be reminded. Words are reminders, and then they are themselves: and there is a store of veracity the interested wish to return to—after reading work which has aspired vaingloriously to the past and vaguely over the future, and omitted of the present those situations which are pertinent to both what has occurred and what will follow. Ignorance is no excuse, so that it may be said, "that writer" has been sincere in his desires, not in his efforts at rendering himself as it is rendered in words. Judged by this standard, most "accepted" contemporary writing retains barely a suggestion of competence largely filling page-numbered areas. At best there is the hurried look over a locale, the haste which penetrates for a moment and shuts the eyes, shuts them unfortunately to do more writing, since somehow repetition pays tho it has become repetitious; at worst, there is the dating littleness connected with the salesmen of letters and rambling dealers in word bric-a-brac.

In sincerity—which is a representation—shapes appear concomitants of word combinations, precursors of, if there is continuance, completed sound or structure, melody or form. There occurs writing which is the detail, not mirage, of seeing, of thinking with the things as they exist, and of directing them along a line of melody. Shapes suggest themselves, and the mind senses and receives awareness. Parallels sought for in the other arts call up the perfect line of occasional drawing, the clear beginning of sculpture not proceeded with.

Presented with sincerity, the mind even tends to supply in further suggestion, which does not attain rested totality, the totality not always found in sincerity and necessary only for perfect rest, complete appreciation. This rested totality may be called objectification—the apprehension satisfied completely as to appearance of the art form as an object. That is: distinct from print which records action and existence and incites the mind to further suggestion, there exists, tho' it may not be harbored as solidity in the crook of an elbow, writing (audibility in two dimensional print) which is an object or affects the mind as such. The codifications of the rhetoric books may have something to do with an explanation of this attainment, but its character may be simply described as the arrangement, into one apprehended unit, of minor units of sincerity—in other words, the resolving of words and their ideation into structure. Granted that the word combination "minor unit of sincerity" is an ironic index of the degradation of the power of the individual word in a culture which seems hardly to know that each word in itself is an arrangement, it may be said that each word possesses objectification to a powerful degree; but that the facts carried by one word are, in view of the preponderance of facts carried by combinations of words, not sufficiently explicit to warrant a realization of rested totality such as might be designated an art form. Yet the objectification which is a poem, or a unit of structural prose, may exist in a very few lines. Three examples—one of sincerity, and two of objectification—are cited from Reznikoff:

1.   Aphrodite Urania

The ceaseless weaving of the uneven water
                              (*Third Group of Verse*)

2.   Hellenist

As I, barbarian, at last, although slowly, could read Greek,
At "blue-eyed Athena"
I greeted her picture that had long been on the wall:
The head slightly bent forward under the heavy helmet,
As if to listen; the beautiful lips slightly scornful.
                              (not yet published)

3.

How shall we mourn you who are killed and wasted,
Sure that you would not die with your work unended,
As if the iron scythe in the grass stops for a flower.
                              (*First Group of Verse*)

The first example illustrates sincerity, not objectification. Each word in the line "The ceaseless weaving of the uneven water" possesses remarkable energy as a representation of water as action. The title carries much connotative and associative meaning in itself and in relation to the line. Yet the line and title together, tho interdependent, have not been arranged as a unit which appeals to the mind in the condition or relation of an object. What the mind is attracted to is rather the veracity of the particular craft, the validity of writing apprehending the most energetic constituents of possible objectification.

The second and third examples are objectification. In the second, the purposeful crudity of the first line as against the quantitative (not necessarily Classic) hexameter measures of the others, the use of words of two syllables (greeted, picture, slightly, forward, heavy, helmet, listen, slightly, scornful) with suitable variations of words of four and three (barbarian, beautiful), the majority of the words accented on the first syllable, all resolve into a structure (which incidentally translates the Hellenic) to which the mind does not wish to add; nor does it, no more than when it contemplates a definite object by itself. The mind can conceivably prefer one object to another—the energy of the heat which is Aten to the benignness of the light which is Athena. But this is a matter of preference, rather than the invalidation of the object not preferred.*

The second example is so much an object that the title, "Hellenist," is a mere tag not even necessary for designation. The third example also needs no title and has none. The fact that it was originally an epitaph for Gaudier Brzeska may compel the attention of a few but adds nothing to the poem as object. Objectification in this poem is attained in the balance of the first two lines; the third line adds the grace of ornament in a simile, as might the design painted around a simple bowl.

At any time, objectification in writing is rare. That is: the poems or the prose structures of a generation are few. Properly, no verse should be called a poem if it does not convey the totality of perfect rest. In contemporary writing, the poems of Ezra Pound alone possess objectification to a most constant degree; his objects are musical shapes. Objectification is to be found in Poems VIII, X, XVIII, XXIII, XXVI in Wm. Carlos Williams' *Spring and All*. With the exception of Marianne Moore's poems beginning "An Octopus" and "Like a Bulrush" and T. S. Eliot's "Mr. Appollinax" [*sic*], progressions of sincerity and not objectification are to be found in these poets. It is interesting that the work of Marianne Moore is largely a portrait of the writer's character intent upon the presentation which is sincerity, rather than the revealed rest of objectification which

---

* It is assumed epistemological problems do not affect existence, that a personal structure of relations might be a definite object or vice versa.

is, for example, "An Octopus." In the work of T. S. Eliot it is often the single quatrain (or whatever the unit of composition may be) which possesses objectification; together, his quatrains are a series rather than the entirety of a poem. Whatever objectification the writings of E. E. Cummings possess (i.e. *Him*; Song III, Amores VII, Unrealities V in *Tulips and Chimneys*; at least a half dozen poems in *Is 5*) is an equilibrium between the extremely connotative speech of an energy of five senses which are vitally young and an aptness of purposeful print and musical rhetoric weaving this energy into an interlacing (sometimes, unfortunately astray). To what extent objectification bearing the trade mark of the Americas may be expected out of a geography and humanity constantly shifting is indicated with ironic evenness in Robert McAlmon's *North America, Continent of Conjecture* (1929): mock historicalness, positing that "in the justness of her undertakings [America] had a strict resemblance to other countries and still has it," joins isolate attenuations—chorus blues of a possible "American Songbag"—and offers not merely North America's but the race's "Unfinished Poem." More objectification cannot be expected from writing than from its subject matter—whatever exists. Still humans live alongside of objects and those interested assume poems are such. The degree of objectification in the work of Charles Reznikoff is small.

It is questionable, however, whether the state of rest achieved by objectification is more pertinent to the mind than presentation in detail. Probably deferring to an ideal of perfection, Reznikoff has called his writings in cadence not poems, but verse. They are actually almost constant examples of sincerity. For, of writing one may at least expect not the meretricious—a contact with concepts which does not result in, but misses, presentation.

A Tapestry

Isolde of the white Hands and her knights, holding their noses and
    laughing
At prisoners whose bellies soldiers open, pulling the guts into basins.
                    (X—*Fourth Group of Verse*)

            •   •   •   •

        - - - - we boys would walk
slowly

To the lots between the streets and the marshes;
     - - - - - - -   the
ball game—
In a noisy, joyous crowd, lemonade men out in the fringe tinkling
    their bells beside the yellow carts.

                    (XVII—*Fourth Group of Verse*)

         •   •   •   •

Love, let us lie down here
On the warm grass,
Glad that we are so near.

Watch on the shores of sleep
The still waves pass,
Feel that sea's languid air
Move in our hair,

And turn at times to trace
In quiet wise,
Each other's smiling face
And sleepy eyes.

                    (XXV—*Fourth Group of Verse*)

There is to be noted in these lines the isolation of each noun so that in itself it is an image, the grouping of nouns so that they partake of the quality of things being together without violence to their individual intact natures. The simple sensory adjectives are as necessary to the presentation as the nouns. If Reznikoff has written elsewhere of the "imperious dawn," the single abstract adjective occurs without the pang of reverie. The metaphor, as in all good writing, has been presented with conciseness in a word. Another writer would have at least a distended clause on "Necessity with ruling arm." The disadvantage of strained metaphor is not that it is necessarily sentimental (the sentimental may at times have its positive personal qualities) but that it carries the mind to a diffuse everywhere and leaves it nowhere. The belief that writing should not do the last is not assumed a moot point. A writer will not pile on metaphor, no more than a musician sensitive to declamation will destroy Shakespeare's line in an arrangement like "Co-ome away, co-ome away, death." One is brought back to the entirely of the single word which is in itself a relation, an implied metaphor, an arrangement and a harmony.[*]

> Ships dragged into the opaque green of the sea,
> Visible winds flinging houses apart—
> And here the poplar lifting the pavement an inch.
>
> (XX—*Third Group of Verse*)

. . . .

> A white curtain turning in an open window.
>
> A swan, dipping a white neck in the trees' shadow,
> Hardly beating the water with golden feet.
>
> Sorrow before her
> Was gone like noise from a street,
> Snow falling.
>
> (*Second Group of Verse*)

The economy of presentation in this writing is a reassertion of faith that the combined letters—the words—are absolute symbols for objects, states, acts, inter-relations, thoughts about them. If not, why use words? The words, for example, render the equivalent of the sounds of things, sometimes of birds:

---

[*] Note: The creation of new words, as in Joyce's *Work in Progress*, obviously does not violate the old; he is merely creating new arrangements and new harmonies. Incidentally, Gertrude Stein does the opposite: i.e. she uses old words for all the possible connotative and grammatical associations she can get out of them.

The traveller
Whom a bird's notes surprise
His eyes
Search the trees—

(not yet published)

and, of birds, sometime with covert irony:

Our nightingale, the clock
Our lark,
Perched on the mantel
Sings so steadily:
A bird of prey!

(not yet published)

In a work most indigenously of These States, and beginning perhaps a century of writing, as Wordsworth's preface of 1800 began it in England, in *Spring and All* (1923), Wm. Carlos Williams writes:

Crude symbolism is to associate emotions with natural phenomena such as anger with lightning, flowers with love[;] it goes further and associates certain textures with

- - - - - - - -

It is typified by the use of the word "like" or that "evocation" of the "image" which served us for a time. Its abuse is apparent. The insignificant "image" may be 'evoked' never so ably and still mean nothing.

An excellent specific for writers: yet the correction of the contemporary fault does not necessarily dictate the use of the bare catalog, tho' the last may be used more effectively than in Whitman—Whitman himself did it; the simile can be not a wandering ornament, but a confirmation of the objects or acts which the writer is setting down. "Likes" have often been seen together, or have been strongly felt together, as in Reznikoff's:

From the bare twigs
Rows of drops, like shining buds are hanging.

(First Group of Verse)

i.e. "The rain is over"—and each rain drop is close to where a bud might be—on the twigs.

The Idiot.

With green stagnant eyes,
Arms and legs
Loose ends of string in a wind,

Keep smiling at your father.

(Second Group of Verse)

The arms and legs may be uncontrolled as are the loose ends of string in a wind; but, the idiot may also be holding a string of which the ends are loose in the wind. What is equivocal here confers distinction upon method.

Evening

The trees in the windless field like a herd asleep.

(Fourth Group of Verse)

To confuse trees with a herd at evening is not an unusual fata morgana.

The green slime—a thicket of young trees standing in brown water;
With knobs like muscles, a naked tree stretches up,
Dead; and a dead duck, head sunk in the water as if diving.

(Fourth Group of Verse)

a tree—"knobs like muscles" ... "naked" ... "stretches up": the anthropomorphism seems natural—muscles are also like knobs—it is such observation which was perhaps responsible for the early tree myths of the race. "As if diving": the duck may have been diving.

> The white edges of the clouds like veining in a stone.
> *(Fourth Group of Verse)*

"Veining"—suggests an edge which surrounds the white which may be stony.

> Old men, wrinkled as knuckles, on the stoops.
> *(Fourth Group of Verse)*

Both the faces and the knuckles of the old men are wrinkled: the stoops may be built of a few stairs which are arranged in a composition of lines with the lines of the knuckles and the wrinkles.

> The fingers of your thoughts
> Are moulding your face
> Ceaselessly.
>
> The wavelets of your thoughts
> Are washing your face
> Beautiful.
> *(First Group of Verse)*

This is not the crude symbolism of "your thoughts are fingers"—the thoughts are actually thinking of fingers, of wavelets, which react upon the face. The repeated durations of the two successive thoughts each measured by the same number of syllables to the line, the equivalence of the line forms in the first stanza to those of the second, make for a symmetrical structure which is a poem.

• • • •

This preoccupation with the accuracy of detail in writing—which is sincerity—is evident on a larger scale in Reznikoff's narrative verse, perhaps the most neglected contribution to verse writing in America in the last ten years. Avoiding the subterfuge of those who have "written narrative poems" with an eye on the glory which was Greece (Sophocles or *The Anthology*), or the glamour which was Arthurian romance, or the agility which was Chaucer, etc., etc.,—a subterfuge which has tended to confirm a suspicion that narrative poetry is perhaps not easy to our age—Reznikoff, in his third and fourth groups of verse, has again looked about him (in the boroughs of New York) and written down verse which is definitely his own and thus *sincerely* contemporary.

Among these poems there is this example of objectification:

> The shoemaker sat in the cellar's dusk beside his bench and sewing
>> machine, his large, blackened hands, finger tips flattened and
>> broad, busy.
> Through the grating in the sidewalk over his window, paper and dust
>> were falling year by year.
>
> At evening Passover would begin. The sunny street was crowded. The
>> shoemaker could see the feet of those who walked over the grating.
> He had one pair of shoes to finish and he would be through.
> His friend came in, a man with a long, black beard, in shabby, dirty
>> clothes, but with shoes newly cobbled and blacked.
> "Beautiful outside, really the world is beautiful."
> A pot of fish was boiling on the stove. Sometimes the water bubbled
>> over and hissed. The smell of the fish filled the cellar.
> "It must be beautiful in the park now. After our fish we'll take a walk in
>> the park." The shoemaker nodded.
> The shoemaker hurried his work on the last shoe. The pot on the stove
>> bubbled and hissed. His friend walked up and down the cellar in
>> shoes newly cobbled and blacked.
>> (XXXXVIII—*Fourth Group of Verse*)

For the rest there is sincerity—in the rendering of character and speech:

> When the club met in her home, embarrassed, she asked them not to begin: her
>   father wanted to speak to them.
> The members whispered to each other, "Who is her father?"
> "I thank you, young men and women," he said, "for the honour of your visit. I
>   suppose you would like to hear some of my poems." And he began to chant.
>   (XXXXVI—*Fourth Group of Verse*)

in the rendering of speech of our time singular enough to be recorded in a poem:

> "I hope you get it."
>   (XXXII—*Fourth Group of Verse*)

in the tension of tragedy:

> She sat by the window opening into the airshaft,
> And looked across the parapet
> At the new moon.
>
> She would have taken the hairpins out of her carefully coiled hair,
> And thrown herself on the bed in tears;
> But he was coming and her mouth had to be pinned into a smile.
>
> If he would have her, she would marry whatever he was,
> She who, slim and gentle once, would soon become clumsy, talking harshly.
>
> A knock. She lit the gas and opened her door.
> Her aunt and the man—skin loose under his eyes, the face slashed with wrinkles.
> "Come in," she said as gently as she could and smiled.
>   (XI—*Third Group of Verse*)

From where she lay she could see the snow crossing the darkness slowly,
Thick about the arc-lights like moths in summer.

She could just move her head. She had been lying so for months.

Her son was growing full and broad-shouldered, his face becoming like that
    of her father,
Dead now for years.

She lay under the bed-clothes as if she, too, were covered with snow,
Calm, facing the blackness of night,
Through which the snow fell in the crowded movement of stars.

Dead, nailed in a box, her son was being sent to her,
Through fields and cities cold and white with snow.

(XIII—Third Group of Verse)

In the last two quotations, melody has been stopped (see Pound's *Cathay*, in which melody is continuous—even a line such as "Emotion is born out of habit" is melodious in the context) and monodies of recurrent prose paragraphs have been substituted. The total rhythm has been lulled to emphasize each word's particular hush, with the result that objectification, inevitably recognized as the complete satisfaction derived from melody in a poem, is missed. Yet the lives of Reznikoff's people slowly occur in the sincerity of the craft with which he has chosen to subdue them. One returns in the end not to the aging girl at the window, nor to the sick mother who does not know that her dead son is being sent to her thru the snow, but to sincerity which has seen, considered, and weighed the tone these things have when rendered in only necessary words.

Analogies sidetrack, but in an explanation of the elementary they are convenient elements. The cabinet maker can say this much I know: this is craft; one begins here to go further; you don't know a square edge when you see it, do you expect these pieces crookedly nailed together to withstand dust—take a look at that space. The same is true of words and the shortcomings of writers. To the vulgar utilitarian a bookcase rocks perhaps, but a preponderance of verbal carelessness does not even wobble. Moreover, one is fooled by the "vested interests" into the belief that "everybody is writing." To attract these interests, the "purple passages" in Reznikoff might be quoted:

> These inconsiderable seconds fill
> The basins of our lives to overflowing,
> And we are emptied
> Into the sink and pipes of death.
>
> (*Fifth Group of Verse*)

"I have a quarrel with the clock" and "How furiously it ticks this fine morning" is more worthy of notice.

Perhaps what is bad in Reznikoff's verse might be pointed out. But where sincerity in writing is present there is enough content so that the insincere may be cut out at will and information not ignorance remains. Sincerity among authors differs with the range of their sensations and apperceptions, but what is negative to sincerity remains negative to all who are sincere. So much that is vicious, as writing, is omitted from all of them, and of these there are probably no more than can be counted on the fingers of both hands in a generation. Reznikoff is included among these. One speaks of sincerity as of that ability which is necessary for existence if one is a writer. Naturally, the bubble does not know what a more actual body brushing past it may do to it, and in a minute it is not even a bubble.

III

> Showing a torn sleeve, with stiff and shaking fingers the old man
> Pulls off a bit of baked apple, shiny with sugar,
> Eating with reverence food, the great comforter.
>
> (*Third Group of Verse*)

It is a salutary phase of Reznikoff's sincerity that the verbal qualities of his shorter poems do not form mere pretty bits (American Poetry, circa 1913) but suggest (as in the quotation heading this paragraph) entire aspects of thought: economics, beliefs, literary analytics etc. This fusion of concise writing with implicit thinking is hardly accidental. At any rate, if his short poems recall the Japanese and Chinese lyric, his plays recall the *Noh*.

Religion having long ago ceased being naturally effective in the west, it cannot be exactly said that Reznikoff's plays have that religiosity of the Noh which are for a "stage where every subsidiary art is bent precisely upon holding the faintest shade of a difference" (W. B. Yeats). But the direction of their poetry is very similar to that of the Noh:

> The rain will stop any day now . . .
> I was in the garden this morning. The inner leaves of the tree are turned brown . . .
> You have been too long over the Bible, Brother.
> Take the horse and splash through the puddles of the road
> The way Father used to . . .
> There's a puddle in Father's coffin, I suppose.
> Death is so trite and yet—
> But we should be the happier
> That Father has left this bubble, Earth, for Paradise.
>   - - - - - - -
>
> I know all the cracks in the walls:
> Which divide and which run into the floor or stop,
> An inch from the ceiling . . .
>   (*Uriel Acosta*)

> But day by day we journeyed on, and sun and moon were friendly, sun and stars;
> Until it seemed our journey might last centuries and centuries,
> While lands covered with grain became desert and cities field again,
> And rivers changed their courses and seas their beds,
> But we, unsubdued by any tribe, journey on
> Across all deserts and all seas.
> But it ends:
>
>   (*Abram in Egypt*)

Canynge. The marble flooring of my vault had fallen in,
And into me, waist-deep in sand, an elm
Stuck its twisted roots.

- - - - - - -

Chatterton. No wonder you ghosts cry out against
The clamp of death,
Lord Mayor Canynge, Lady Mayoress, and Priest Rowley:
Any weather is fair weather to a warm coat.

(*Chatterton*)

The unusual appearance of these ghosts as part of the drama in *Chatterton* is not a ritual with Reznikoff, yet the latent resemblance to the Noh ritual is striking. And essentially, Reznikoff's plays, like the Noh, are poetic expressions centering in superior sensitized minds naturally involved in religion. It is not the particular situations which are important, but the way things affect these minds and make for tragedy or irony, and, in turn, the peace which they manage to make with this tragedy or irony. Superior sensitized minds do not always succeed at making peace with things, or do in a way which is suicide (Meriwether Lewis, Marianne in *Captive Israel*, John Brown and Lincoln in *Coral*).

The expression of these minds being the important thing, stage directions may be dispensed with. The longest play need be no more than 27 pages (i.e. *Chatterton*, incidentally, the earliest written and not as good as the others as examples of poetic craft); the Civil War may be rendered in 12, the sojourn of Abram in Egypt in 3—the superior Pharaoh need not even appear, it is enough that his messengers can say to Abram:

Pharaoh from whom no thing is hidden knows
That Sarai is your wife,

- - - - - - -

The liars Pharaoh has inherited are his,
But you go!

In fact, the flat stage, with its usual stuffed sets, may be dispensed with; the words in these plays are the stage. To be acted—and these plays should be, for the superior minds in them are not discussions of ideas but characters (personae) in concise dramatic situations, tangible in the speech of poetry rather than amid scenic lumber—they would demand, of course, performers and a stage of their own. The Noh cannot be deferred to directly: the *Nine Plays* have an individual rather than national source. But, as in the Noh performance, consideration would deal with a stage in which all the elements of good writing are brought into the round, and in which the significance of sensitized minds "amid things," not merely immediate scenes, are emphasized. Perhaps a round stage—natural to all poetic drama, since the spectator is there given the opportunity to be more intimate all around with the performer—suggests itself: a stage surface across and around and within which anything can happen—the world, to quote Reznikoff's *The Black Death*, from which one dream may have gone, "not what caused the dream."

Of course, Reznikoff indicates: "President Lincoln at a desk"; "A theatre gallery"; but he indicates also: "Night. The Pacific surf is heard" and "the heat of day." In *Abram in Egypt*, the scene is indicated only in the dialogue. In *Rashi*, time, without being mentioned as a stage property, moves thru the play with a perfect lyrical order. In five pages the scene intrinsically shifts three times, characters appear and fall into their place in the action, and are absorbed in the movement of a poem whose continuity never halts till the end.

Speech is the main control in the drama of the *Nine Plays*. To those interested in a native American drama this fact should be important, especially as illustrated in the plays dealing with native themes: *Coral*, which in its synopsis of the Civil War poses the implied question as to whether men, like coral, would be able to build on their skeletons dry land at last (cf. *Waters of Manhattan*); and *Meriwether Lewis*, which deals with the development of material pathways at the expense of the driven, isolate spirit. In justice to the plays, the themes should not be stated. It is more pertinent that the negro Nat Turner should be heard speaking:

> "Nat Turner isn't caught easily.
> Served them right, wouldn't listen to the Lord,
> Filled their bellies with cider, swilled and swilled.
> But I listened,
> O yes Lord,
> Ever since that morning I stood behind the plough and
> heard You."

The rhythm of the negro chant is accurate here (compare examples in Adams, *Congaree Sketches*, North Carolina Press).

Lincoln speaks to an old neighbor of Sangamon County:

> Poor Berry ...
> You get to know people and to—like them,
> Then ... (*The attendant shows in a Quaker who looks like Lincoln*)
> Sometimes they come back like you, Joe. (*Lincoln and Joe shake
> hands and Joe goes out.*)

The stage directions merely serve to show how really tacit Lincoln's speech is. Again, Meriwether Lewis, with another, both hungry, dragging off the head of a dead horse in the snow: "Come on now, and we two Salomes help each other with this head." The speech implying the isolation of the speaker gives the American scene: poetically, the speech is as significantly American as the poetry of the Noh is significantly Japanese.

IV

Reznikoff's prose, *By the Waters of Manhattan*, a fragment of a novel, and the several stories, "Apocrypha," "Nudnik," "Salesman" and "Passage at Arms,"* is an extension of the subject matter of the narrative verse. For that matter, all of Reznikoff's prose might be called apocrypha: i.e. these are stories of doubtful religiosity in the more or less canonical history of his race. This happens to the Jew outside the Bible: "Lot became one of the men that wander through the city, that late at night lie down on newspapers in the hall of a tenement or on the porch of a public building. - - - - Abraham was happy. His son was a better business man than even he had been. - - - - Nahor, too, was doing well, but in a quiet way: nobody heard much of him." In this prose, Reznikoff's Jews have strayed as far from their traditional history as Joyce's "Dubliners" from the Celtic myths. In both cases, moreover, they remain "a stubborn and stiff-necked people."

As in Joyce, writing here is not merely the story of the characters of a people, but the prose. There is more room for detailed story-telling in Reznikoff's prose than

---

* The first three of the four stories appeared in *The Menorah Journal*, respectively in Feb. 1928, Nov. 1929, Dec. 1929. The last is not yet published. *By the Waters of Manhattan* has since been published in revised form as a complete novel by [Charles Boni] Paper Books, New York, 1930.

in the short narrative verse, but there are never spaces in the prose which sincerity, observable in the data of presentation, has not filled. And there is variety:

> "I've lots besides Japanese paintings. Here is something from the Chinese. Hold one end of the scroll, please. Now," and Joel made believe he was unrolling it, "look at this prairie fire. What a sweep of flames! See the blackened skeletons of trees left behind. The flames are coming down on this field of large feathery stalks of grass. Here is a gazelle in front of the flames, its head lifted in agony. Here is the white tail of another, diving into the grass. The sky in back is golden with fire, in front black with smoke." He waved the scroll aside without troubling to roll it up.

> (Pg 45—*By the Waters of Manhattan*)

> He made a cup of his hands: the water from the faucet, even though he let it run a long time, had tiny flakes of black in it. He decided not to drink.

> (Pg 47—*By the Waters of Manhattan*)

> As for the barber-shop, he was not so accustomed to dissect his feelings as to be able to explain why he liked that very wait which his son thought a waste of time. Really, when his "next" came, he was sorry. There were, to begin with, the other customers, neighbors and friends; they talked over the news, how work was coming on in their shops, news of the union, news of the world, all spiced with witticisms. There he would sit in the comfortable cane-bottom chair and rest. During a lull in the talk he would read a newspaper. All the newspapers were there, he did not have to buy any. This little saving was pleasant. The barbers, too, were always polite: he was a customer; and that made him feel important. And the shop had such a good smell: bay rum and the violet perfume of talcum powder. Now and then a customer ordered a hair tonic. This sent a sharp pleasant odour into the air. And

then the luxury of stretching out and, utterly passive, to feel the blade take a week's growth of beard from his face. How could he explain all this to his son who in a contemptuous voice was urging him to use a safety-razor?

(Pp 94–95—*By the Waters of Manhattan*)

He came to City Hall Park. The morning newspapers were out. In the morning he would have to grab his bag of millinery to join the rest in the hunt for orders, more orders, never enough: the maw of the shop would stretch to hold all he could bring. The trade would be coming to town; his spring line must be ready. Hoods of that woolen stuff were played out, dead as last year; new styles, but the same business, the old futility.

(Pg 100—*By the Waters of Manhattan*)

Tweedlesky—a squeaky name, he thought, like a pair of new shoes or twelve mice playing in a cupboard, but Tweedlekoff ends softly with a polite bow. They saw a bald head over a book—Tweedlekoff thought of Martial's verse—I hate a hairy, bald man. . . . "He comes in here everyday," the girl went on. "If that seat is taken, he cannot work. He waits till it's empty."

"This place is full of lunatics," said Tweedlekoff. He himself thought best walking backwards and forwards . . . and he could even write that way—of course only a few words at a time. Lately he trained himself to read while walking about.

("Passage at Arms")

In English—Reznikoff does for the Jews what Joyce did for the Irish in *Dubliners*. As with Joyce, Reznikoff's art is a conscious effort, perhaps a tacit assertion that the more contemporary writing has to compete with other and newer interpretations of present day living, the more conscious contemporary writing must become. Unless one trusts that events themselves (as in the past) will be powerful and new enough to create a new way of saying things which sees, hears, does, and thus comments, but not by way of discursive discussion. Anticipating the "advanced guard" of social upheaval, Reznikoff, in his prose and verse, has written of shops, of pedlars frequenting them and smelling the apples they sell, of men shouting above the noise of machines, the subway, factories, salesmen, and the business of making a living. At the same time, certain also that this matter must be rendered in words, he has set about learning their craft—which is sincerity as it has been defined here. Interested in craft, he has not found it derogatory to his production to infuse his care for significant detail and precision into the excellent verbalisms of others. He has, therefore, recorded his mother's autobiography (vide pages by Sarah Reznikoff in *By the Waters of Manhattan*) and edited passages of the Bible. In "Editing and Glosses" he has given the main narrative and verbal substance of most of the Pentateuch and of the episodes connected with the life of David. For the most part, the "Glosses" are quotations out of the King James' Version, verified or altered by a study of the Hebrew. The narrative has been rendered concisely in emphasized cadence and given the condition of Reznikoff's mental bearings and literal art.

It is more important for the communal good that individual authors should spend their time recording and objectifying good writing wherever it is found (note the use of quotations in Marianne Moore from Government Guide Books, Pound's translations and quotations in the *Cantos*, Wm. Carlos Williams' passages out of Spanish and Early American sources in *In the American Grain*, etc.) than that a plenum of authors should found their fame on all sorts of personal vagueness—often called "sophistication."

Recording—

> I have run through a troop,
> And jumped over a wall;
> He teaches my hands war,
> To bend the bow;
> He has given me my enemies:
> I made them as dust before the wind,
> I threw them away as dirt in the street.

—Reznikoff has done better than improvising on "David and Michal." Admitting in conversation that he would now have this final passage of the "Glosses" omitted, Reznikoff's defense of his lapse may well be the continual strain of thinking about these mental things to oneself amid the practical strain of having to publish one's own work for a "literary" market not interested in sincerity as craft. And yet, sincerity, even in isolation,* persists.

---

*   In this connection it is necessary to note two exceptions:

      I - Mr. Malcolm Cowley commented briefly but favorably on an early collection of Reznikoff's verse published in 1920, but since then revised.

      II - Mr. Ezra Pound has expressed the opinion that Reznikoff's Verse and Prose are "good"; also, "after reading Reznikoff's work, suspicions as to

           1. whether the next wave of literature will be jewish

           2. whether the lack of prose in german is due to drawing off the idiomatic energy into yiddish."

Imagisme

L'Influence du Symbolisme Français sur la Poésie Américaine (de 1910 à 1920), by René Taupin. Paris, Librairie Honoré Champion, 1929.

M. Taupin's book should be translated into English. With the essays on the French symbolists and the new poetry in Pound's *Pavannes and Divisions* and *Instigations*, whose influence M. Taupin acknowledges, and the pertinently fired improvisations in Williams's *Spring and All* and other of his occasional critical assaults, it forms perhaps the only printed literature worthy of respect in this matter, which, after all, is: what is poetry?

The crux of M. Taupin's subject is the Imagist Movement (1913) which destroyed the sentimental ornamentation of American verse-writing of 1910 and earlier by reacting with the method employed by French symbolism. M. Taupin, however, knows better than to erect another cenotaph of literary history. Escaping the pigeon-holed generalities of historians of letters, he qualifies thirty pages on Imagist theories:

"It is more accurate not to consider Imagism a doctrine, or even a school of poetry, but the gathering of certain poets who, for several weeks rather than several months, found themselves in accord on a few important points, and wished to prescribe their ideas on how to rescue poetry from the germs of decadence, which for so long a period had been enervating it."

M. Taupin's prime concern is with the individuality of these poets, despite their "human interest" as a group. The matter of an influence acting in common upon individual temperaments results, therefore, in differences which have variegated it and been variegated by it in accordance with: (1) its presence in the air: sometimes the proximity of a poet's edified literary acquaintances, however conscious or unconscious a poet may be of the almost literal drafts around him; (2) coincidence of temperament affected and the temperament only apparently, not actually affecting; since the modality of events of a period of fifty or seventy-five years may show, at any time of their calendar, two similar individuals, different as to locale, and contemporary or anachronistic as to their birth and mortuary dates; (3) conscious choice or rejection of a literary tradition.

M. Taupin's examples are more to the point than generalizations: (1) William Carlos Williams does not, as M. Taupin suggests, "flatter himself with being under cover of Europe." If its cover, to Williams, has not been a constant chagrin, he would, nevertheless, much prefer the appreciation of his own Americans. It is true, however, that Williams has been conversant "with people, like Pound, who have extracted from French poetry all which they thought necessary to the development of American literature." (2), Eliot, in "Sweeney," recalled André Salmon in "Les Veufs de Rose" (1910). Also, in *Prikaz*, "Salmon realized, in something not unlike a film, an indefinable sentiment stronger than any *information* on the most poetic matter of the time: the Bolshevik Revolution"; to transcribe with similar precision a sentiment of the same order, Eliot wrote *The Waste Land*. Furthermore, Eliot found in Mallarmé and Laforgue qualities of the English metaphysical poets: and the process of assimilating them was peculiar to Eliot.

(3), As for Pound: "He has looked for the necessary perfection of technique among the French who have best preserved the Latin virtues. He has been reproached with changing his models too often, but it has not been difficult to show that he has always remained the same. When he found a new model, he accepted him only if he complied with his tradition, which is that of Villon, Gautier and Corbière."

From these examples it is evident that M. Taupin does more than trace influence. The question of influence as the conscious acceptance of a literary tradition borders on the second term in the title of M. Taupin's book.

Determining T. S. Eliot's relations, M. Taupin makes several distinctions:

"He allied himself with French symbolism, not the vague symbolism of Samain, not the symbolism of forms and colors of Henri de Régnier, but that of Baudelaire, when he expresses a definite torment by concrete images, of Corbière when he makes an object visible, of Laforgue when he dresses in irony an emotion which has submitted to decorum and the world."

Like Pound, not interested merely in "a smack at chaos," but in literature and models of literature, M. Taupin is also aware of the distinction between Rimbaud, the rapidity of whose images carries over the tactility of words (in "Vénus Anadyomène," not in the *Illuminations*), and Mallarmé whose verbalism still floats in a dream.

It is obvious that what is important to M. Taupin is not *symbolism* in general, but distinctions between the work of various writers commonly called symbolists, between image and haze, direct verbal description and hallucination. Unlike the literary historians who are naturally respectful and praise the wrong things, M. Taupin is a critic who is interested in those processes of symbolism which are poetry.

He judges American poetry, between 1910 and 1920, by the same standards. The contributions of Pound, Williams, Eliot, Marianne Moore and H. D., comprising M. Taupin's preference, are the only possible contributions: image, music and verbalism. He recognizes that the French influence was only one among many: the French qualities found in the new poetry were obtained by the study of other literatures and almost always from the old poets who know all that it is necessary to know of rhythm, concentration and image.

Naturally the values poets deal with are alike for all of them. "Bare ruined choirs where late the sweet birds sang": omit the word "sweet" and read: "Bare ruined choirs where late the birds sang"... and the line's poetic substance is not very different from Rimbaud. Not that Shakespeare's line has not more tonal value—and certainly more value of cadence—than the "the twitter of birds" or some other expression; but omitting "sweet," one thinks of the English line as it might possibly sound in French: i.e. "Moi, l'autre hiver, plus sourd que les cerveaux d'enfants" (*Bateau Ivre*).

American Poetry
1920–1930

A Sequel to M. Taupin's Book, 1910–1920[*]

1

About the most recent events in American poetry, M. Taupin writes: "Eliot should be considered as forming the transition between pure imagism and the new symbolism which is more complex; between a first generation which sought sincerity of expression and of rhythm, and a new generation of poets taking from the world of their conscience forms and sounds to combine them according to the laws of harmony and sensibility and to express the movements of their brain" (p. 287). Given one collective brain which M. Taupin's statement qualifies, the brain and conscience of Joyce are that of his literary generation. After him: his visible influence on Cummings (of course, Cummings might have existed of himself)—"mil(lions of aflickf)litter ing brightmillion ofS hurl;edindodg:ing"; on what is fairly readable in Hart Crane—*smithereens*; on the newest generation of *Blues* (edited by C. H. Ford, Columbus, Miss., 1929), mainly via Cummings.[**]

"No man ever writes much poetry that matters" (Ezra Pound). Yet if a man once does, one likes to see him continue, for at least twenty years. Deviating, then, from M. Taupin's possibly evolutionary implications of statement (though his word 'complex' does not necessarily suggest improvement on what preceded) one may study the progress of individual work rather than its use in an 'evolution' of poetry.

---

[*] *L'Influence du Symbolisme français sur la Poésie américaine (de 1910 à 1920)*, par René Taupin. Paris, 1929.

[**] Cummings' Elizabethan *in american* became Chaucerian *in american* in Ernest Walsh's Poems, *This Quarter*, No. 3: at times curious amoretti, at time poetry. The influence of Joyce is also evident, but then Walsh too was Irish. Joyce's simultaneity of various connotations is paralleled in Williams, but strangely enough Williams' work shows also a kinship with the work of Gertrude Stein, which in it simplified analysis is Joyce's opposite. Kenneth Rexroth—out of Williams' *The Great American Novel*; thus, out of Joyce and Stein. But new writers had perhaps better be given a chance to find their own forbears.

The first generation, then, developed, after 1920 or shortly before, as did Joyce, literary mechanisms for expressing the movements of individual brains. An accurate consideration of the matter of influence may even have to deal with the relation of Pound's "First Canto," opening with the voyage of Ulysses, and of the process of immediately shifting from one fact to the next in the other *Cantos*, to Joyce. Pound's first three *Cantos* preceded Joyce's *Ulysses* by some years.

Pound, Williams, Eliot, Marianne Moore (not H. D., whose later work, with the exception of "Lethe," "Hymen" and very few other poems, suffers from an Anglicized dilution of metric and speech value, defeating her double effort towards emotional expanse and condensation) did not stop with the monolinear image; they extended it to include "a greater accessibility to experience" (Marianne Moore, "N. Y."). For that matter, they never started merely with the image (1913). They are thus not a gang-plank for a younger generation to step onto. Or if they are, their individual rungs matter, and Cummings is maybe on shore or sometimes certainly on board.

Of the younger generation and those five or seven years older present: several of the younger generation have been published by Mr. Pound in *The Exile* 2, 3 and 4 (Carl Rakosi, Payson Loomis, Zukofsky). Robert McAlmon in *Unfinished Poem* has recalled in its inclusiveness of the American mock-historical, geographical scene, the scope of Marianne Moore's "An Octopus," retained an isolate individualism similar to hers while communizing quotation, hardly ever reached her incisiveness—the definite hardness of perhaps Whitman when he writes of a stallion "Head high in the forehead, wide between the ears"—and added the indigenous cynicism of American song blues. Ezra Pound's conversation of American personae in the *Cantos* is much better than the conversation of similar personae in McAlmon's *Portrait of a Generation* (1926) and *Unfinished Poem* (1929).

Charles Reznikoff (b. 1894), in *Five Groups of Verse 1918-1927* and *Nine Plays*, has shown a capacity for becalmed accuracy of concrete idea in cadence; as, also, in the unpublished "After Rain":

> The motor cars in the shining rain move in
> semicircles of spray, semicircles of spray.

In "The Shoemaker," *Rashi* and the unpublished "Landing at Jamestown," after Edward Arber's sources, *The Works of Capt. John Smith* (*The English Garland*), he gives the composite of objectified fact which makes a poem:

The English in Virginia April 1607

They landed and could
    see nothing but
    meadows and tall
    trees—

Cypress, nearly three
    fathoms about at the
    roots,

Rising straight for
    sixty or eighty feet
    without a branch.

In the woods were
    cedars, oaks, and
    walnut-trees;

Some beech, some elm,
    black walnut, ash,
    and sassafras; mul-
    berry trees in
    groves.

Honey-suckle and
    other vines hanging
    in clusters on
    many trees.

They stepped on
  violets and other
  sweet flowers,

Many kinds in many
  colors; straw-
  berries and rasp-
  berries were on
  the ground.

Black birds with red
  shoulders were
  flying about.

And many small birds,
  some red, some blue;
The woods were full
  of deer;

And running
  everywhere
  fresh water—
  brooks, rundles,
  springs and creeks.

In the twilight,
  through the thickets
  and tall grass,

Creeping upon all
  fours—the
  savages! their
  bows in their
  mouths.

Reznikoff attains here a poised balance of picture in the resultant equilibrium of a conflict between stress and counting syllables so that they give an image—precision and concision. The principle of varying the stress of a regular meter and counting the same number of syllables to the line is thus transferred from 'traditional' to cadenced verse. Williams began this procedure in Spring and All: that is, not that he made each line of a stanza or printed division carry absolutely the same number of syllables—neither in his case nor in Reznikoff's "Jamestown" does the practice appear to have been intended—but there seems to have been a decided awareness of the printed, as well as the quantitative, looseness of vers libre. Obviously, what counts is quantity; print only emphasizes—yet, printing correctly, a poet (Williams or Cummings) shows his salutary gift of quantity.*

If, as M. Taupin has shown, *La poésie en Amérique aujourd'hui parle français*— Americans do not need to blush if it is 'la poésie'—Reznikoff's poetry, singularly, does

---

* Zukofsky, in two Dedications, "Tibor Serly" and "Diego Rivera," counted the number of words to the line, in this manner necessarily restricting the number of syllables but allowing for variations that might make the quantity interesting:

from "Tibor Serly":

Bodies
Of waves
Whose crests

Spear air
Here rolls

The sea
Go chase

It—a
Salt pact

Ranged over
Bars—white

Ribs pervade
In constant

Measures the
Rounds—etc

from "Diego Rivera":

Executives of industry,

Rich stone heads
Conferring at tables
We peasants and

Workers, our faces
Becoming us more
Than frescoes of saints

Marshal to say:
We are the
Heads over industry.

Williams seems also, perhaps not too consciously, to have counted the number of words to the line in the poems of *Spring and All*. The printed arrangement of two lines or three lines, in the manner of couplets and terza rima, derives also from Williams and was used by Z. because it makes for emphasized clarity of image. At this point the matter under discussion goes back to the feeling for image in handwriting and type—vide Pound's translation of Fenollosa, *The Chinese Written Character*.

not speak French; but neither does it speak immemorial English in so many light-stress syllables of regular verse, or speak prettified octopus-Whitman, as Carl Sandburg when he says *Good Morning, America*, and but for one or two poems on butterslips or some other kind of flower, really says Goodbye, Carl Sandburg.

Naturally, there may be poems lying around unpublished. New work by Wallace Stevens, with the exception of his recent "Academic Discourse at Havana" (1929), has not appeared since 1924. He returns with the same resonant elegance of precision—at least with "Jehovah and the great sea-worm," "a peanut parody for peanut people," "the thickest man on thickest stallion-back," and "How full of exhalations of the sea." His return, however, is marked by an attenuated "accessibility to experience" characteristic of the latest Eliot ("Animula," "A Song for Simeon," "Ash Wednesday"),* perhaps because, like Eliot, he has purposely led his rather submerged intellectual excellences (as contrasted with Pound's rebelliousness and awareness of changing forces) to a versification clambering the stiles of English influence.** Stevens'

> Speak and the sleepers in their sleep shall move,
> Waken, and watch the moonlight on their floors . . .

is good, but is too obviously Milton:

> That sing, and singing in their glory move
> And wipe the tears forever from his eyes.

The work of the new formalists—Allen Tate, Crowe Ransom, Malcolm Cowley—seems also to droop from the stem of English influence; perhaps via Eliot. In any case, their linear and stanzaic impalings do not even possess Eliot's spark of craftsman's

---

*   The cadences and conversational overtones of "The Journey of the Magi" which show the influences of Pound's *Cantos* are more interesting.

**   This article was finished before the appearance of Eliot's latest poem, "Marina" (No. 29, *The Ariel Poems*, London). Its lyrical unison—the fine handling of approximately equally spaced vibrations of tone, the accord of Classical quantities with English accent, the musical progress of the lives defined by the internal rhymes furthering, and agreeing with, the end rhymes—is such as perhaps justifies a complete redaction of this article's reference to "submerged intellectual excellences." Technically, and without question emotionally, whatever personal symbols this song may lead one to infer give nothing but a simple statement of objective fact and image in musical shape—"the hope" this new poem sings of. At its best, and it is all best, "Marina" is the important Eliot—perhaps his most fruitful product to date.

accomplishment. Their steadiness is that of truncated emotions. Their poems are not metaphysical in the seventeenth century sense of constructions mentally alive, precise, and ramified and sub-ramified as to meaning, despite a unified emotional source. The poetic emotion is lacking, and the product is 'intellectual,' from which blurred tangibilities hang disjointed:

> waiting
> An empty sacrificial vessel waiting
> Without patience to be filled with God
>
> . . .
>
> But you shall hear the thunder
> Of bursting walls, the gates of night swing wide,
> And journeys will be set against the sunrise.
> (Malcolm Cowley.)

The work of Hart Crane (including *The Bridge*), whose technical regularities tend to place him in a class with this last 'group,' is emotionally preferable. He, at least, has energy. Yet it is an energy too often pseudo-musical and amorphous in its conflation of sense values. His single words are hardly ever alone, they are rarely absolute symbols for the things they represent, e.g.,

> The incunabula of the divine grotesque.

The result is an aura—a doubtful, subtle exhalation—a haze. All of which is more to the bad than the good, unless a kind of 'heat proper' gets across:

> Take this sea, whose diapason knolls
> On scrolls of silver snowy sentences
>
> . . .
>
> Mark how her turning shoulders wind the hours,
> And hasten while her penniless rich palms
> Pass superscription of bent foam and wave.

"*Snowy* sentences" are not "knolled." By itself the second line is pretty metaphor. On the third line, Ezra Pound with reference to the Wagnerian ideal might be quoted: "You confuse the spectator by smacking as many of his senses as possible at every possible moment, this prevents his noting anything with unusual lucidity, but you may fluster or excite him to the point of making him receptive" (*Antheil*, p. 44). The line has interesting anthropomorphic feelings, but for this reason it is not the latest word in 'modern' writing, and it is too much of a metrical rocker to be primitive. Line 4, the sea has rich palms but no pennies in them, is rather a paltry idea. Granted line 2, line 5 is a good echo.

To what extent Crane's music which is often Elizabethan drive—iambic in the grand manner—helps an indefinite language and prolongs verbal indecision past the useful necessity of meaning is indicated by the poverty of his unrhymed work in recent numbers of *transition*. In these poems his words are obviously ineffectual. Their spirals of conceit are difficult to no good purpose, and the musical twisters of his metrical form are not present to carry them.

These strictures do no apply to Crane's "O Carib Isle" (*transition*, and not included in his published volumes) which, but for a minimum of haze and a melody drummed by a kind of linguistic pedal, leaves the sensationally classic and is, with distinction, of the senses. His other poems are mystical, filmy. If fish were a dead metaphor, the sea-film they wear is the logic surrounding these poems: the result is rhetoric—"noon's tyranny," "sulphur dreams."

Crane is not unique erring on the side of mysticism. There is Elinor Wylie:

> Fear not, pathetic flame,
> Your sustenance is doubt.
> Glassed in translucent dream
> They cannot snuff you out.
>
> Wear water, or mask
> Of unapparent cloud;
> Be brave and never ask
> A more defunctive shroud.

These verses addressed to the soul are not metaphysical, but a repeated shifting from one feeling-tone (one kind of ecstasy) to another. But it is evident that the substratum of idea is vague, for the soul must be one thing of several or nothing, i.e., pathetic flame, or doubt's sustenance, or translucent dream, or water, or unapparent cloud. That there is a pseudo-substratum of idea contrasting with the feeling-tone is unfortunate in the first place. In Donne, the idea was also his feeling-tone and was also a particular metaphysical concept of his time—emotion propelling the crowding on of metaphysical things:

> For, nor in nothing, nor in things
> Extreme, and scatt'ring bright, can love inhere;
> Then as an Angell, face, and wings
> Of aire, not pure as it, yet pure doth weare
> So thy love may be my love's spheare;

Strangely enough, the criticism of dialecticians inclined to think of Wm. Carlos Williams as a mountain goat butting among crags, has never stopped to analyse the metaphysical concept behind his reiterated improvisations. But it is a definite metaphysical concept: the thought is the thing which, in turn, produces the thought. Williams' feeling-tone, as Donne's, groups an order of tangible objects:

> Say it! No ideas but in things. Mr.
> Paterson has gone away
> to rest and write. Inside the bus one sees
> his thoughts sitting and standing. His thoughts
> alight and scatter—
> who are these people (how complex
> their mathematic) among whom I see myself
> in the regular ordered plateglass of
> his thoughts, glimmering before shoes and bicycles—?
> They walk incommunicado, the
> equation is beyond solution, yet
> its sense is clear—that they may live
> his thought is listed in the Telephone
> Directory—
>
> "Paterson"

Of its time, but definitely the rare inheritance of metaphysical poetry. It is obvious why Williams should prefer the intellectual specifications, even dryness, of Mina Loy (see *Contact Anthology*) to the pseudo-ecstatic work of a half dozen "lyricists of her sex" and as many roundabout males.

2

Mr. Yvor Winters and the humanists among whom he does not count himself are right when they attempt to reintegrate the human spirit in poetry and in general, but their models excite only scepticism: instead of Pound, Winters chooses Frost; instead of chastising their own caudae equinae they attempt to apply their college fraternity initiation paddles to personalities who are fortunately vital.

It is in the nature of things that poets should want to live; and ethically living cannot be a Wordsworthian

> throwing back,
> As if regret were in it and were sacred
> (Frost's "West-Running Brook"),

but—

> This beats me
> Beats me, I mean that I do not understand it
> This love of death that is in them.
> (Pound, Canto XXIX).

Of course, Mr. Frost intends "the fall of most of it to be always raising a little, sending up a little," but his thought as well as his versifying involved in the allegorical dies at the hearth. What is present is the middle-aged seducing, inventing ontological proofs of God. Or, occasionally, there is a sign of storm and we see his flowers "lodged—though not dead"—and then, "I know how the flowers felt." Mr. Frost, admittedly comparing his race to a lumbering bear, does not save his own poetic processes. He is just too cutely pastoral, too cutely rampant to be alive, to be true.

As for contemporaneousness, one goes back to Herrick's "Divination":

> When a Daffadill I see
> Hanging down his head t'wards me
> Guess I may, what I must be:
> First, I shall decline my head;
> Secondly, I shall be dead;
> Lastly, safely buryed.

This is not death, or if it is "we do not sell and buy things so necessary" (Cummings).

Ultimately, poetry is a question of natures, of constitutions, of mental colorings. But it is understood that if the author of Canto XXX (*The Hound & Horn*, Spring 1930) were incapable of the distinction of an ethical commonplace by Spinoza, it is not likely that he would have written the composite of internal rhyme, repetition of word, repetition of line with one word altered, delayed and rapidly extended cadence, and tendency towards wrenching of accent:

> Now if no fayre creature followeth me
> It is on account of Pity,
> It is on account that Pity forbideth them slaye.
> All things are made foul in this season,
> This is the reason, none may seek purity
> Having for foulnesse pity
> And things growne awry;
> No more do my shaftes fly
> To slay. Nothing is now clean slayne
> But rotteth away.

In contrast, it cannot be said that the 'idea' in these lines is the substance of Robinson Jeffers' works, for his melodrama has vitiated all idea as expression. His one poem, "Continent's End," excepted, the result of his pursuing the Greek furies is a negative Goethe. The contribution of the great Romanticist has already been gaged in Wm. C. Williams' *The Descent of Winter* (*Exile* 4)—"Goethe was a rotten dramatist." Compared with Jeffers, the sad, honest work of Archibald MacLeish (much, too much, overburdened with Eliot) is at least an obvious attempt at meaning.

For bearings this essay returns to the several poets it started with. Its portmanteau bibliography of poetry after 1920 is brief: Pound's *Cantos*; Eliot's *The Waste Land*; Marianne Moore's *Observations*; Williams' *Spring and All*, *Primavera* (the edition in the new *Imagist Anthology* is incomplete, yet anything but the fiasco which the rest of this Anthology is); Cummings' *Is 5*; references to earlier volumes by Cummings, Stevens' *Harmonium*, McAlmon, Reznikoff, *Exile* 3 and 4. Traditions and influences of one upon the other aside, it is to be noted that these poets come out of a country which after a great deal of versified mess produced Emily Dickinson and the raw Whitman who occasionally giving "the soul of literature" the cold shoulder "descended upon things to arrest them all" and "arrested" then "all faithful solids and fluids."

One proceeds with aesthetic principle (Ezra Pound's *Pavannes and Divisions*, or *Instigations*, or *How to Read*, or all three). "Emotion is an organizer of forms" (Pound). The image is at the basis of poetic form. In the last ten years Pound has not concerned himself merely with isolation of the image—a cross-breeding between single words which are absolute symbols for things and textures—

> The sand that night like a seal's back
> Glossy beneath the lanthorns
>> (Canto XXIX)

but with the poetic locus produced by the passage from one image to another. His *Cantos* are, in this sense, one extended image. One cannot pick from them a solitary poetic idea or a dozen variations of it, as out of Eliot's *Waste Land*, and say this is the substance out of which this single atmosphere emanates.* The *Cantos* cannot be described as a sequence. A synopsis may no more be given of them than of a box, a

---

*   Zukofsky's "Poem Beginning 'The'" (1926), written as a reply to people concerned with the end of the world, the dedication and attendant numbers intended as a kind of hors d'oeuvre not as an aid to digestion, is obviously more of a thought sequence than *The Waste Land* is from movement to movement. The images in "The" are incidental and its intention is hardly an atmosphere. The result is certainly not an improvement on *The Waste Land* but something different—something perhaps nearer to an intellectual control (one doubts its value), to statement than to pointilism. For the rest, since there is probably no relationship one should distinguish differences—i.e., Z. perhaps uses stress and consonance too much, with too little relief of the lighter vowel qualities characteristic of the French hexameter which Eliot adapted for English use.

leaf, a chair, a picture: they are an image of this world, "an intellectual and emotional complex in an instant of time."

In Williams, the advance in the use of image has been from a word structure paralleling French painting (Cézanne) to the same structure in movement—*Della Primavera Transportata Al Morale*.

Marianne Moore has allowed the "neatness of finish" of her "octopus of ice" to clarify ubiquitously the texture of at least a hundred images with a capacity for fact. Cummings is less nominalistic, more sensuously evocative, sometimes fanciful ("after all white horses are in bed") but continually interested in something like capillaries, "everything which we really are and never quite live," the sources where images begin—

> if scarcely the somewhat city
> . . . . . . in considerable twilight

and are known perhaps only negatively—

> touch (now) with a suddenly unsaid
> gesture lightly my eyes?

His typography, illustrated by the use of the parenthesis around 'now' also suggests the image, by doubting it.

*
*   *

> "A new cadence means a new idea" (Pound).

Naturally in a poem image, cadence and idea are inseparable. The passage from Pound on Pity, quoted above, is effective because the cadence of the word 'pity' itself is never perfectly expected. The versification is not a matter of each syllable finding its usual place in an iambic pentameter, as in Frost's

> One bird begins to close a faded eye

or

> I have been one acquainted with the night.

There is, of course, melody in the passage on Pity. Melody, with Frost, is by now almost a dead issue. There was melody in the Frost of *A Boy's Will*, a melody often on a par with R. C. Dunning. There will be when the *Cantos* are finished the complete music of the *Cantos*, and it will include successfully those conversational overtones which Frost seems to have labored over for about 20 years, only to falsify them with Simple Simon naiveté. The main drawback was, of course, his continued tinkering with accent. Pound's contribution is quantity, and the dealers in stock and trade sonnets and iambs have never taken up his challenge. They have also dissipated the sonnet as a form; it is time someone resurrected it. Cummings has partly done so in those attempts in which he is not palpably Shakespearean—with lines like

> moon's bright third tumbling slowly
>
> (sonnet IV—*Is 5*)

Occasionally his music has recalled Pound's with a difference in print and somewhat loosely:

> Cats which move smoothly from neck to neck of bottles, cats
> smoothly willowing out and in between bottles, who step smoothly
> and rapidly along this pole over five squirming
> mice; or leap through hoops of fire, creating smoothness
>
> (*Is 5*: Three—III)

But for the most part, excepting a quatrain now and then in the manner of Eliot, he has been himself, the cadence approximating the actuality:

> the very swift and
> invisibly living
> rhythm of your Heart possibly
>
> (*Is 5*: Four—XVII)

and—

> bring on your fireworks, which are a mixed
> splendor of piston and of pistil; very well
> provided an instant may be fixed
> so that it will not rub, like any other pastel
>
> (*Is* 5: One—XXXIX)

Eliot has always been more interesting in his effects with quantity than in his effects with accent:

> Lord, the Roman hyacinths are blooming in bowls and

as against

> Kept faith and fact, provided for the poor

—both lines from "A Song for Simeon."

The music of Marianne Moore's *Observations* varies from the quantitative couplets in "An Egyptian Pulled Glass Bottle in the Shape of a Fish" (she does not, like Robert Frost, seem to say, "Look, I am writing couplets") to the complex stanza of "Those Various Scalpels" (compared to which Donne's "A Valediction of Weeping" seems easy), to the energy of her longer poems:

> in which action perpetuates action and angle is at variance with angle
> till submerged by the general action;
> obscured by "fathomless suggestions of color,"
>
> .   .   .
>
>   ocean of hurrying
> consonants
>
> .   .   .
>
> crashing itself out in one long hiss of spray.
>
> ("Novices")

The resonance of her "Fear is Hope," the length of its rhetorical periods carried over despite the fall of the rhymes, are worthy of John Donne:

> ...round glasses spun
> To flame as hemispheres of one
> Great hourglass dwindling to a stem.

Williams' extremely important revisions and condensations of vers libre, his contribution to an emphasis of word and stress in *Spring and All* and *Primavera*, have already been discussed in this essay. *Primavera* contains this perfect lyric:

> as love
>   newborn
> each day upon the twig
>   which may die
>
>   springs your love
> fresh up
>   lusty for the sun
> he bird's companion

also this original stanzaic pattern with effective stress variations:

> Trundled from
> the strangeness of the sea—
> a kind of
> heaven—
>
> Ladies and Gentlemen!
> the greatest
> sea monster ever exhibited
> alive

the gigantic
sea-elephant—O wallow
of flesh where
are

there fish enough for
that
appetite stupidity
cannot lessen?

Music of word in a poem is to a great extent a matter of diction. The sedate will likely reject the last quotation from Williams and will admire the uncertain Elizabethan virtues of Cummings' "my very lady," or an extension of it, "your crisp eyes actually," rather than his "why are these pipples taking their hets off?" (*Is 5*: One XVIII), or the straightforward diction of

And send life out of me and the night
absolutely into me
(*Is 5*: Five I)

Whatever one's preferences, the diction of these poets remains their fully varied material, which includes quotations from sources apparently useful to a kind of communistic interest in preserving poetry wherever it is found—but hardly ever dead. Pound's Canto XXVIII contains:

Joe hittin' the gob at 25 feet
Every time, ping on the metal
(Az ole man Comley wd. say: Boys! . . .
Never cherr terbakker! Hrwwkke tth!
Never cherr terbakker!)

also—

If thou wilt go to Chiaso wilt find that indestructible female
As if waiting for the train to Topeka

Canto XXIX:

> Phoibus of narrow thighs,
> The cut cool of the air.

The only diction which is dead today is that of poets who, as some one has said of Matthew Arnold, have put on singing robes to lose themselves in the universal. Anent this matter, a paragraph from Roger Kaigh's "Paper" (still unpublished—the state of criticism in American is very low, as perhaps elsewhere) is not inappropriate:

"The bias of paper, to this day, most radically affects logicians and philosophers. Logicians will admit that a word may have more than one meaning, but each must be definite and thus distinct. Infinite shades of meaning cannot be recognized, for the instrument of formal logic depends upon static or categorical meanings, that is, definitions, for its operation. Otherwise the logician detects the fallacy of four terms. But categories which appear distinct upon paper derive an infinity of variations in speech. 'Yes' and 'No' are categorically distinct upon paper, but either may mean anything from emphatic 'Yes' to emphatic 'No' when spoken. For the context, gesture, intonation and pronunciation give words a stamp of meaning which a written form will lack."

The diction employed by Pound, Eliot, Williams, M. Moore and Cummings has always tended towards the most definite connotation and to a varied play of connotation. The devices of emphasizing cadence by arrangement of line and typography have always been those which would clarify and render the meaning of the spoken word specific. The things these poets deal with are of their world and time, but they are 'modern' only because their words are energies which make for meaning. Back of their poetry is certainly not a desire of "gentlemen of fifty" to "let things remain as they are" (Canto XXIX), but an effort to register what their several comprehensions have experimented or worked with and interrelated.*

---

* Contrast, as a case in point, H. D.'s formal, English translation of the choruses of Euripides' *Bacchae*, in which Euripides' ideas seem unduly naked, not of the poetry, and Cocteau's ironic reliving of the choruses of the *Antigone* with the telling prowess of a young man mocking in his very imitation something like a political speech heard over the radio.

3

By Way of Finale

A Note on the Work of William Carlos Williams

He is of rare importance in the last decade (1920-1930), for whatever he has written the direction of it has been poetry—and, in a special sense, history. History, or the attractions of living recorded—the words a shining transcript.

He has written:

On the oak-leaves the light snow lay encrusted till the wind turned a leaf over.

No use, no use. The banality wins, is rather increased by the attempt to reduce it. Better to learn to write and to make a smooth page no matter what the incoherence of the day, no matter what erasures must be sacrificed to improve a lying appearance to keep ordered the disorder of the pageless actual.

A Novelette (1929)

He has looked around—the dimensions of writing like those of music continually audible to him (somehow in a discussion of writing today, after his discussions, the word 'dimension' gets in): "I think these days when there is so little to believe in—when the old loyalties—god, country, and the hope of Heaven—aren't very real, we are more dependent than we should be on our friends." Isolation. Yet he has imagined "each step enlarged to a plain"—known, in facts, "his intimate, his musician, his servant."

The aesthetics of his material is a living one, a continual beginning, a vision amid pressure; *The Great American Novel* (1923), the only one because it is the product of the scene given its parallel in words. America, the shifting, as one hurriedly thinks of it or sees it perhaps as one changes from street car to street car, resulted in this book in the swift hold of art on things seen, in the sudden completeness of the words envisioning them. "He could see the red tail-light still burning brightly with the electricity that came from the battery under the floor boards. No one had stolen the spare tire." (Chapter II). "Corners of rooms sacred to so many deeds. Here he had said so and so, done so and so." (Chapter XIII). Such things are seen and recorded not as notes, but as finished, swiftly trained deliberations of the mind between leaps to other work or the multiplicity of living scenes.

Therefore, his exclusion of sentimentalisms, extraneous comparisons, similes, overweening autobiographies of the heart, of all which permits factitious 'reflection about,' of sequence, of all but the full sight of the immediate, in *Spring and All* (1923). A collection of his works should contain only *the facts of his words*, even those which jar as they brighten in the composition—for these, too, illuminate, as against the personally lyric padding, the idly discursive depressing stages of writing not the product swift out of the materiel. In this he is almost unrelated: in a kind of morality which is his visioned impact against the environment; in a complete awareness of values in the living broken down for others by sentimentalisms.

The critics who are at this late date first beginning to see him as the poet of *The Tempers* (1913), *Al Que Quiere* (1917), *Sour Grapes* (1922) do not know him. There are in these books much that will stay—even poems—though line after line must go invalidated by his subsequent criticism. It is salutary that many of the lines may be omitted and still leave a number of structures. The process of rehabilitating the good to its rightful structure is always possible with writing in which something was seen, a quantity heard, an emotion apprehended, to begin with.

One is faced with the same difficulties in the *Improvisations* [*Kora in Hell*] (1920), and the same outlet: what he learned later to exclude may be omitted in the reading. The element is often not seen from the emanation, or as he has said, the paper is not felt from the glaze—the substance of his words is referred to, of course, not the paper. But at best the writing in the *Improvisations* attains a Shakespearean verbalism: "When beldams dig clams their fat hams (it's always beldams) balanced near Tellus' hide, this rhinoceros pelt, these lumped stones—buffoonery of midges on a bull's thigh—invoke, what you will: birth's glut, awe at God's craft, youth's poverty, evolution of a child's caper, man's poor inconsequence. Eclipse of all things; sun's self turned hen's rump." (XI, 2). At best, there is a continual friskiness, the writing is a fugue, comparable to the scene in *Twelfth Night*, in which the Clown proves Olivia a fool. (Incidentally, in *The Descent* of *Winter* (1928) and in a few other scattered notes, he has written about the best Shakespearean criticism there is—at least, it is no more nor less serious than the incidental.)

"Porpoises risen in a green sea, the wind at nightfall bending the rose-red grasses and you—in your apron running to catch—say it seems to you to be your son. How ridiculous! You will pass up into a cloud and look back at me, not count the scribbling foolish that put wings to your heels, at your knees." (1920). To prove: "there is no thing that with a twist of the imagination cannot be something else." (*Improvisations*, XXVII, 2).

He has, however, since 1923, printed his poems differently—used print as a guide to the voice and the eye. His line sense is not only a music heard, but seen, printed as bars, printed (or cut as it were) for the author—the sentimentalisms which might possibly have encroached brushed off like flies as at those clear times when the dynamic feeling of a person is not disturbed. One does not think of line-ends in him but of essential rhythm, each cadence emphasized, the rhythm breaking and beginning again, an action, each action deserving a line:

> the harried
> earth is swept.
> >   The trees
> the tulip's bright
> >   tips
> >   sidle and
> toss
>
> >   (*Primavera*)

nouns: acts as much as verbs.

He has apparently even broken with his own stylistic standards when the power behind the words demanded it. Thus, the conceit of his "Botticellian Trees" (unpublished part of *Primavera*): but one feels "the alphabet of the trees" identified with roots and growths which make the alphabet of his actual writing. The conceit does not stick out of the verse, but builds it: his kinship with Donne, with Shakespearean metaphor.

For these attainments, he has had no need to make concessions to the 'obstinate rationalists.' Yet he has come across, and retained, more learning than he himself may be satisfied to allow he has: *In the American Grain* (1925) and *A Voyage to Pagany* (1929).

History is in these pages and in the poems—history defined as the facts about us, their chronological enlivening for the present set down as art, and, so, good for the next age and the next. "The pure products of America go crazy" is the poem it is through its realization of points of aesthetic, living values, social determinism of American suburbs in the first thirty years of the twentieth century. The poem could perhaps be realized only by one who has vicariously written, rather than painted as he has always wished to do, but, in any event, it has been realized by one vitally of his time. Remarkable that no outside program has influenced his social awareness. It is the product of the singular creature living in society and expressing in spite of the numb terror around him the awareness which after a while cannot help be but general. It is the living creature becoming conscious of his own needs through the destruction of the various isolated around him, and, till his day comes, continuing unwitnessed to work, no one but himself to drive the car through the suburbs, till they, too, become conscious of demands unsatisfied by the routine senseless repetition of events.

Ezra Pound's XXX Cantos

A Draft of XXX Cantos by Ezra Pound.
Paris: Hours Press, 1930.

Ezra Pound's dwelling in the human provinces has conditioned an accurate expression of them. Yet the numerous dramatis personae in Pound's *Cantos*—exceeding the number in his short poems—, his consideration of the "osmosis of persons," penetrating or passing each other in the world or its reflected idea which might be called history, combined with an adeptness for "slaying things clean," such as "and that was the revolution . . . as soon as they named it" (passages, in the *Cantos*, on Russia 1917, on the War, on Zenos Metevsky reminiscent of Basil Zaharof) have been the cause of mental bafflement. The other than musical, imagistic, and various speech material of Pound's short poems, when not lyrical in the exact definiteness of their forms (Pound has for over 20 years been a student of the "old" music, musical declamation as the "old" song writers, as also Bach and Mozart, knew it), or epigrammatic in the manner of the satiric sketch, is a reliving of dramatis personae not with obvious didactic palpability but still in the tradition of Browning—Pound's immediate master. It is but natural that Pound, like all great poets, should have desired to express even while he was writing his short poems their basic content which was himself and his interests in one, long, definitive poem, more inclusive than ever of all he knew and felt, more complex in detail, but essentially as simple and instantaneous in spite of its length as any of his single line images. Pound is still writing this poem. The *XXX Cantos*, however, are enough material for an estimate of their contents. As a volume they form the only long poem of value in English since Browning's *Ring and the Book* (it is true other long exercises in verse have been published)—Eliot's *Waste Land* is not much longer than any one of the *Cantos*—and as a contribution to writing they are to poetry what Joyce's *Ulysses* is to prose.

Yet a comparison of the two works is not implied. For beyond an aptitude for saying a full number of things at a time in a very few words—an attribute which might be called modern if it were not for the fact that Dante in his *Commedia* said at least three things at a time as he explained in a well known letter—comparison is inconsequential. In both works anachronisms do not exist, because the words can pass from one time to another, live over all times at once. But while *Ulysses* is still bound by the classical unities of time and place—a day and Dublin—the *Cantos* have completely discarded these unities. The difference is symptomatic of two individual mentalities: Joyce's essentially Catholic training and Pound's capacity for disassociation of ideas which has led him to see the need (realized by scientists and the initiators of symbolic logic) for thought forms and language structures other than those used by monolinear mediaeval logic inherited from Aristotle.

In the *Cantos*, time is the instant which is a complex large enough to include the past and present and even indicate further direction. Place is the poet's mind, and action is the coordinate movement of his lines. If Pound seems at an instant to be travelling in a railroad train, the reader must not be duped by his past habits that this will be Pound's unity of place forever (i.e. as long as the poem lasts); the next instant Pound may be on top of the world in the guise of his *choros nympharum*, singing of the vegetation and change everywhere and making no zealot's distinction between "the down and the up."

No synopsis of the *Cantos* is therefore possible for they deal with no simple, successive sequence of time. The only progress is an almost tacit autobiographical order of events not always strictly chronological accompanying Pound's more objective interests in history and poetry never a matter for chronology, and—which is more important—the inevitable progress of the lines such as Pound's mental idea of the entire music has conceived (tho the poem is still unfinished) it should be. The line in the *Cantos* is what the melody is to the completely developed musical composition. Mr. T. S. Eliot has written on what a fund of finished practice Pound's line offers to the poet and student of prosody—quantity especially. By analogy the lines are to Pound's total poetic product what successive squares of film are to the reflected screen pictures—progressively they compose an extended image of Pound's world.

Of a world no synopsis is possible except if it be connected with a theologian's superimposed story upon it. The scope of an index, however, may be indicated. Pound is no theologian, but his mentality has interrelated his various personae, their several planes of living for better or for worse, his opinions of them which are not didactic but the observed consequences of his people's acts, in the world of his poetry which is at once a verbal, imagistic and musical process. Whether this process be called epic or not is immaterial. In terms of poetry, however, it is concerned with direct presentation by means of translated passages and paraphrase of a history of poetic styles, (thus the *Cantos* becomingly begin with a translation of Andreas Divus' Latin version of the *Odyssey*—the journey to the Dead and onward); with formulations in poetry on musical practice; with root ideas (studies of origins, habits, customs—vide Canto II after Ovid, Canto XXII the passage on the synagogue—human intentions and contrivances become history—Sigismundo Malatesta's sponsoring of art, Francesco da Bologna's contribution to printing, the railroad, radium, etc., etc.) related to sociology—production and distribution—and ethics (cf. Canto XIII after Confucius). Pound's preoccupation with the Renaissance for example is not merely that of the scholarly poet but an attempt at getting across the intensities of individuals and a distinguished civilization and relating them to contemporary national and international qualities—"to-day against the past." Pound's women have their historic as well as physical status and are not merely subjects of miasmic passional writing. All this pertinent material occurs as incident and situation, and recurs in different guises much as the resolutions of chords; also, simultaneously, as polyphony, in music. The mirror fugues of Bach are perhaps the kind of writing which a not entirely pertinent analogy may discern in Pound's renewals, or mutual reflections of movement.

Adverse criticism of Pound's *Cantos* must, however, be answered. It will consist of an objection to his quotations to which the answer is not every one can quote significantly so that the quotations themselves become a different reality in the context they are used. Another objection will be that Pound's multitudinous references are at best traps of obscurity characterized by vague personal allusions. The answer is that Pound is, at least on the surface, the least subjective of poets. For one personal, lyrical statement he marshals any number of lyrical facts of cadence and idea. In his poem he is but another persona, never an index pointing at himself. His so-called obscure references are easy enough in their context to anyone with an average reader's knowledge and two grains of wit to relate one seemingly removed fact and another. No one quarrels with Browning for writing of Galuppi, or with Dante for ransacking the names before his time. Moreover, the specific names Pound refers to will eventually mean more than names, since the poetry in which they occur is of distinction.

A third objection to the *Cantos* will be Pound's use of foreign languages. The justification is of the same order as those which explain his use of quotations and his varied information. They make for entirely new connotative and denotative values.

If the reader does not know these languages it is unfortunate because no concepts and sounds in English can adequately be substituted to articulate to the same degree certain junctures in Pound's poem (cf. Cantos XVI—a persona's record of the war in conversational French, designated "exact"). Curiously, Pound has also been admonished for his use of Americanisms. Yet Pound's use of phonetics to present American spoken is always revelatory: "Hu er 'you?" As characteristic of its subject as his phonetic renditions of continental and English types: "O-hon dit que'qe fois au vi'-a-ge..."; "Thass a funny lookin' buk... Ah... Wu... Wu... wot you goin' eh to do with ah... ah read-it?"

A more indefinite objection will be Pound's lack of intensity. The basis for it will be a perverted taste, for Pound never confuses the function of the several senses in words to impress, or adds unnecessary verbal arpeggios to the single word which is the absolute symbol for thing and texture. As for his music it has the seeming simplicity of melodic, and melodiously developed, structure, but it is never simple. Neither is it merely monolinear, for there is the movement of verse paragraphs, cantos, and the entire *Cantos*. Yet it may be expected that one who finds adequate mentality and emotional make-up in currently favored vacua and confusions will speak of Pound's *Draft of XXX Cantos* as of a superfluous aristocracy.

"London or Troy?"
"Adest"

Redimiculum Matellarum by Basil Bunting.
Privately printed, Milan, Italy.

Mr. Bunting's poetic care is measure. He is aware that quantity has naturally to do with the tones of words. His diction, as a result, tends to a classical selection, even when his themes are modern, as in his epigram to Narciss and in the sonnet beginning "An arles, an arles for my hiring." At the same time, reversing this relation, the past meets the present as in "Against Memory":

> Ten or ten thousand, does it much signify, Helen, how we
> date fantasmal events, London or Troy? Let Polyhymnia
> strong with cadence multiply song, voices enmeshed by music
> respond bringing the savors of our sadness or delight again.

The diction often seems to collect no more than the experience of classical poetry: "The distant gods . . . abstracts of our spirit," at the end of "While Shepherds Watched," themselves "rabbits sucked by a ferret"; the preoccupied but outwardly integrated mythology of the "Chorus of Furies—Overheard—*guarda, mi disse, le feroce Erine*":

> Let us come upon him first as if in a dream,
> Anonymous triple presence,
> Memory made substance and tally of heart's rot:
> Then in the waking Now be demonstrable, seem
> Sole aspect of being's essence,
> Coffin to the living touch, self's Iscariot.
> Then he will loathe the year's recurrent long caress

Without hope of divorce,

Envying idiocy's apathy or the stress

Of definite remorse.

He will lapse into a half-life lest the taut force

Of the mind's eagerness

Recall these fiends or new apparitions endorse

His excessive distress.

He will shrink, his manhood leave him, slough self-aware

The last skin of the flayed, despair.

He will nurse his terror carefully, uncertain

Even of death's solace,

Impotent to outpace

Dispersion of the soul, disruption of the brain.

But Mr. Bunting would not be among the isolate instances of Englishmen concerned with poetry in this time, were his content only the product of a classical ear directing a polished manner. All his poems, and especially the "Villon," are grounded in an experience, though the accompanying tones of the words are their own experience:

Let his days be few and let

His bishoprick pass to another,

For he fed me on carrion and on a dry crust,

Mouldy bread that his dogs had vomited.

I lying on my back in the dark place, in the grave,

Fettered to a post in the damp cellarage.

Whereinall we differ not. But they have swept the floor,

There are no dancers, no somersaulters now,

Only bricks and bleak black cement and bricks,

Only the military tread and the snap of the locks.

His indictment of Bertillon in this poem is violence that an intelligent man confronted with historical fact has had to express, even if the name has joined the decorative scheme of his poem. The coda of the "Villon"—

> How can I sing with my love in my bosom?
> Unclean, immature and unseasonable salmon—

is the logical humility consequent on Mr. Buntings bitterness. The rhetorical wrench of the last line is self-mitigated because the writer's metaphor has become the objective equivalent of his personal irony.

Mr. Bunting's adaptation of Lucretius' invocation to Venus even indicates a safer art and a more certain direction:

> Therefore, since you alone control the sum of things
> And nothing without you comes forth into the light
> And nothing beautiful or glorious can be
> Without you, Alma Venus! trim my poetry
> With your grace; and give peace to write and read and think.

So much so that the French epigrams opening and closing his volumes and laying restraint on the extent of his expression (*Bornons ici cette carrière*) are unnecessary.

Mr. Kagawa, Mr. Winters, Mr. Blackmur

Hidden Flame by Bunichi Kagawa, with a foreword by Yvor Winters. The Halfmoon Press, Stanford, California, 1930.

Mr. Bunichi Kagawa writing

> The silence above the moonlit lucent
> Air hammered me to a special logic
> That I could not easily change
>   (We Used To Meet)

evidently wishes to be accepted literally. Poetry, has, however, to do with Mr. Kagawa's other lines, with—the analysis of craft—

> we are emotionless
> With the simplicity of our strength—
>   (February)

and with—wholeness, synthesis, composition—

> All clear things are a vision
>   (This We Touch)

Mr. Winters' pointing out of two of Kagawa's qualities not to be overlooked—namely, "his slow and elaborate tempo" and his "definite rhetoric"—is not acceptable. For one, because the movement may not be abstracted since the words as unanalyzable symbols not meaning objects or states interfere with the reading; for the other, because the unanalyzable words are merely a vague aggregate of "rhetoric" (deprecatory sense).

It would be interesting to show that Mr. Kagawa is not, as Mr. Winters thinks, "a writer cut off from tradition," but a writer very close to Mr. Winters and others carrying on an ineluctible *symbolisme* (Frenchmen of the eighties not always clear—even Maeterlinck—, Hart Crane, and Shakespeare—once compared to the Belgian—when he is merely drumming metaphorical complications). That is: "dark flame of will," "noiseless death of light," "eats into my body left mostly alone" (the use of the adverb, Cummings'), "flood of time," "mist-fall of infinity." These phrases have nothing to do with any particularization of a philosophy or science, thing observed or, for the space of a poem, adequately felt.

It would be also interesting to apply Mr. R. P. Blackmur's creditable standard ("E. E. Cummings' Language," *The Hound and Horn*, Winter, 1931), "a word used in a poem should be the sum of all its appropriate history made concrete and particular in the individual context"—to show of a selection of Kagawa's words that they do not form a context; also, that Mr. Blackmur has, for the most part, been wasting his time applying his judgment to the wrong example. Cummings' "prisms of sharp mind" refers *in* its context to prisms—objects in painting—produced on a canvas by certain painters *of* "sharp mind," such as certain Cubists of several years ago. The instances can be multiplied—Mr. Winters glosses a collusion of English; Mr. Blackmur cannot, or refuses to, read the English of an original, but precise, context. Cummings' repetitiousness of subject is another matter; his saving, intelligible irony still another.

On the other hand, Mr. Kagawa has to a minor degree solved his own problem of conveying meaning in such representative metaphor (of Oriental origin?) as

He is a shadow put aside by a light.

Prose Cantos
XX–XXI

XX. "THERE *Is* No Time ..."

The Gates of the Compass by Robert Hillyer.
The Viking Press, 1930.

Naked Heel by Leonora Speyer. Alfred A. Knopt, 1931.

Mr. Hillyer is obviously a better craftsman than Mrs. Speyer, a craftswoman, but their poetic programs are essentially the same. That is, here is the expected social entertainment, the stanzaic dehiscence, the disquisition through unnecessary verses: leading ultimately to the vulgarity of the drawing room, the conceptual blind-alleys of artistic professors during and between classes, the chit-chat of reception rooms introductory to the business offices of elite publishers.

Mr. Hillyer's case is especially unfortunate,—if he is bothered by poetry,—since in some of the concluding lines of his "Summer Night" there is substance. He might use them as a starting point, and realize more than accidentally that words attain contextual meaning only after they have individually, and in the phrasing, signified experimental content; and that when he says "There is no time not even for this rhyme" he is not observing the 20th century, but merely sitting pretty,—in contradistinction to Eliot, for instance, who when he writes "HURRY UP PLEASE ITS TIME" is observing movement, the character of an era, and the precision of a particular voice.

As for Mrs. Speyer, she is embarrassing when she fills pages with false cadence and rambling banality ("Enfold it heart, and lift!") and calls the whole an elegy; or pretends with sentimental restatements of what originally were emotional, exact narratives and myth (*Monk and Lady*,—Chaucer was amiable but he particularized historical data, hence really amiable, fulfilling a function . . .); or syllabically counts out sonnets which have forgotten how to sing. "Let there be hills" says Mrs. Speyer (no objections) and "Where are the poets?" (Mr. Hillyer); "These are the men who will turn from their business to ponder the hillside." Suggested: less pondering, and that both Mrs. Speyer and Mr. Hillyer read and find out, and stop hatching irrelevancies. For if Mrs. Speyer's symbolish mermaid means Poesy,—like her Old Doc Higgins she better get a good look at the fish-lady because she may never "git thet chance again."

XXI. SOMETIMES...

Ten Poems by Kathleen Tankersley Young. New York: Parnassus Press, 1930.

Miss Young is evidently more conscientious and has seriously investigated the work of *poets* around her, but obfuscated her matter by an inability to hide her derivations: "Sometimes O, often, we fell," "because I have not existed in your mind perhaps," poem number 9; (all possibly Eliot uncomprehended because not integrated). Poem number 4 (again, possibly Cummings uncomprehended because incapable of his verbal distinctions). Miss Young might refer to the criticism in Williams' *Spring and All* and Pound's *Dont's* to avoid further confusion of the senses in her next. On the other hand, there are isolated in this volume "biting on bitter twigs," "tomorrow, a morning and it is swallowed," "a confusion of sleep, orchids, I," "a Christmas tree with yellow lights," "we descending into the lake," "we moved and read the hands of clocks," "blue breath of horses" (the horses admittedly somewhat bluish themselves for the word "blue" to be more than ornamental), "a heavy wind comes without birds," "filtered green." All this is information to any sensible person: even of serious import to the welfare of a possible writer's gild?

"Completely and Accurately"

Shakespeare and Music by Edward W. Naylor, with illustrations from the music of the seventeenth and sixteenth
centuries. First published 1896. New edition. E. P.
Dutton & Co., 1931.

The Poems by Wilfred Owen. A new edition, with notes on his
life by Edmund Blunden. The Viking Press, 1931.

Strict Joy and Other Poems by James Stephens. The Macmillan Co., 1931.

Edward W. Naylor's test for Shakespeare's treatment of music—"completely and accurately"—is a correct test for poetry. Mr. Naylor affords the pleasure of quotation: "The study of this one feature (music) of the 'age and body' of Shakespeare's time, with the view of clearly grasping the extreme accuracy of the 'abstract and brief chronicle' to be found in his works—argues very much indeed in a writer's favor, that the 'layman' has managed to write the simplest sentence about a specialty without some more or less serious blunder."

Mr. Naylor's illustrations from sixteenth and seventeenth century music—technical terms, instruments, musical education, songs and singing, serenades, dances and dancing, Pythagoreanism, use of musical stage directions—are continuously interesting notes forming a full bibliography to his subject. His photographs of old instruments are well printed. His translations from old manuscripts, Arbeau's *Orchèsographie*, 1588, sets perhaps his most gracious example, are delectable in an antique and fine sense. The reader of poetry enjoys this writing on music and takes away several facts special to the poetic craft.

"No one could be admitted to primam tonsuram except he could first bene le bene con bene can, as they call it, which is to read well, to conster (construe) well and to sing well."

"Modern 'time' is rather a matter of accent; the ancient 'proportion' was more concerned with relative lengths of notes."

· · · ·

James Stephens's ability to sing well—to suggest the accompaniment of a tune by his words—in his new volume is its best in the last stanza of "Sarasvati":

> Fly to thy talent! To thy charm!
> Thy nest, thine hive, thy sheltering arm!
> Who can to sing,
> There let him flee,
> This is, naught else is, certainty.

This recapitulation of three preceding digressive metaphors each given one stanza of Irish sentiment—"as bird to nest," "as bee to hive," "as child to mother running"—is also Stephens's best as a poet. For his remaining intellectual efforts to read and construe well lead him in his own words not "to sing for singing" but "to write too little or too much" and "smudge" more than "somewhat" the subject he touches.

His perhaps one strict image—the last three lines of "Theme"—follows lost after an abstract metaphrase of Plotinus. A consistent handling throughout Mr. Stephens's volume of the craft displayed in the shifting of accent to suggest musical quantity, as in the last stanza of "Sarasvati," would have been preferable to his wistful Celtic associations, brooded ponderings, fluttering interjections and not fully apprehended neo-Platonic meditations already well treated by Yeats and Blake, and with the definiteness of a poetic philosophy in Stephen MacKenna's translation of Plotinus himself. Mr. Stephens should at least not have approached the thought of the English romantics in his rendering of this precise philosophy. Shakespeare's "discord in the spheres," Mr. Naylor notes, reworded Pythagoras accurately. It is to be added that when Mr. Stephens's other spiritual cares lead him to imitate Gerard Manley Hopkins metrically, as in "Where naught is but which would, and utter cannot" the meters are Hopkins's without Hopkins.

.   .   .   .

The new and enlarged edition of the poems of Wilfred Owen—who was, according to Edmund Blunden's preface, apart from Mr. Sassoon, the greatest of the English war poets—again impresses one with the sincerity of Owen's sacrifice of his subject matter—poetry—to the pity of his subject—war. Owen's intention, as expressed in his preface to the 1920 edition, "All a poet can do today is warn," was commendable. The bluntest and best expression of this intention was in his prose—in letters to his mother: "I can see no excuse for deceiving you about these last four days. I have suffered seventh hell. I have not been at the front. I have been in front of it—it was of course dark, too dark, and the ground was not mud, not slopping mud, but an octopus of sucking clay, three, four and five feet deep, relieved only by craters full of water. Men have been known to drown in them. Many stuck in the mud," &c.

The verses of Owen's "Exposure" are, by comparison, literary. The figurativeness of his language, despite himself, led him to sidetrack his true matter into the relief of ornament. Most constantly present is the discursive unraveling of descriptive melodrama as opposed to the inferno of intense occasional phrasing, like "I saw their bitten backs curve, loop and straighten." Traditionally, he began as a poet whose ornament made for color, as well shown in his "Fragment: a Farewell." His poetic intelligence compelled him to list his best lyric in this manner, "Greater Love," as doubtful. The sonnet "Anthem for Doomed Youth," for all its resonant tonality, suffers from current English cadences. His reading in Old French and its use of assonance prompted him to revive consonance (end riming of like consonant sounds with a play on the vowels). His persistent inventiveness in these strains now seems stubborn even in his best poem, "Strange Meeting."

.   .   .   .

It is possible that had the war permitted experiment, the use of the quantitative line instead of the syllabically regular might have relieved the harsh expectancy of his end sounds and subdued his consonants to the quiet essentially demanded of his concept. Owen's poems as a rendering of the very form and pressure of the time in any case never approach several of Hardy's war lyrics, Ezra Pound's "These fought in any case," "There died a myriad," or the body of Canto XVI. The pity Owen intended as poetry is precisely a matter to be presented as poetry—completely and accurately.

The Transition

The Doom of Youth by Wyndham Lewis. New York: Robert M. McBride & Co., 1932.

Mr. Wyndham Lewis is "not one of those who believe in the ultimate 'triumph' of *any* class in these class-wars. All equally will be defeated," he thinks. "But it is the interim conditions—the 'Transition'"—that occupies him in his political studies and nothing else.

"Really what the 'doom of Youth' means is the erecting of 'Youth' into a *unique* value, and by so doing abolishing Youth altogether. For something that is *everything* in human life cannot be anything so limited as 'Youth' as understood upon the merely emotional plane.

"For the 'Youth-politician' there is, strictly speaking, *no Youth*. There are only different degrees and powers of an abstract energy. There is one long *adult* life, if you like. No life is worth considering, for the 'Youth-politician' except adult life. And adult life is not worth while, of course, once the person is no longer active and capable of creative or at least useful work."

"This appears," to Mr. Lewis, "to be not at all a bad ideal. On the other hand, the use of the term 'Youth'—as a result of the technique of 'Youth-politics'—for this inclusive valuation, is confusing." He irritably proceeds, therefore, with the realization of the Aristotelian entelechy, to expose the predatoriness of the "Youth-politicians" who have destroyed the European's "certain fixed conception with regard to the leisurely growing-up of a human being and made of him at ten today a little 'adult.'" Mr. Lewis' exhibition involves an exposé of the "slave-literature" of the popular press and the political tacticians behind it: the individualists working in the interest of fanatical democracy and the dictator-minded. Their destructiveness is translated in terms of the class-wars—sex-war, age-war, rich-and-poor-war, etc., and the seemingly peaceful manifestations of the Cult of the Child, the boy scout, "the most motherable man in London" riding a rocking-horse, etc., and since Mr. Lewis finds it impossible to define certain aspects of these reversals too sharply he adds to these the child-art of the German, Klee, Miss Gertrude Stein, and Charlie Chaplin.

"In fact," to Mr. Lewis, "all men are fairly unpleasant." Himself, he happens "to be an individual (not, however, an 'individualist'): and as such" he is "not a 'group' person. The very notion of the 'group' must be suspect, unless it is integrated on behalf of mankind, and not against mankind—on behalf of exceptional talents, and not in order to enable a small herd of talented persons to masquerade as 'geniuses,' under the wing of some Zeitgeist."

"In fine, it is THE INDIVIDUAL, and his *individuality*, in whatever shape or form that is marked down for extinction. And what is 'genius,' after all, but an excess of individuality? And what is an excess of individuality but an excess of power? And is not *power* substantially the same thing as money?

"Again: is the mass-midget person preferable to the 'free' western *individual*? For myself, nothing interests me at all outside the *individual*. But since I do not mean by that *any* individual, I am open to conviction that the best way to protect the *best* individual is to eliminate the interference and futile competition of *all the myriad* 'individuals' of which the human herd is composed. The objectionable results of unchecked 'individuals' is apparent upon all hands."

From the point of view of analysis and pertinent translation Mr. Lewis' use of the Aristotelian entelechy would seem to be limited to the assertions of italics and single quotes. "The whole idea of 'fulfilment,'" he says, "is alien to our time." But elsewhere he also says, "I am sure that ultimately (and if we really push beyond every sentimental value of both religion and aesthetics) only the *useful* is the *beautiful*, and vice versa, and that ugly and well-worn heresy is not only true but beautiful." Mr. Lewis as an *individual* (his own italics) may at least be suspect of an excess of power against exceptional talent, while the assertions of his italics and quotes fall short of the completed realization as distinguished from formative causes or energy. At least, giving 266 pages (besides 29 of introduction) to a subject admittedly not too sharply defined, he does not seem "to prevent the mere destructive technique of the *transition* (Youth-politics) from being taken too seriously," as he would wish.

His fault would seem to be that he does not really push beyond every sentimental value of aesthetics in his implied definition of analysis, for in distinguishing between a work of science pure and simple and a work of literature he escapes the analysis of the beautiful and loses the realization of the useful.

The fact is that Mr. Lewis' subject matter would be worth analysis, perhaps not 266 pages besides 29 of introduction, but as the subject matter of an individual who is perhaps not suspect of an excess of power against exceptional talent. The guess is that, as in the matter of *paintableness* (Mr. Lewis' italics), the validity of such subject matter would be the realization of the occasion, or the occasion become art. The resulting book might probably be of the nature of an old magazine evolving out of Futurism instigating the verb Blast; or if the *transition* of a 'group' (Mr Lewis' single quotes) were not taken too seriously it might be like the humor of Apollinaire's *Les Mamelles de Tiresias*, or like the laughs and driving fiction of Mr. Lewis' own *Tarr*, *The Wild Body*, and his *Apes of God*, in which talk as an art seems at times an even more expressive and particular evidence of the facts than good fiction, because the occasion has been realized.

"The Open Mind" — Physiology and a Poem

Of "the open mind" Spinoza's ethics proved by geometry would perhaps imply that in contemplation the natural processes are seized, are still. For "the open mind" is not so much characterized by the results of thinking which have attained a state of quietus, a form in repose, but by the processes of seizure and letting go: the impact of the blow, as well as the early aftermath of contemplating that which has received the blow, as well as the relinquishment of the object which has received the blow—so that the object of thought in turn takes on whatever impact is left it—contemplating being over. The drift of this entire process involving not the play of a dialectic but the interaction of a physiology with objects has been tragically understood by all earnest historians. So Henry Adams: "the historian must not try to know what is truth, he is certain to falsify his facts." Or the opposite of this principle which, like all paradoxes, really offering no element of overwhelming surprise, is the same principle—Frobenius' approach to a historical morphology of cultures, for example. He begins by recognizing the need for replacing the encompassment of force in extension by the idea in profundity.

The faith of Frobenius is the tragedy of Henry Adams; the skepticism of Adams, the positivism of Frobenius. Both say the same things: there is the myth, the idea, the dialectic, the truth; all these replace, have their impacts upon, the facts. Could both of these historians, in imaginations resembling theirs, dissociate themselves from the attained forms of their thinking—their quietus of history stretched out as story, as analyzable dialectic—they would perhaps face nothing but memories of their original vitality of approach—their respective physiologies and their respective interactions among objects.

In the history written by skeptics, or even positivists, the elation of physiologies among objects, if a trace of it is carried over, exists only in the immediate gratuities of style. All important writers thus write a poetry which is a history of objects, ideas, facts, which as men, they have tried to seize. Examples: the autobiographical detail of Henry Adams' *Education*, the African stories which Frobenius translates to replace an abstract explanation of the life of a culture.

So much for "the open mind" of historians: the occasional gratuities of their style, their styles, (platitudinously) the men. Or perhaps a reader with "an open mind"—reading itself a process of seizure and its resultant quietus—may trace a constant gratuity. For few historians constantly give the flavor of poetry. In poetry the skepticism itself becomes liberation. I translate from an essay ("Pour Dada") by that poetically charged temperament, André Breton: "What right has anyone to declare arbitrarily his place in the formation of works and ideas? That which usually touches us is less willed than one may believe. A happy formula, a sensational discovery, are miserable enunciations. No thing attains its end except as it is outrun by something else. And the history of intellectual hesitations, the psychology of literature, explains nothing. Despite its pretensions, a novel has never proved anything. The most illustrious examples are never worthy enough to be placed under our eyes. The greatest indifference would be the proper fashion. Incapable of at once embracing the canvas of a painting and an unhappiness, where do we get the permission to judge? . . . I affirm only for the pleasure of compromising myself. It becomes a confusion to appeal to the doubtful modes of discourse. The most convinced is not the most authoritative, as one may think. . . . The obscurity of our word is constant. The divination of sense is left to children. To read a book in order to know denotes a certain simplicity. The few who apprehend their author and their reading have found that the most reputed works quickly dissuade them from this experience. It is the thesis, and not the expression which deceives us. I regret passing thru the badly lighted windings, regret receiving confidences without object, regret proving at each instant by the default of a babbler the impression of the already known. Poets who know all this hopelessly run off from the intelligible. They know that their work has everything to gain by this escape. More lovable than any other of a woman's qualities is her madness."

"The open mind" as this essay, by its intelligibility, turns upon itself, we see, is more than somewhat dependent on physiology.

Res animae:—who knows their sources.

Note: The above "theme" was "presented" by a "freshman" ("1931") to his "instructor" in a New York City college. It received the grade of C- (minus), with this comment: "Not illiterate, but like a series of literary hiccoughs, this form of writing obscures ideas in themselves not difficult. Clarity is not infantile, nor is complex opacity profound. Stop stuttering."

The words "the open mind" are obviously the imposed "contribution" of the "instructor." Mr. Louis Zukofsky sends us this essay, with the recommendation that "it would be unfortunate if this fine informal prose—sensible and naturally rare—were squelched because of the 'oversight' of an instructor." The student is still, if unfortunately, registered at the New York City college hinted at, and must for obvious reasons remain anonymous.

A Further Note on *XXX Cantos* by Ezra Pound

Reading (by which is meant here, going thru supposedly familiar material, one *sees* for the first time)—And re-reading the *Cantos*—

Emphasis, if not specifically placed so before,* may be on their poetic achievement in three respects:

I—in respect to the writing of History.

II—in respect to the writing of Narration.

III—in respect to the functioning, by concrete example, of literary criticism.

I—the poetry of the *Cantos* is a history. The writing (technique) proceeds towards a living museum of facts about man and his world which displays the validity of his successive positions as against the unwieldy detail of all of his story.

> *XXX Cantos*, II:
>
> God-sleight then, god-sleight:
>
> Ship stock fast in sea-swirl
>
> Ivy upon the oars, King Pentheus
>
> (Mythological, B.C.)
>
> The ship landed in Scios,
>
> men wanting spring-water,
>
> And by the rock-pool a young boy loggy with vine-must,

---

* The undersigned:
Échanges, vol 1, no. 3, Paris, 1930; *The Criterion*, London, April 1931; *Front*, no. 4, Amsterdam, June 1931; "American Poetry 1920-1930," *The Symposium*, New York, Jan. 1931; Preface and Dedication to *An "Objectivists" Anthology*, Le Beausset, Var, France and New York, 1932. René Taupin, *Quatre Essais Indifférents, pour Une Esthétique de l'Inspiration*, Paris, 1932—the fourth essay.

"To Naxos? Yes, we'll take you to Naxos,

Cum' along lad."

      (The same myth receiving a Roman handling.)

XXV:

    ... because of the stink of the dungeons.

                           (1344.)

stone stair,

        (1415.)

XXXIII (*Pagany*, vol. 2, no. 3, Summer 1931):

    ... was in the minds of the people

    and this was affected from 1760 to 1775

    in the course of fifteen years ... before Lexington ...

XXXI (do.):

    ... or paupers, who are about one fifth of the whole ..."

           (on the state of England in 1814)

XXXIII (do.):

        (*Das Kapital*) denounced in 1842 still

    continue (today 1864) report of '42 was merely chucked into

    the archives and remained there while these boys were

    ruined and became fathers of this generation ...law for workshops

XVI:

    Liste officielle des morts 5,000,000.

        (Europe, the last war.)

    Guns on the top of the post-office and the palace,

        (Russia, October 1917.)

XXII:

    And C. H. said to the renowned Mr. Bukos:

    "What is the cause of the H. C. L.?" and Mr. Bukos,

    The economist consulted of nations, said:

                "Lack of labour."

    And there were two millions of men out of work.

        (Almost contemporary.)

XXXIII (*Pagany*, do.):

        150 millions

yearly, merely in usurious discounts . . .

(Contemporary.)

The arts achieve historical status at those times when they consciously, or by means other than consciousness, forcefully realize the purposes of their particular actions

XXV:

"as the sculptor sees the form in the air
before he sets hand to mallet,
"and as he sees the in, and the through,
the four sides
"not the one face to the painter

The mentality of the human organism functioning in poetry can bear specifically on an account of the various logics of various times: contemporary expression includes the past of the human organism and the poet's present become significant. In Pound's *XXX Cantos*, each line of the poem, relative to the whole matter, involves in its thought, approach or impetus, the just outcome of man's story. The technique proceeds by leaps to well-calculated landmarks. These are so aptly placed and arranged for related reference as to make a swift and concise history readable.

II—Narration.

The XV. Bookes
of P. Ouidius Naso, entytuled
Metamorphosis, translated oute of
Latin into English meeter by Arthur Golding Gentleman,
A worke very pleasant
and delectable. 1567

The Third Booke:

Acetis is my name:
Of Parentes but of low degree in *Lidy* land I came.
- -

Now as by chaunce I late ago did toward Dilos sayle
I came on coast of Scios Ile, and seeing day to fayle,
Tooke harbrough there and went a lande. Assone as that the night
Was spent, and morning gan to peere with ruddie glaring light,
I rose and bad my companie fresh water fetch aboord.
And pointing them the way that led directly to the foorde,
I went me to a little hill, and viewed round about
To see what weather we were lyke to have eresetting out.
Which done, I called my watermen and all my Mates togither
And willed them all to go aboord my selfe first going thither.
Loe here we are (*Opheltes* sayd) (he was the Maysters Mate)
And (as he thought) a bootie found in desert fields a late,
He dragd a boy upon his hande that for his beautie sheene,
A mayden rather than a boy appeared for to beene.
This childe, as one forelade with wine, and dreint with drousie sleepe
Did reele, as though he scarcely could himselfe from falling keepe.
I markt his countnance, weede and pace, no inckling could I see
By which I might conjecture him a mortall wight to bee.
I thought and to my fellows sayd: what God I can not tell
But in this bodie that we see some Godhead sure doth dwell.
- -

And with that worde I stept
Uppon the Hatches, all the rest from entrance to have kept.
The rankest Ruffian of the rout that *Lycab* had to name,
(Who for a murder being late driven out of *Tuscane* came
To me for succor) waxed wode, and with his sturdie fist
Did give me such a churlish blow because I did resist,
That over boord he had me sent, but that with much ado
I caught the tackling in my hand and helde me fast thereto.
The wicked Varlets had a sport to see me handled so.

Then Bacchus (for it Bacchus was) as though he had but tho
Bene waked with noyse from sleepe, and that his drousie braine
Discharged of the wine, begon to gather sence againe
Said: what a doe? what noyse is this? how came I here I pray?
Sirs tell me whether you doe meane to carie me away.
Feare not my boy (the Patrone sayd) no more but tell me where
Thou doest desire to go a lande, and we will set thee there.
To *Naxus* ward (quoth Bacchus tho) set ship upon the fome
There would I have you harbrough take, for Naxus is my home.

⸌ ⸌

Now even by him (for sure than he in all the worlde so wide
There is no God more near at hande at every time and tide),
I sweare unto that the things the which I shall declare,
Like as they seem incredible, even so most true they are.
The ship stoode still amid the Sea as in a dustie docke.
They wondring at this miracle, and making but a mocke,
Persist in beating with their Ores, and on with all their sayles:
To make their Galley to remove, no Art nor labor fayles,
But Ivie troubled so their Ores that forth they could not row:
And both with Beries and with leaves their sailes did overgrow.
And he himselfe with clustered grapes about his temples round,
Did shake a Javeling in his hand that round about was bound
With leaves of Vines: and at his feete there seemed for to couch
Of Tygers, Lynx, and Panthers shapes most ougly for to touch.
I cannot tell you whether feare or woodnesse were the cause,
But every person leapeth up and from his labor drawes.

⸌ ⸌

This *Licabs* chappes did waxen wide, his nostrils waxed flat
His skin waxt tough, and scales thereon began to grow.

⸌ ⸌

Of twentie persons (for our ship so many men did beare)
I only did remaine nigh straught and trembling still for feare
The God could scarce recomfort me,

⸌ ⸌

His Chaplaine I became. And thus his Orgies I frequent.

The smooth, connected manner which redounds to the praise of Golding's narrative translation of Ovid is not in Pound's.

> *XXX Cantos*, II:
>> And an ex-convict out of Italy
>>> knocked me into the fore-stays,
>> (He was wanted for manslaughter in Tuscany)
>>> And the whole twenty against me,
>> Mad for a little slave money.
>>> And they took her out of Scios
>> And off her course . . .
>>> And the boy came to, again, with the racket,
>> And looked out over the bows,
>>> and to eastward, and to the Naxos passage.

The significance of the narrative here is in the focus of historical light: in relation to all of history (*Mad for a little slave money*), and in relation to all of writing. The smoothness is in the order of lately civilized disconnections, so that the narration introduces a historical perception. But the particular incident in Ovid's story must keep all of the original emotion in Pound's words and in Pound's setting of his poem (his mind become his printed page).
Then, Pound's

> And looked out over the bows,
>> and to the eastward, and to the Naxos passages

instead of Golding's

> There would I have you harbrough take, for Naxus is my home

Yet the arrangement of the vowels used to express nostalgia in English in 1567 and Pound's vowels tend to like ends—translation of Ovid, poetry, the materials of writing.

Sometimes Pound adds an image which as poetry makes history in its own right: as in the description of Bacchus' beasts—"a furred tail upon nothingness."

Sometimes the lines, less innovation than delicate paraphrase, reduce themselves to decor for the rest of his long poem:

> Lynx-purr, and heathery smell of beasts,
> where tar smell had been,
> Sniff and pad-foot of beasts,
> eye-glitter out of black air.

To the thinking gentleman's query: "What does Mr. Pound believe?" Mr Pound believes all of the quotations under I of this note, all of the quotations under II of this note. He believes them for the light they shed on things (history) and sometimes for the things the quotations are themselves, in so far as they are productive acts of a human organism.

Involving the use of symbols which operate, he believes the well-meant allusiveness of:

> *XXX Cantos*, II—
> And you, Pentheus,
> Had as well listen to Tiresias, and to Cadmus,
> or your luck will go out of you.

He believes that poetry, by its own concrete example, can take care of the functions of

III—Literary Criticism

> *XXX Cantos*, VII:
> "Si pulvis nullus" said Ovid
> "Erit, nullum tamen excute"
> Then file and candles, e li mestiers ecoutes;
> Scene for the battle only, but still scene,
> Pennons and standards y cavals armatz
> Not mere succession of strokes, sightless narration,
> And Dante's "ciocco," brand stuck in the game.

Un peu moisi, plancher plus bas que le jardin.

"Contre le lambris, fauteuil de paille
"Un vieux piano, et sous le baromètre . . ."

Which means that the examples quoted in this passage are *not* sightless narration. The examples quoted have also become the presentation of his own music and his own thought sense.

Considering

150 millions

yearly, merely in usurious discounts

further exegesis of other parts of *XXX Cantos* may be left to the 21st century. This note merely commemorates their printed appearance in the U.S.A. in 1933 (Farrar and Rinehart $2.50).

One's Own Taste

The Root and the Flower by L. H. Myers. Harcourt Brace & Co., 1935.

Explained by his own preface the author of this unfinished novel (already a trilogy of 583 pages) is a connoisseur in character. His respect for such moral taste as he himself may possess causes him to discern the deep-seated spiritual vulgarity that lies at the heart of our civilization. Counting upon the comfortable, normal ignorance of the reader, he has chosen as his scene India at the end of the sixteenth century and as his action the decay of Akbar's court. He has distorted or purposely ignored facts when they were inconvenient, in order to obtain an attention undistracted by the social and economic problems of our day. For between the novel as a description of persons and philosophy as a description of the universe there is, he thinks, a natural connexion.—Sic.

It is unfair to identify a novelist with his characters. But when Mr. Myers uses them to contribute something to a description of the universe they may be used in turn to reveal some problems which concern him. Perhaps the most meditative of them is Gokal, the Brahmin: "Man is under an obligation to act—under a psychological necessity that is also a spiritual obligation. And somehow in his action he must reconcile the pursuit of his own small, definite, and rightful ends with the working out of an inscrutable purpose." Mr. Myers' characters, tho a good many of them achieve an effect of manuals on the history of philosophy and esoteric guides to Oriental religions, are not—it may be granted him—abstractions personified. They do their parts in the pursuit of their own small "rightful" ends in a decaying empire. How in whose name their different ends will ultimately succeed in making Mr. Myers' definition of a "spiritual sense" less inscrutable, only the reader whose interest if he has any, as Mr. Myers says in his preface, will be of the kind that is accompanied by patience, can guess.

Different people, Marx noted in *The Criticism of the Gotha Program*, are not equal one to another; and, therefore, "equal right" is really a violation of equality, and an injustice. And he formulated a basis for morals. The author of *The Root and the Flower*, like one of his characters, seems to consider loyalty to one's own taste even more important in the moral sphere than in the aesthetic, and the result of his entire taste is personal: an achievement of detective story torsion present in his handling of plot and suspense, which has very little to do with morals, and only superficially with aesthetics.

Muriel Rukeyser's Poems

Theory of Flight by Muriel Rukeyser, with a Foreword by Stephen Vincent Benét. Yale University Press, 1935.

In *Theory of Flight*, Muriel Rukeyser hints at several orders—poetic, scientific and revolutionary—but rarely with the conviction that language is a social factor, and as such its main function is to be understood. With this in mind, communists, as poets, can do two things:

1. Write the poems everybody can understand—for example, the strike-songs which Miss Rukeyser only mentions;

2. Deal with precise fields of knowledge (science, etc.,) so as to confirm revolutionary theory in sensory values. Communists who specialize in these fields can understand this writing and explain it to the masses who under capitalism obviously find it almost impossible to pursue such fields of study by themselves.

Miss Rukeyser has *tried* to write of the proletariat and to grasp the imaginative substance of historical materialism, and this effort takes her out of the class of poets who have not. Nevertheless her method, intimated in her line "Breathe-in experience, breathe-out poetry" (from "Poem Out of Childhood"), has not served her well. To breathe is not in one's control; to be thorough in the facts one writes about is, a matter requiring sincere application. Her technique is bad, because her thought is inaccurate. The emotion of her language, turgid, because she confessedly falls back on "cerebral titillation" ("Wooden Spring"), when she does not know.

Despite her skill in metrical composition, she has not given introspection an outward content. No sooner does she tackle a problem of poetics in any one line than she leaves it unresolved and follows it with another and another unsolved in the next line and the next. Her numbers never add up because her poetic quantities remain indeterminate. Or why should an "expanding universe" have a "cheek," a "hub" be "inevitable," "speed" be "black," a "wave shocked to motion" (it is moving or it isn't a wave!). Miss Rukeyser has heard something about "clocks" in connection with the theory of relativity, and she immediately transmutes their scientific definition into vagueness.

Or, again, is she addressing the picket-line when she writes "I give you cats"? From her forcedly lyrical, suffering point of view, "poetry" and "picket-line" are "conflicting graces," but one doubts their moving dialectically "to one end" in her poem, as she asserts. The picket-line, not understanding her symbol, would only suffer from an embarrassment of riches if presented with her gift. Then, there are the redundant abstractions following a perfectly communicable word: "fields of change," "grief's awful violet," "blue-print of birth," etc., etc., against which the directness of her prose quotations from Orville and Wilbur Wright, on flying, is a comfort to the reader even if it has not been admonishment to her.

And because of her confusion of detail, her elegiacs—both amatory and mournful—interfere with her communist intention. The three—love, grief and the class struggle—are hopelessly submerged in an uncommonly vague mysticism. The poems that her readers among the intelligentsia will praise, like "Breathing Landscape" and "Hundreds of Days," convey a feeling of an objective subject matter not felt; of thought construed beyond her content and denying it at the same time. Possibly she intends to convey in these poems contradictions like those in the development of modes of production—contradictions synthesized in historical materialism. But one can only guess at her purpose. The gaps in understanding are the consequence of her inability to pause and comprehend the possible meaning to workers of each individual fact, *before* she emotionally rushes to anticipate relations to other facts.

What can Miss Rukeyser do to improve her future work? She can begin very simply by avoiding a solecism like "thought among the childhood"—certainly not as amusing as the comic cartoonists "Ignatz among the jail." She can learn to present her subject matter progressively and not spring a surprise on her New York reader, in a foot-note explaining that she has been writing all the time about the New York Public Library, after making him wade through a dozen incomprehensible lines. What if we had to read a paragraph on political tactics by Lenin and at the bottom of the page find the foot-note—revolution!

She can continue to experiment with the ballad which she often does nicely, but not so well as Sterling Brown in "Black Worker and White Worker." She can forget the effete metaphor of Wallace Stevens, and the hazy effulgence of Hart Crane, influences which exist in her work like archaic remains and are undeniably the result of an economy constituting the material worlds which affected these poets. But, as Marx noted, *there has been history*. And there have been examples of poetic art and invention—technics.

On the few occasions when she writes clearly she attests the existence of these things, and they attest hers:

> Tomorrow's Mayday.—How many are we?
> We'll be everyone.
> - - - - - - - - - - - -
> O, we are afflicted with these present evils,
> they press between the mirror and our eyes. . .
> We focus on our times, destroying you, fathers

Finally, Miss Rukeyser need not be decoyed by the praise of Stephen Benét who balmily writes in the foreword to her book: "I do not intend to add, in this preface, to the dreary and unreal discussion about unconscious fascists, conscious proletarians, and other figures of straw which has afflicted recent criticism with head noises and small specks in front of the eyes." *She* is still young.

Matter That Thinks, Or Notations towards Action

Not "topics of the times," etc. Lenin said: "Nothing but an objective account of the sum total of all the mutual relationships of all the classes of a given society without exception, ... as well as an account of the mutual relationship between it and other societies, can serve as the basis for the correct tactics of the class that forms the vanguard."

.   .   .   .

The vigorous caption arresting the reader at the head of this writing is from Engels' *Historical Materialism*: "It is impossible to separate thought from matter that thinks. This matter is the substratum of all changes going on in the world. The word infinite is meaningless, unless it states that our mind is capable of performing an endless process of addition."

.   .   .   .

The slick, old boys go on adding mechanically without reference to "final aims." Not knowing what existence is (read the quotation from Engels again), how can they aim? So they write notebooks, the family skeletons of ideas which will never be given bodies. With bleary eyes on a bodiless infinite, "Looking only at that part of the motion which is directed *backwards*" (Lenin).

.   .   .   .

Notations towards action, then, since the abbreviations of our discussions should integrate all discussions and form a workable calculation.

.   .   .   .

The best buy for a nickle (5¢) to-day is the *Manifesto of the Communist Party* by Karl Marx and Friedrich Engels (International Publishers, New York).

.   .   .   .

You can only find out about "motion," by "looking" upon it "not only from the point of view of the past, but also from the point of view of the future."

.   .   .   .

Lenin again, with the force of a composer who recognizes a theme and where it will lead him.

.   .   .   .

"Now the present *status musices* is quite different from what it was, its technique is so much more complex, and the public *gusto* so changed, that old-fashioned music sounds strangely in our ears. Greater care must therefore be taken to obtain *subjecta* capable of satisfying the modern *gustum* in music, and also instructed in its technique, to say nothing of the composer's desire to hear his works performed properly. It is astonishing that musicians should be expected to play *ex tempore* any music put before them, just as if they were the *virtuosi* for whom it was written, men who therefore have had opportunity to study it, indeed almost to learn it by heart, enjoy moreover large salaries to reward their labour and diligence, and have leisure to study and master their parts. People do not bear this in mind, but leave our players in a position merely to do the best they can, the necessity to earn their daily bread allowing them little leisure to perfect their technique, still less to become *virtuosi*. A single *exempel* may be given: let anyone observe how the royal musicians are paid."

. . . .

Johann Sebastian Bach, writing August 30th, 1730.

. . . .

And already looking forward to the present status of music. Don't the unemployed and the underpaid among our musicians know!

Two Related Notes

1.–Program: "Objectivists" 1931

An Objective (Optics)–The lens bringing the rays from an object to a focus. (Military use)–That which is aimed at. (Use extended to poetry)–Desire for that is objectively perfect, inextricably the direction of historic and contemporary particulars.

Historic and contemporary particulars may mean a thing or things as well as an event or a chain of events: i.e. an Egyptian pulled-glass bottle in the shape of a fish, oak leaves, and the performance of Bach's *Matthew Passion* in Leipzig, or the Russian revolution and the rise of metallurgical plants in Siberia.

2.–1936

The critical position is never entirely separate from the poetic: and, therefore, is virtually "the union of realities" not isolated from "practical life," reached in the materialist dialectics. (quotes Marx to P. V. Annenkov, 1846).

Most "Marxist" criticism could be avoided if it went back to Marx:

". . . men, who fashion their social relations in accordance with their material method of production, also fashion *ideas* and *categories*, that is to say the abstract, ideal expression of these same social relations. Thus the categories are no more eternal than the relations they express. They are historic and transitory products. For M. Proudhon, on the contrary, abstractions and categories are the primordial cause. According to him they, and not men, make history. The *abstraction*, the *category taken as such*, i.e. apart from men and their material activities, is of course immortal, unmoved, unchangeable, it is only one form of the being of pure reason; which is only another way of saying that the abstraction as such is abstract. An admirable *tautology*." (Marx. Ibid.)

"... the philosophy of every epoch, since it is a definite sphere in the division of labour, has as its presupposition certain definite intellectual material handed down to it by its predecessors, from which it takes its start." (Engels to Conrad Schmidt, 27 October 1890.)

All of the following statements avoid the tautology of the abstraction and pertinently analyze *historic and transitory products*:

I—"Weight, grandeur, and energy in writing are very largely produced, dear pupil, by the use of 'images.' (That at least is what some people call the actual mental pictures). For the term Imagination is applied in general to an idea which *enters the mind from any source and engenders speech* . ." (Longinus, *On the Sublime*, XV, 2.)

II—"Now canzone, according to the true meaning of the name, is the action or passion itself of singing, just as *lectio* is the passion or action of reading." (Dante, *De Vulgari Eloquentia*, Book II, viii.)

III—"Men became accustomed in explaining their actions to start from their thinking and not from their needs (which are of course reflected in the head, perceived) . ." (Engels, *The Role of Labour*.)

IV—In *Historical Materialism*, Engels suggests that the dialectic was already on its way when Duns Scotus asked the question whether it was "impossible for matter to think?"

V—Marx said somewhere: "The philosophers have only interpreted the world in various ways; the point, however, is to change it."

UN-
COLLECTED
LATER PROSE
(1956-1973)

The Summing Up

The summing up: *Rock-Drill*, Canto 90—Trees die ... Ubi amor, ibi oculus—about sums it up. And the opening lines of Canto 91 and of 93. But let's see what 96 to 100 will bring.

A Preface?

—I do not think so
—Never believe it

as much as the parenthesis of your *Fifty-One High-Coup Syllables* and all that title honor—

Dear Jonathan,

   Amen/Huzza/Selah disseminated in three languages. While some of your friend David's psalms end with *selah*, the word-colporteurs decided its meaning cannot be certainly explained, taking it for 'a pause.'

   Very good: *Hymeneal.*

   I like to think some will know to pause after "you" in that poem, then harry "yo-yo" for the sacred fire. Cherokees down there? Or be led to think "agite ite ad alta"—GAI VALERI CATULLI VERONENSIS LIBER

In fair Verona

Hark! how around the hills rejoice
And rocks reflected *ios* sing—

Congreve whose ladies' nights from the grass stared at the moon—as in Buncombe.

   But I can't help thinking as I did not say to two of your friends, off in my next book, that someone reading its dedication will think maybe of Herrick's *The Vision.*

Barely
   and
      widely
love

they say—
in these words—

of Paul
"barely
twelve"

and of me
"widely
published

throughout
a long
career"

So unknown

Celia
you are the peer-
ess of this
song

making the news notes
sing
as there

our music is called—
smiling
"Make sure

call your next book—
*Barely and
widely*"

dear.

Or, not to sidetrack for a minute as you're worried perhaps,

"A-bomb and H-," as Aristotle articulated to the First Fisherman

The implicit alchemy in the atomic table of the human animal is his residual perceptive *stand* in the *rout* of an original formation of flesh-and-blood life . . .

In the thinking stand of process, in which want or desire or love persists, each tongue still speaks with others by means of the heat of life; or the alternative to this is to see all individual bodies buried—a singularly visual future which, if in nature happens to all at once, may by someone imaginably surviving be thought of only as the common death that has forgotten to know what each has been or *seen*.

Those alive love when thought springs back to sense from some ratio that has cast too far in thought—to the eyebright first fisherman in *Pericles*:

> Die, ke-tha; now Gods forbid't, and I have a Gowne heere,
> come put it on, keepe thee warme.
>
> II i 82

So the quarto reads, tho Malone read *quoth-a* for *ke-tha* (a dialect form current in the 17c, says the glossary). But thought that distils from sense may as well play with as little Greek as it finds in Feyerabend's pocket dictionary or as maybe the writer of *Pericles* had: **kéthe** = **ekéthe** = **eké** = . . . there; thither; then; in that case—*keepe thee warme."*

And you know where that's from

Your friend,

Louis Zukofsky

Apr. 7/56

"What I Come To Do Is Partial"

The Whip, by Robert Creeley. Migrant Books (Jonathan Williams, Highlands, North Carolina). $1.00

As he says in his preface, Robert Creeley's honest metaphysical intention is: "–there is no use in counting. Nor more, say, to live than what there is, to live. I want the poem as close to this fact as I can bring it; or it, me." It is like Spinoza's definition of honesty–"I call that honest which men who live under the guidance of reason praise and which is not opposed to the making of friendship." With some disposition like that in mind Creeley can happily say: "I write poems because it pleases me, very much–I think that is true."

That one guiding and reasonable fact "Nor more to live than what there is," whatever way he "stumbles into" particular examples, should assure Creeley that these cannot be "hopeful and pompous." Considering the one fact moves all of his poems, it is understandable that Creeley–if he writes for anyone–may seem "now" to "know less of these poems" than the possible reader he imagines, who also knows it and sees the poems made by it:

> & the head could not
> go further
> without those friends

. . . .

> I mean, graces come slowly

. . . .

perpetuity
        (which is not reluctant, or if it is,
it is no longer important.

                    .   .   .   .

friendship, the wandering and inexhaustible wish to
be of use, somehow
to be helpful

when it isn't simple

                    .   .   .   .

        behind her there were
flowers, and behind them
nothing

                    .   .   .   .

        there
is the rock in evidence . . .

What I come to do
is partial

                    .   .   .   .

Where fire is, they are quieter
and sit, comforted . . .
    If they speak
I have myself, and love them

       • • • •

The poem . . . addressed to
emptiness—this is the courage

Necessary.

       • • • •

    If quietly and like another time
There is the passage of an unexpected thing:

to look at it is more
than it was.

       • • • •

But how account for love even if you look for it?
I trusted it.

a counterpoint

Let me be my own fool
of my own making, the sum of it

is equivocal.
One says of the drunken farmer:

leave him lay off it. And this is
the explanation.

.　.　.　.

Which one sings, if he sings it,
with care.

.　.　.　.

No man shall be an idiot for purely exterior reasons.

The poems are to be praised for not counting up to the "conceit" of rhetoric, which a generation of so ago misnamed "metaphysical," whose thought presumed more hope than the voice of a limited body.

Prose passages from
Autobiography

I too have been charged with obscurity, tho it's a case of listeners wanting to know too much about me, more than the words say.

—Little

As a poet I have always felt that the work says all there needs to be said of one's life.

.   .   .   .

C. Z.

music for poems by

Louis Zukofsky

the poem ... the completed action of one writing words to be set to music. For all the good sense one must owe to Dante, these twenty-two settings to eighteen poems ("Song 8" from *55* has two versions, "Song 29" from *Anew* three, and "que j'ay dit devant" again two) have always acted to complete the words for me. I find some notes intended for comment at a reading, going back some twenty years,* which point to the final intention of the words: "madrigal," "plain chant," "organum," "Adoration" (no doubt in the medieval sense), "for one voice," "for several" and so on. The composer set the words to the "forms" I asked for—to which I had perhaps no right, unable to compose them myself; but in following my wish or whim she also did something else—showing me that apart from my impositions on my words and her, the words had potentially their own tunes which she followed even more carefully to complete for me.

L. Z.

February 17, 1962

New York, January 23, 1941

. . . .

But the bare facts are: I was born in Manhattan, January 23, 1904, the year Henry James returned to the American scene to look at the Lower East Side. The contingency appeals to me as a forecast of the first-generation American infusion into twentieth-century literature. At one time or another I have lived in all of the boroughs of New York City—for over thirty years in Brooklyn Heights not far from the house on Cranberry Street where Whitman's *Leaves of Grass* was first printed.

. . . .

My first exposure to letters at the age of four was thru the Yiddish theaters, most memorably the Thalia on the Bowery. By the age of nine I had seen a good deal of Shakespeare, Ibsen, Strindberg and Tolstoy performed—all in Yiddish. Even Longfellow's *Hiawatha* was to begin with read by me in Yiddish, as was Aeschylus' *Prometheus Bound*. My first exposure to English was, to be exact, P.S. 7 on Chrystie and Hester Streets. By eleven I was writing poetry in English, as yet not "American English," tho I found Keats rather difficult as compared with Shelley's "Men of England" and Burns' "Scots, wha hae."

. . . .

My poems first appeared in print in 1920 and continued to appear in more than one hundred "little" magazines, national and international. The appearances led to friendship with Ezra Pound and William Carlos Williams beginning in 1927. I wrote the first extended essay on Pound's *Cantos 1-27*, which appeared in French in *Échanges* (Paris) 1930. It was thru Pound's efforts that Harriet Monroe invited me to edit the February 1931 issue of *Poetry* (Chicago). But it was not until 1965 that an easily accessible volume of my poetry appeared on the American scene. My thanks for this fact are due to W. W. Norton & Company.

. . . .

As for subsistence I can only quote with affection e. e. cummings: "no thanks."

. . . .

My wife Celia and son Paul have been the only reason for the poet's persistence. She has collaborated with me in my work on Shakespeare and Catullus. Paul is a violinist and composer. I trust, considering his gifts, that his art will be welcomed sooner than mine.

Reply to Questionnaire: On Rhythm from America

The purpose of this questionnaire is to seek practical answer from poets concerning their methods and intentions in the disposition of their poems upon the page. We are not investigating the absolute nature of rhythm so much as the rhythmic intention behind the print. Because of the variety of rhythmic systems, numbers of questions may seem irrelevant to your practice. Please ignore these and treat the questionnaire as a guide; we would prefer a straightforward account of your practice in continuous prose.

GENERAL POINTS

1. Apart from the obvious differences, such as of accent on words like "temporary" and "civilization," do you recognize in your work a distinction between English and American sufficient to entail new systems of rhythm of metre?

1. Privately always; the world's more important.

2. How conscious are you of rhythmical considerations? Are poems of yours ever triggered off by a purely rhythmic suggestion?

2. Always.

[Question 3, apparently regarding the visual appearance of the poem on the page, is missing.]

3. Both together.

4. How do you regard the line-end:

>   *(a) as a minute pause inevitably,*
>
>   *(b) as a pause only when punctuated, or*
>
>   *(c) as a pause, any way, but one lengthened by punctuation?*

4. (a)

5. For what purpose would you run a sentence from one stanza to the next?

5. Continuity (&/or) variety.

6. Do you ever split words at the end of the line and for what purpose?

6. See 4(a) above.

7. What sound-effects are you conscious of using or seeking?

7. Transliteration (as in C. & L. Z. *Catullus*).

VERS LIBRE

8. Are you conscious, like Eliot, of a constant approach towards and retreat from some norm? If so, what are your usual norms?

8. Like T. S. E. but wary of usual.

9. Do you compose instinctively, for the ear alone, seeking like Lawrence the effect of spontaneous speech?

9. Both.

10. Does the line-end indicate your rhythmic intention or unit or is it a result of punctuation and sense alone?

10. Unit.

11. What use do you make of caesuras in your vers libre?

11. Infinite, I hope.

12. *Do you use in your verse any principle of alternating syllables counterpointed against the rhythms or speech?*

12. Sometimes.

SYLLABICS

13. *Do you do anything to obviate the placing of unimportant words at the line-end?*

13. Consciously.

14. *How do you define for your own purposes "a syllable"? What do you do about the slurring of syllables that occurs in speech?*

14. "consonants with-without vowels quaver

        larynx and syrinx" (self quote); slur 'em.

15. *Do you pay any attention to syllable length, or stress, or consonant content?*

15. Constantly (all).

16. *How do you distinguish, except typographically, between, say, a three-lined stanza of six syllables and a two-line stanza of nine syllables per line?*

16. Let the reader decide.

METRICAL VERSE

17. *How dead is the pentameter? What do you do to re-animate it?*

17. The general practice—very, but I try.

18. *Do you use a modification of, or the traditional Saintsbury type of system?*

18. G.S.' sensitivity for detail as fine as Sam Johnson's—their dogmas weren't or aren't.

19. Do you counterpoint your metre against the normal speech-rhythm or do you attempt a coincidence?

19. Both, depending on the sense.

20. Do you use rhyme of any sort, if so, which and for what purpose?

20. Unavoidably to further the poem.

21. Do you pay any attention in your metrical verse to length as opposed to stress of syllable or to syllable count?

21. All 3 as (or since) I count words: cf. H. J.'s preface to *The Golden Bowl* (N. Y. edition)—which I read long after my early practice (1924-1931), but see "Influence," 1930 in my collected criticism, *Prepositions*.

Respondents: Donald Davie, Richard Eberhart, Donald Hall, Daryl Hine, Robert Lowell, Christopher Middleton, George Oppen, W.D. Snodgrass, William Stafford, LZ.

MUSICAL A
OF "A" (1964

PART V

APTATIONS

967)

"A" Libretto

CHORUS:

A

Round of fiddles playing Bach.

Come, ye daughters, share my anguish—

Bare arms, black dresses,

See Him! Whom?

Bediamond the passion of our Lord,

See Him! How?

His legs blue, tendons bleeding,

O Lamb of God most holy!

NARRATOR:

Black full dress of the audience.

. . .

The autos parked, honking.

. . .

The lights dim, and the brain when the flesh dims.

Hats picked up from under the seats.

Galleries darkening.

"Not that exit, Sir!"

. . .

MALE:

And as one who under stars

Spits across the sand dunes, and the winds

Blow thru him, the spittle drowning worlds—

I lit a cigarette, and stepped free

Beyond the red light of the exit.

. . .

It was also Passover.

The blood's tide like the music.

A round of fiddles playing

Without effort—

As into the fields and forgetting to die.

299

The streets smoothed over as fields,
Not even the friction of wheels,
Feet off ground:
As beyond effort—
Music leaving no traces,
Not dying, and leaving no traces.

. . .

"I heard him agonizing,

. . .

As if it had not kept, flower-cell, liveforever,
    before the eyes, perfecting.

. . .

. . .

CHORUS: Existence not even subsistence,

. . .

great numbers idle, shiftless, disguised on streets—

. . .

Dogs cuddling to lamposts,
Maybe broken forged iron,
    "Ye lightnings, ye thunders
    In clouds are ye vanished?

    Open, O fierce flaming pit!"

["A"-2]

FEMALE: Ankle, like fetlock, at the center leaf—
Looked into the mild orbs of the flower,
Eyes drowned in the mild orbs;

Hair falling over ankle, hair falling over forehead,
What is at my lips,
The flower bears rust lightly,

   . . .

I walked on Easter Sunday,
   This is my face
   This is my form.

   . . .

In a style of leaves growing.

CHORUS:

A train crossed the country: (cantata).
A sign behind trees read (blood red as intertwined
   Rose of the Passion)
        Wrigleys.
Boy and girl with crosses of straw for their nosegays
Impinged upon field as on ocean;
Breath fast as in love's lying close,
Crouched, high—O my God, into the flower!

   . . .

NARRATOR:

The song out of the voices.

["A"-3]

1ST FEMALE:

At eventide, cool hour
Your dead mouth singing,

2ND FEMALE:	Ricky,

Automobiles speed
Past the cemetery,

No meter turns.
Sleep,

With an open gas range
Beneath for a pillow.

1ST FEMALE:	The cat, paw brought back

Over her seat, velvet,

Puss—.

2ND FEMALE:	"Who smelt gas?"

1ST FEMALE:	"—Would I lie!"

"No crossin' bridges,
Rick'—
No bridges, not after midnight!'

2ND FEMALE:	"—God's gift to woman!"

1ST FEMALE:	Out of memory

A little boy,

It's rai-ai-nin',

Ricky,
Coeur de Lion.

Lion-heart,

A horse bridled—

Trappings rise,
Princelet
Out of history.

1ST FEMALE: Trappings
Rise and surround

Two dark heads
Dead, straight foreheads,

The beautiful
Almost sexual

Brothers.

2ND FEMALE: I, Arimathaea,
His mirror,
Lights either side—

        Go,
        Beg His corpse

1ST FEMALE: —Wish I had been broken!

1ST AND 2ND FEMALES: In another world
We will not motor.

Dead mouth
(Cemetery rounded

By a gastank)

The song reaches home

'Here are your dead,

Not yours—
A broken stanchion.

Of leaves,

Lion-heart, my dove,
Pansy over the heart, dicky-bird.'

["A"-4]

NARRATOR: Tree of the Bach family
               Compiled by Sebastian himself.
               '   Veit Bach, a miller in Wechmar,
               Delighted most in his lute
               Which he brought to the mill
               And played while it was grinding.
               A pretty noise the pair must have made,
               Teaching him to keep time.
               But, apparently, that is how
               Music first came into our family!'
                    . . .

FEMALE: "I will gather a chain
               Of marguerites, pluck red anemone,
               Till of every hostile see
               Never a memory remain."

["A"-5]

CHORUS: An animate still-life—night.
Leaves, autumn.
Thread the middle.

MALE: A cigarette,

FEMALE: Leaf-edge, burning
                            obliquely urban,
                            the branches of trees air
                                      comfort.

                  . . .

CHORUS: And past the leaf's edge
(Not in the central heart)

1ST MALE: Our voices:

1ST FEMALE: "How? without roots?"

2ND FEMALE: "I have said *The courses we tide from.*"

2ND MALE: "They are then a light matter?"

1ST FEMALE: "Let it go at that, they are a light matter."

1ST MALE: "Isn't it more?" "As you say."

2ND MALE: "You write a strange speech." "This."

NARRATOR: One song
Of many voices:

The words Matthew weeps
(Plaint, clavicembalo)—
      Chorale, the kids in the loft
        (*O love untold*, love lying close);
Or say, words have knees
      water's in them, all joints crack,—
(New York, tonight, the rat-lofts
             light
                with the light of a trefoil);

["A"-6]

CHORUS: Natura Naturans—
                Nature as creator,
                Natura Naturata—
                Nature as created
                    . . .

MALE: To find a thing, all things.

                On that morning when everything
                    will be clear,
                . . .
                One will see
                    gravel in gravel
                . . .

CHORUS: Schweight still—plaudert nicht—
                Quiet—cut the gab—
                No "please" in the German—
                That to his audience.

["A"-7]

1ST MALE:

Horses: who will do it? out of manes? Words
Will do it, out of manes, our of airs, but
They have no manes, so there are no airs, birds
Of words, from me to them no singing gut.
For they have no eyes, for their legs are wood,
For their stomachs are logs with print on them;
Blood red, red lamps hang from necks or where could
Be necks, two legs stand A, four together M.
"Street Closed" is what print says on their stomachs;
That cuts out everybody but the diggers;
You're cut out, and she's cut out, and the jiggers
Are cut out. No! we can't have such nor bucks
    As won't, tho they're not here, pass thru a hoop
    Strayed on a manhole—me? Am on a stoop.

1ST FEMALE:

Am on a stoop to sit here tho no one
Asked me, nor asked you because you're not here,
A sign creaks—LAUNDRY TO-LET
    (creaks—wind—)—SUN—
(Nights?) the sun's, bro', what months rent in arrear?
Aighuh—and no manes and horses' trot? butt, butt
Of earth, birds spreading harps, two manes a pair
Of birds, each bird a word, a streaming gut,
Trot, trot—? No horse is here, no horse is there?
Says you! Then I—fellow me, airs! we'll make
Wood horse, and recognize it with our words—
Not it—nine less two!—as many as take
To make a dead man purple in the face,
Full dress to rise and circle thru a pace
Trained horses—in latticed orchards, (switch!) birds.

2ND FEMALE: Just what I said—Birds!—*See Him! Whom?*

                    The Son

Of Man, grave-turf on taxi, taxi gone,

Who blabbed of orchards, strides one leg here, one

Leg there—wooden horses? Give them manes!—

                    (was on

A stoop, *He found them sleeping*, don't you see?

See him! How? Against wood his body close,

Speaks: My face at where its forehead might be,

The plank's end's a forehead waving a rose—

CHORUS: Birds—birds—nozzle of horse, washed plank in air . . .

For they had no manes we would give them manes,

For their wood was dead the wood would

                   move—bare

But for the print on it—for diggers gone, trains'

   Run, light lights in air where the dead reposed—

   As many as take liveforever, "Street Closed."

1ST MALE: "Closed"? then fellow me airs, We'll open ruts

For the wood-grain skin laundered to pass thru,

Switch is a whip which never has been, cuts

Winds for words—Turf streams words, airs untraced

                  —New

The night, and orchards were here? Horses passed?—

   There were no diggers, bro', no horses there,

   But the graves were turfed and the horses grassed—

Two voices:—Airs? No birds. Taxi? No air—

2ND MALE: Says one! Then I—Are logs?! Two legs stand "A"—

Pace them! in revolution are the same!

Switch! See! we can have such and bucks tho they

Are not here, nor were there, pass thru a hoop

(Tho their legs are wood and their necks 've no name)

Strayed on a manhole—See! Am on a stoop!

IST MALE: See! For me these jiggers, these dancing bucks:
Bum pump a-dumb, the pump is neither bum
Nor dumb, dumb pump uh! hum, bum pump o! shucks!
(Whose clavicembalo? bum? bum? te-hum . . .)
Not in the say but in the sound's—hey-hey—
The way to-day, Die die, die, die, tap, slow,
Die, wake up, up! up! *O Saviour*, to-day!
Choose Jews' shoes or whose: anyway Choose! Go!

CHORUS: But they had no eyes, and their legs were wood!
But their stomachs were logs with print on them!
Blood red, red lamps hung from necks or where could
Be necks, two legs stood A, four together M—
    They had no manes so there were no airs, but—
    Butt . . . butt . . . from me to pit no singing gut!

IST MALE: Says you! Then I, Singing, It is not the sea
But what floats over: hang from necks or where could
Be necks, blood red, red lamps (Night), Launder me,
Mary! Sea of horses that once were wood,
Green and, and leaf on leaf, and dancing bucks,
Who take liveforever! Taken a pump
And shaped a flower. "Street Closed" on their
                        stomachs.

IST FEMALE: But the street has moved; at each block a stump
That blossoms red, and I sat there, no one
Asked me, nor asked you. Whom? You were not there.
A sign creaked—LAUNDRY TO-LET—creaked—
              wind—)—SUN—
(Nights?) the sun's, bro', no months' rent in arrear—
    Bum pump a-dum, no one's cut out, pump a-
    Ricky, bro', Shimaunu-Sān, yours is the

Clavicembalo—Nine less two, Seven
Were the diggers, seven sang, danced, the paces
Seven, Seven Saviours went to heaven—
Their tongues, hands, feet, eyes, ears and hearts,

each face as
Of a Sea looking Outward (Rose the Glass
Broken), Each a reflection of the other.
Just for the fun of it. And 't came to pass

CHORUS: (Open, O fierce flaming pit!)

three said: "Bother,

Brother, we want a meal, different techniques."
Two ways, my two voices . . . Offal and what
The imagination . . . And the seven came
To horses seven (of wood—who will?—kissed

their stomachs)
Bent knees as these rose around them—trot—trot—
Spoke: words, words, we are words, horses, manes,

words.

["A"-8]

MALE: Light lights in air,
                         on streets, on earth, in earth—

                         . . .

NARRATOR: By the green waters oil
                         The air circles the wild flower; the men
                         Skirt along the skyscraper street and carry weights
                         Heavier than themselves;

                         . . .

The machines shattering invisibles

. . .

May is, Airs wreathe (times): and they mirror:

. . .

(Times): that dug under the set hymns, *tonus
Contrarius*—

. . .

MALE: Luteclavicembalo—bullets pursue:
Labor light lights in earth, in air, on earth.

["A"-9]

FEMALE: Hands, heart, not value made us, and of any
Desired perfection the projection solely,
Lives worked us slowly to delight the senses,
Of their fire shall you find us,

. . .

MALE: Light acts beyond the phase day wills us into
Call a maturer day, the poor are torn—a
Pawl to adorn a ratchet—hope dim—eyeing
Move cangues, conjoined the coils of things they thin to,
With allayed furor the obscurer bourne, a
Stopped hope unworn, a voiced look, mask espying
That, as things, men want in us yet behoove us,
Disprove us least as things of light appearing
To the will gearing to light's infinite locus:
Not today but tomorrow is their focus.
No one really knows us who does not prove us,
None or times move us but that we wake searing
The labor veering from guises which cloak us,

As animate instruments men invoke us.

. . .

NARRATOR: We are things, say, like a quantum of action
Defined product of energy and time, now
In these words which rhyme now how song's exaction
Forces abstraction to turn from equated
Values to labor we have approximated.

. . .

MALE: Virtue flames value, merriment love—any
Compassed perfection a projection solely
Power, the lowly do not tune the senses;

. . .

FEMALE: Love acts beyond the phase day wills it into—
Hate is obscure, errs, is pain, furor, torn—a
Lust to adorn aversion, hope—love eyeing
Its object joined to its cause, sees path into
Things the future or now, that poorer bourne, a
Past, a step, a worn, a voiced look, gone—eyeing
These, each in itself is saying, "behoove us,
Disprove us least as things of love appearing
In a wish gearing to light's infinite locus,
Balm or jewelweed is according to focus.
No one really knows us who does not love us,
Time does not move us, we are and love, searing
Remembrance—veering from guises which cloak us,
So defined as eternal, men invoke us."

CHORUS: A wise man pledging piety unguarded
Lives good not error. By love's heir are asserted
Song, light obverted to mind, joy enjoined to
Least death, act edging patience, envy discarded;

Difficult rare excellence, love's heir, averted
Loss seize the hurt head Apollo's eyes point to:
Ai, Ai Hyacinthus, the petals in vision—
The scission living acquiescence, coded
Tempers decoded for friendship, evaded
Image recurring to vigilance, raided
By falsehood burning it clear to the vision,
Derision transmuted by laughter, goaded
Voice holding the node at heart, song, unfaded
Understanding whereby action is aided.

Love speaks:

MALE AND FEMALE: "in wracked cities there is less action,
Sweet alyssum sometimes is not of time; now
Weep, love's heir, rhyme now how song's exaction
Is your distraction—related is equated,
How else is love's distance approximated."

["A"-10]

NARRATOR: Paris
        Paris
        Of your beautiful phrases
        Is fallen
        The wire services halted

        Go ahead Paris
        London tunes in the Nazi broadcast already on
        New York feels the raid over Tours
                in the noon-hour cafés
        Cannot hear Paris
        Come over the air

Stares as into a bomb crater
At all the announcements
Of baseball scores that matter
Or do not matter a damn
The song passed out of the voices
As freedom goes out of speech

All the people of Paris
Mass, massed refugees on the roads
Go to mass with the air
      and the shrapnel for a church
    . . .

CHORUS: *Kyrie eleison*

MALE: They sang
                  The song passes out of the voices
                      one whisper

Cry louder
People   people   people
Alone each one is a whisper
A mess sucked out
No substance

Cry out in the streets of New York
But cry out in the streets of London
Cry loudest in the streets of Paris

People   people   people
There is no whisper but vibrates
Your body
No voice alone but that *you*
Speak it

NARRATOR:

Poor songster so weak
Stopped singing to curse
A mess sucked out
No substance

People   people
But you record it
Christ!

Glory on high

and in earth peace

Battered France halts her railroads
To freeze the flight south of her millions
From the Germans still advancing

. . .

You common people in the blackout

. . .

CHORUS:

Credo   I believe

Shame

Ashamed of all people put to shame
And all planets emit light
and indeed all bodies do

. . .

MALE:

The Rhino is a lovely beast
He has two horns or one at least
And neither horn is just a horn
Provoking a dictator's scorn
His surest backside venting scorn

He sits upon the Rhino's horn
And corporate spumes up a yeast
The Rhino such a lovely beast

Empaled beneath the Rhino's knee
People foul in its wet majesty
It feels them with a heavy paw
The spittle dribbles from its jaw
He mires their bleeding overalls
The loveliest of animals

. . .

CHORUS: *Go ahead Paris*
There'll be famine next winter

. . .

Blessed is the new age-old effervescence

Till the sailors who mistook their planet
                              for a light
And took the wrong soundings
Come back

And the people
Grant us the people's peace.

["A"-11]

MALE: River that must turn full after I stop dying
Song, my song, raise grief to music

. . .

> song, sang the blest is delight knowing
We overcome ills by love. Hurt, song, nourish
Eyes
>
> . . .
>
> Graced, your heart in nothing less than in death, go—
I, dust—raise the great hem of the extended
World that nothing can leave;
>
> . . .
>
> the river's turn that finds the
Grace in you,
>
> . . .
>
> song sounding

FEMALE: The grace

["A"-12]

CHORUS: *Out of deep need*

NARRATOR: Four trombones and the organ in the nave
A torch surged—
Timed the theme Bach's name,
Dark, larch and ridge, night:

. . .

MALE: Who tells time on all fours, yet moves
Shape, love—

. . .

FEMALE: How comes this gentle concord in the world?

. . .

"Speak to me in a different anguish

. . .

MALE: While you're partly right you're all wrong—

. . .

Love looks not with the eyes but with the mind

—is blind

. . .

FEMALE: Did Bach think sometimes like the Chinese—
Reason: the face of sky?

. . .

MALE: If love exists, why remember it?

. . .

NARRATOR: Facing south, I looked
At the ferry at South Ferry
At night, the ruins of Castle Garden
Where Jenny Lind sang
Before my time—with the diamonds
Of the songs of the nightingale—
Long after the Castle became the Aquarium:
Swung back by my young pulse,
Recalled a seal in teal blue,
A compass in binnacle—
Asleep or sleepless

. . .

The full moon rose. Flowed in the water.

. . .

MALE: Like the sea fishing
Constantly fishing
Its own waters

. . .

Already a little ode:
How I had to ford
To Hungerford,
I can't afford
Another word

. . .

NARRATOR:	I don't know just what is up. Some of the guys say that we will be going to Germany and some say to Korea. . . . We aboarded a train at the camp . . . Friday, April 13, we derk at the port of Yokohama 5,263 miles from San Francisco. We derk about 1 o'clock in the afternoon and stay on the ship until midnight. (What for I don't know)

. . .

MALE:	Wind carried larch to ridge.
	Patience.
	Truest horse.
	—it says—
	May I read your letter?

. . .

NARRATOR:	—A legitimate exchange of ignorance

. . . .

Everyone
Will explain to us
How to do
The wrong things
The right way

. . .

MALE:	—Tell me

NARRATOR:	—Tell *you*

["A"-13]

MALE:	Man in the moon stand and stride
	On his forked goad the burden he bears

It is a wonder that he does not slide,
For doubt less he fall he shudders and sheers.
When the frost freezes much chill he bides
The thorns are keen to tear his tatters to shreds.
Is no one in the world knows when he sees,
No but it be the hedge, what weeds he wears.
Whither trusts this man what the way takes?
He has set one foot and his other before
For no behest he hastes can he see me nor move
He is the slowest man that was ever borne.
Where he was of the field and pitched stakes
In hope his thorns would stop up his doors
His twibill had other cuttings to make
Or all his day's work would be there forlorn.
This same man up high ere he was there
Where he was born and fed in the moon
Leans on his fork as a grey friar
This crooked canard sore in his dread
It is many a day gone that he was here.
I know of his errand, he has not sped
He has hewn somewhere a burden of brier
Therefore some hayward has taken his pledge.
If the pledge is forfeit bring home the brush
Set forth thy other foot, stride over sty
We shall beg the hayward home to our house
And put him at ease for our mastery
Drink to him dearly of foul good booze
And our Dame Dowse shall sit by him
And when he is drunk as a drenched mouse
Then we'll redeem the pledge from the bailiff.
This man does not hear me tho I cry to him
I know the churl is deaf the Devil take him.
Tho I yell up high he will not hie
The lost lazy lout knows nothing of law.

Hop out Hubert in your hose magpie!
I know you are marshalled up to your craw
Tho I rage at him till my teeth are on edge
The churl will not down ere the day dawn.

. . .

NARRATOR: No one in history of legend
Died of laughter

. . .

MALE: Oldish man, frail, a
Yellow slip of paper
On which a song buds,

. . .

NARRATOR: mi-

nus-

cule on odd

scrap paper

["A"-14]

CHORUS: moon
loon
bless
light

. . .

NARRATOR: Ranger VII
photos landing
on the

moon
how deep
its dust?

crater whose
base is
shoal?

. . .

MALE: 'Fly which
way shall
I fly

whose eye
views all
things at

one view
in the
precincts of

light

. . .

space may
produce new

worlds, landscape
snow or
shower—

. . .

CHORUS: what thou
seest what

there thou
seest thyself
with thee

it came
and goes
but follow

me. Whom
fliest thou?
whom thou

fliest of
him thou
art.
  . . .
     how
shall we
breathe in

air
bent on
speed black

gurge human
from human
free so

many laws
argue so
many sins

till over
wrath grace
shall abound

hope no
higher tho
all the

stars thou
knew'st by
name

. . .

en canimus listen

we are singing
claruit semper urbs
nostra musica, our

city set forth
in music—

MALE: in
the dark backward

glib as who
when thing or
life was good

chattered 'it sings'
drew up facile—
doubt true skeptic

MALE: your *everyday* is
doubt, better not
know the family

tree, be spared
a feeble smile
eulogy lights on

Bach's necrolog from
half-wit aunt
aging child 'knew

not right hand
from left, brothers
the Lord glorified.'

["A"-16]

FEMALE: An

            inequality

                    Wind flower

["A"-17]

MALE: a
                    high
                    voice

                    as with
                    a lien
                    on
                    the sky

                    that becomes

                    low now

. . .

That song
        is the kiss
it keeps

    . . .

the crest of passion quieted

["A"-20]

CHORUS:	oh ivy green, so soft and green
	thou that do cover the earth and wall,
MALE AND FEMALE:	I pray to know what makes me worship thee,
	Thou that do cover do make travelers stand
	While Robins do nest in thy leaves
	While crickets do hum their song
	and bees do fly around thee
	What is it, I wonder that makes thee
	so loved

"A"

Cantata

13   v

CHORUS:

Naked sitting and lying awake

Quiet held near to speak,

Walking past each other not to step

Over their own bodies

Slender summit most night

Envelope of floral leaves'

Twilight when all seams sun

The same either night or day

Travels the raised blind

Lights the view.

And comes to:

Behind the five windows

The light let to no hour

Becomes all neighborhood

TENOR:

Always between the pattern of roofs

       there is water hidden and open below

That brings the bridges to span it

       piers and boats,

Whole

Quiet

SOPRANO:

So brief is not brief

Not brief is so brief

TENOR:

Quiet once taught to speak

DUET	The embrace
(TENOR AND	Of the beloved
SOPRANO):	That know
	Nothing else
	Within or
	Without,
	Incapable of
	Conspiring
	Together
CHORUS:	Only the image of a voice:
SOPRANO:	*Love you*

THE UNCOLLECTED LOUIS ZUKOFSKY

ACKNOWLEDGMENTS

For the various archival materials, journals and books consulted for this volume, we thank the following: Harry Ransom Center at the University of Texas at Austin, Beinecke Rare Book and Manuscript Library at Yale University, Richard L. D. and Marjorie J. Morse Department of Archives and Special Collections at Kansas State University, New York Public Library, and the Paul Zukofsky estate. We also want to thank New Directions and Faber and Faber for permission to reprint Ezra Pound materials, as well as Daniel Nordby for the estate of Carl Rakosi.

NOTES

Note on the Texts

The majority of works in this edition were published during Zukofsky's lifetime, and in these cases, the printed versions have served as copy texts, with only clear misprints or errata corrected. In most cases, there are also manuscripts and/or typescripts, which have been checked as well. Significant differences have been noted below, but overall there are few consequential textual complications.

For unpublished materials, typescripts have been preferred over manuscripts whenever available. Zukofsky did not type, so usually he had his works typed up only when he was satisfied that they were finished and ready to be sent out for publication, although this did not rule out further revisions in some cases.

Both manuscripts and published texts exhibit considerable inconsistency in spelling and punctuation (much of this would today be considered by Americans as "British," but this distinction was far from clear in the first half of the twentieth century). These have been regularized to current American practice, except to maintain his preferred spellings or that of his quoted sources. The punctuation of titles can be especially variable (underlined, single or double quotation marks, all capitals or standard capitalization). These have been regularized throughout.

These notes do not offer an exhaustive register of the differences between printed, typed and autograph versions of the texts, but only record substantive variants.

Annotations

Dates of composition are given when known, followed by information on the initial publication or other copy text used, in the following format: [date] / [first publication/ copy text]. Composition dates are taken from Zukofsky's manuscripts and typescripts, which he was in the habit of dating; in most cases, we have an accurate idea of when each work was completed. Unless otherwise specified, all manuscripts, typescripts, letters, and personal copies of journals referred to in these notes are held at the Harry Ransom Center, University of Texas at Austin.

In addition, background and contextualizing information has been provided where helpful, along with some identifications of quotations, names and titles, as well as cross-references with other Zukofsky works.

Abbreviations Used

LZ	Louis Zukofsky
MS	manuscript
TS	typescript
HRC	Harry Ransom Center, University of Texas at Austin
Yale	Beinecke Rare Book and Manuscript Library, Yale University
"A"	"A" (New Directions, 2011)
CSP	Anew: Complete Shorter Poetry (New Directions, 2011)
Prep.	Prepositions+: The Collected Critical Essays (Wesleyan University Press, 2000)

PART I. Arise, Arise

27 June 1936 / *Kulchur* 6 (Summer 1962)

TS dated 27 June 1936, with a note that the play was revised 30 November 1940. These revisions are not substantive but matters of tightening up and occasional rewording, and this revised text is the basis of the published texts: first in *Kulchur* 6 (1962), then as a book in 1973 by Grossman Publishers. The Grossman publication serves as the copy text here.

The play was given a reading performance by the Dramatic Workshop directed by Erwin Piscator at the New School for Social Research in 1947. In 1950, LZ submitted *Arise, Arise* to the Japanese journal *Shigaku* with a brief preface, as quoted in the introduction. The play was first staged by the Cinémathèque Theatre in New York

City in August 1965 under the direction of Jerry Benjamin. For that performance, LZ placed particular stress on the play's musical aspect, writing out a list of musical works with additional suggestions beyond those specified in the stage directions.

The play incorporates a wide range of quotations, which in many cases are not marked as such but simply integrated into the dialogue:

"At the round earth's imagined corners, blow … : John Donne, "Holy Sonnet 7." One of the two main sources of the play's title, lines from this poem recur periodically throughout (see 4, 7, 21, 29).

There was once a Strictly Anonymous … : this limerick was written in response to another by Ezra Pound directed at LZ, entitled "Formalism."

Le Pauvre Laboureur: traditional French folk song, LZ's translation.

We came to the garden in flower … : LZ's translation of Guillaume Apollinaire's poem "The Gathering" (La cueillette); continuing at 17 **An expansive garden is nipped, my egotist**. … (see Translations 178)

That there comes a time when twenty years are but one day … : from Karl Marx, letter to Frederick Engels, 9 April 1863. Also quoted in "Thanks to the Dictionary" (*Collected Fiction* 279).

He came also still … : adapted from the fifteenth century English carol "I sing of a maiden"; (included in *A Test of Poetry* 13). Most notably, LZ substitutes a sister for the mother (Virgin Mary) of the original poem. See below at 22, where the carol is continued.

We mourn only ourselves, our own earth selves: from LZ's uncollected sonnet, "Someone said, 'earth, bowed with her death, we mourn'" (154).

"Sentimentally I am disposed … : from Charles Lamb, "A Chapter on Ears."

In the time of the Indian war the wife of Van Tienhoven . . . : from *Manual of the Corporation of the City of New York for 1855*, ed. D. T. Valentine. This and other documents on early New York are from materials LZ researched for his work with the W.P.A. in the 1930s.

They wired from Strasbourg . . . : from a colonial era newspaper; where the source has "write" LZ substitutes "wired."

Minuchihr would treat as worse than evil . . . : from the Persian national epic *Shahnameh* by Ferdowsi (940-1020?).

All one's friends . . . : from Henry Adams, *The Education of Henry Adams*, Chap. XXII (1918).

I am no longer myself. I am the fifteenth after the eleventh: LZ's translation from the poem "À la Santé" by Guillaume Apollinaire. See "Sequence from *The Writing of Guillaume Apollinaire*" (180).

We were all there today . . . : adapted from John Donne, "Holy Sonnet 7."

"we understood . . . : from John Donne, "The Second Anniversary: Of the Progress of the Soul."

He came also still . . . : adapted from a fifteenth-century carol, see above.

Passing me on the street today Sam MacVea . . . : LZ's translation from Apollinaire's *Le Pòete assassiné*; see "Sequence from *The Writing of Guillaume Apollinaire*" (180).

Machines—luxury and beauty are only their spray: LZ's translation from Apollinaire's poem "1909"; see "Sequence from *The Writing of Guillaume Apollinaire*" (180).

It is plain, moreover, that work now brutal under suitable conditions...: from Karl Marx, *Capital*; continuing at 32: It is just as stupid to regard the Christo-Teutonic form of the family...

A specter is haunting Europe...: the opening of Marx and Engels, *The Communist Manifesto*.

Debout les damnés de la terre...: the beginning of the socialist anthem, *L'Internationale*, composed by Eugene Pottier to celebrate the Paris Commune of 1871. This song is the second major source of the play's title, along with Donne's "Holy Sonnet 7."

No man sick with ever such sickness...: from Henry Adams' rendition of the thirteenth century French fable, "Aucassins and Nicolette" in *Mont-Saint-Michel and Chartres*, Chap. XII (1905); continuing at 29: **Should you pass her door**...

It is late to ask much of its grace, when we are here: adapted from John Donne, "Holy Sonnet 7"; also "Death's woe."

The land where milk and honey flow...: an early verse description promoting New Amsterdam (New York), adapted from Jacob Steendam, *Praise of New Netherland* (1661).

The moneyed relation that tore from our family its sentimental veil: from Marx and Engels, *The Communist Manifesto*.

And I see the ground on which your aunt stood has been drawn from under her feet...: the Doctor's lines here and on following couple of pages, ending with "... **have produced their own gravediggers**," are adapted from Marx and Engels, *The Communist Manifesto*.

Arise damned of earth!: English translation of the opening line of *L'Internationale*, see above.

The ground's onesidedness ... : this and the following Doctor's speech adapted from *The Communist Manifesto*.

Where is your capital? [. . .] Why, then, there can no longer be wage labor: adapted from *The Communist Manifesto*.

the intellect has become common property: from *The Communist Manifesto*.

Mesquakies, their reservations lowlands ... : from *The New York Times*, 27 April 1936.

What is money? ... : paraphrased from Marx, *Capital*. See quotations from *Capital* on money in *First Half of "A"-9* (59–64).

A certain surgeon had a beautiful garden here: from Adriaen van der Donck, *A Description of the New Netherland* (1655).

Here in New York, the grain sowed in the middle of May ... : from 1626 letter by Peter Schagen, Dutch colonial era official.

a fruit called *forerunners*: from van der Donck, *A Description of New Netherland*, see above. This detail is mentioned in *Bottom: on Shakespeare* 86.

One wrote of an east river: a narrow passage ... : from Daniel Denton, *A Brief Description of New York* (1670).

Morning stars, maritoffles ... : from van der Donck, *A Description of the New Netherland*, see above.

Divers birds chirping harmonious discord .... : from Denton, *A Brief Description of New York*, see above.

tho its trees one time were so laden with peaches . . . : from *Journal of Jasper Danckaerts* (1679-1680).

Small fish are fried . . . : from W. H. Gibson, *Camping for Boys* (1913).

Propped on the earth, and from where, what sleep . . . : from LZ's poem, "(Awake!)" (159).

I've been at Valenciennes . . . : Valenciennes is a major coal producing area in northern France, which played a key role in the General Strike across France in June 1936. *The New York Times* reported that "Miners in the Valenciennes region slept on railroad tracks to prevent movement of cars of coal" (6 June 1936).

Graced, graced, the eyes grow black from dancing: from an early (probably 1923) unpublished LZ poem: *The First Seasons and Other Early Poems 1918-1924*, ed. Jeffrey Twitchell-Waas (Z-site Publications, 2024), 113.

One thing we pray of Diana. Let whoever never loved . . . : from the anonymous Latin *Pervigilium Veneris* (probably second or third century), adapted from the first chapter of Ezra Pound's *The Spirit of Romance* (1910), which uses J. W. MacKail's translation. The refrain appears in *Anew* 31 (*CSP* 94-95).

PART II. First Half of "A"-9

24 Nov. 1939 / privately printed 1940

This work was published by Celia Zukofsky in a mimeograph edition "limited to 55 autographed copies." LZ always insisted that this assemblage was not to be reprinted. "A"-9 (first half) was published the following year in *Poetry* 58:3 (June 1941). In 1966, both halves of "A"-9 were published as a folded broadside alongside the Italian text of Cavalcanti's canzone with an abridged and revised statement on "The 'Form'" (in German) by edition hansjörg mayer (Stuttgart).

The Italian text of Cavalcanti's canzone is from Pound's edition of the complete poems, *Guido Cavalcanti Rime* (Genoa: Marano 1932). LZ's vernacular version ("A foin lass bodders me") was composed intermittently from 9 August 1938 to 1 April 1940. It was never reprinted in LZ's lifetime, and its first readily available publication was by Hugh Kenner in a section of tributes to LZ in *New Directions* 39 (1979) with Kenner's commentary, "Loove in Brooklyn."

Pound's remarks quoted in "The 'Form'" are from the essay, "Cavalcanti," published in its original form in *The Dial* (1928) and then in both *Guido Cavalcanti Rime* and *Make It New* (1934).

As was his characteristic practice, LZ uses a two-dot (. .) ellipsis for his own cuts in the texts from Marx and on physics, but maintains a standard ellipsis whenever these appear within Marx's own presentation of quotations.

PART III. Uncollected Poems and Translations

Uncollected Poems (1923–1977)

A Parable of Time

Summer 1923 / *Two Worlds* 1:1 (Sept. 1925).

Although written while LZ was still a student at Columbia University, this poem, along with "The Sadness After," represents his first significant publication after his graduation and the first in a major little magazine (aside from a conventional sonnet in *Poetry* in 1924). *Two Worlds: A Literary Quarterly Devoted to the Increase of the Gaiety of Nations* was edited by Samuel Roth (1893–1974), who would gain notoriety for publishing unauthorized sections of James Joyce's *Ulysses* in his sequel journal, *Two Worlds Monthly*.

"No sound. But sun."

16 Aug. 1923 / *Blues* 1 (Feb. 1929).

"The people change and the birds in the air"

25 May 1924 / Unpublished (MS HRC)
    MS adds: "Long Beach / (Second Island night)."

"All the stars have filled the heavens"

6 July 1924 / *Poetry* 34:3 (June 1929).

    Published in *Poetry* as part of a group of seven poems under the general title "Siren and Signal": I. "'He Came Also Still'"; II. "All the stars have filled the heavens"; III. "Play lost, banjos!"; IV. North River Ferry; V. "Cars once steel and green, now old"; VI. "Comes a day when the round tracts of sky"; VII. "During lunch hour I shall stretch opposite." III and IV are included in *55 Poems* (*CSP* 24, 31); for the other poems, see below.

"'It is well on this June night'"

7 July 1924 / *Pagany* 1:2 (April–June 1930).

Wickson: almost certainly LZ's Columbia classmate and friend, Whittaker Chambers (1901-1961), whose family home was near the Long Island shore where LZ spent summers and which is the setting of many poems from this period. In *Pagany* this poem was published with two others, "And looking to where shone Orion" and "Only water–," both included in *55 Poems* (*CSP* 29); the former also explicitly addresses "Wickson" and both are set at the seashore.

"Always the May-day sun"

17 Aug. 1924 / *Blues* 9 (Fall 1930).

sub aeternitatis specie: under the aspect of eternity, Spinoza's famous phrase from his *Ethics*.

"September among the headstones"

21 Sept. 1924 / *The Criterion* 8:32 (April 1929).

"Comes a day when the round tract of sky"

18 Feb. 1925 / *The Lavender* 3:6 (Jan. 1926); *Poetry* 34:3 (June 1929)
> See note for "All the stars have filled the heavens" (340).
> In *The Lavender* appears under the title, "February 18, 1925." *The Lavender* was
the student literary magazine of the City College of New York, which was co-edited
by LZ's friend Henry Zolinsky (1901–2001).

"And they rest: the manifold light rays–"

15–16 June 1925 / Unpublished (MS HRC).
> MS notes: "Long Beach."

"Play lost, banjos! Across the areas of ocean's flowing"

23 Aug. 1925 / *Poetry* 34:3 (June 1929).
> See note for "All the stars have filled the heavens" (340).

The Sadness After

Fall 1925 / *Two Worlds* 1:2 (Dec. 1925).

"The sun–"

6 Sept. 1925 / *Blues* 9 (Fall 1930).

"Across the smoke, over all past living"

17 Oct. 1925 / *Blues* 2 (March 1929).

"And about these lights, they are the lights"

8 Nov. 1926 / *Blues* 2 (March 1929).

A TS, significantly revised by hand, matches the printed version except for a typo in l. 9 ("world-whip") and in l. 25 adds a comma and the phrase "jewelled nerve."

"'And the strong men shall bow themselves, and the grinders'"

27 Jan. 1926 / *Blues* 2 (March 1929).

The first stanza quotes from Ecclesiastes 12:3.

(I wait for the train)

10 May 1926 / *Blues* 8 (Spring 1930).

For a Thing by Bach

14 June 1926 / *Pagany* 1:4 (Oct–Dec. 1930).

LZ refers to and quotes bits of this poem in "A"-18 ("A" 391).

A Preface and 18 Poems to the Future

1925–1927? / Mostly unpublished (TS Yale).

LZ submitted this sequence with its preface as a follow-up to "Poem beginning 'The'" in *The Exile* 3 (Spring 1928), but Pound was unenthusiastic. In the end, *The Exile* 4 (Autumn 1928) included an eclectic group of pieces by LZ: a review of E. E. Cummings' *HIM*, "Mr. Cummings and the Delectable Mountains"; two verse-essays, "Preface–1927" and "Critique of Antheil"; a poem in homage to Lenin, "Constellation" (retitled "Memory of V. I. Ulianov" in *55 Poems*); and finally "A Preface" intended for "18 Poems to the Future." Most of the "18 Poems to the Future" are undated and MS do not survive, but the period 1925–1927 is a plausible guess. This sequence of poems exists only in a TS preserved among Pound's papers at Yale, which lacks "A Preface," although the title page indicates it belongs with these poems.

Using quotations from John Bunyan's *Pilgrim's Progress* for epigraphs was quite probably suggested by Cummings' novel *The Enormous Room* (1922), which LZ admired at this time. In *The Exile* 4, the poem to Lenin also included an epigraph from *Pilgrim's Progress*, which suggests it may have been considered for inclusion in "18 Poems to the Future." It is possible the Lenin poem was originally intended as the concluding poem of the sequence, which might explain why the final poem in the typescript has no number, lacks an epigraph and was composed after "A Preface." Only three poems of the sequence were published: #10 "In the Era of Rays" and #14 "During the Passaic Strike of 1926" are both included in *55 Poems*, and the final poem, "N. Y. 1927" was published in *Nativity* 2 (Spring 1931) but otherwise uncollected.

A Preface

17 Oct. 1926 / *The Exile* 4 (Autumn 1928).

Sorel: as LZ indicates the quotations are from George Sorel's *Réflexions sur la violence* (1908), which was translated by T. E. Hulme as *Reflections on Violence* (1914):

> It is a philosophy of conduct rather than a theory of the world; it considers the *march towards deliverance* as narrowly conditioned [...] The pessimist regards social conditions as forming a system bound together by an iron law which cannot be evaded, so that the system is given, as it were, in one block, and cannot disappear except in a catastrophe which involves the whole.
>
> In the total ruin of institutions and of morals there remains something which is powerful, new, and intact, and it is that which constitutes, properly speaking, the soul of the revolutionary proletariat. Nor will this be swept away in the general decadence of moral values, if the workers have enough energy to bar the road to the middle-class corrupters, answering their advances with the plainest brutality.

9. "Nervure-sharp, O tipping tower"

Dated December 21, 1925.

10. In the Era of Rays

MS dated May 3, 1926 / "Poem 11" in *55 Poems* (1941).

In *55 Poems*, this poem lacks the title and the epigraph from Bunyan; also the first line is deleted and the penultimate line revised: "Ours, till again it moves along the sky" (*CSP* 28)—both of these latter alterations are indicated in an MS.

12. "How home-born the engines"

Dated January 25, 1926.

13. "Look it in the face, then, and it will smile as it always has on Caesar–"

The epigraph is from George Bernard Shaw's preface to *Three Plays for Puritans* (Grant Richards, 1901), which includes *Caesar and Cleopatra*: "I have, I think, always been a Puritan in my attitude towards Art. I am as fond of fine music and handsome buildings as Milton was, or Cromwell, or Bunyan; but if I found that they were becoming the instruments of a systematic idolatry of sensuousness, I would hold it good statesmanship to blow every cathedral in the world to pieces with dynamite, organ and all, without the least heed to the screams of the art critics and cultured voluptuaries."

14. During the Passaic Strike of 1926

MS dated April 18, 1926 / "Poem 7" in *55 Poems* (1941).

Textile workers in Passaic, New Jersey, began a strike over wage cuts and better working conditions in January 1926. Eventually 15,000 workers were out on strike, which lasted through most of the year and involved numerous clashes with police and arrests of strikers.

S. T. H.: S. Theodore Hecht (1895–1973), LZ's Columbia classmate and good friend.

18. N. Y. 1927

Sept. 13, 1927 / *Nativity* 2 (Spring 1931).

The somewhat tightened up *Nativity* text has been preferred over the earlier "18 Poems to the Future" TS version, which differs as follows:

Title: N. / Y. / 1927.

line 2: Now song that lipped once

line 5: than one man and men together

line 8: Build them high walls and pyramids, hugeness

line 10: Isolated

line 11: two-footed men

line 13: Up—ah—gullies of air

line 17: en masse

line 19: Sand-color from heaven

line 20: You, my city

line 23: For the many, walkers and steel-shifters

lines 27–29:

> May yet to the builders of them not be the drudgery of their years
>
> sapped out,

> And to the mourner of past Song may be that
> Superfluity of grace enriching a transient stay,
> Man's day of work, as does at times the adornment of a new
> cravat!

(Spinoza in a Winter Season)

26 Jan. 1927 / *The Criterion* 8:32 (April 1929).

This poem was composed three days before the death of LZ's mother, which is clearly the poem's circumstance. The quotation in lines 9–10 is from Spinoza's *Ethics* Part I, Prop. XVI. LZ slightly adapts the translation from the Everyman's Library edition of

Ethics and On the Correction of the Understanding, trans. Andrew Boyle (1910): "Infinite things in infinite modes [...] must necessarily follow from the necessity of divine nature."

"What are these smoke-stacks"

26 Jan. 1927 / *The Left* 1:1 (Spring 1931).

"My watch!"

7 March 1927 / *Blues* 8 (Spring 1930).

"He Came Also Still"

9 March 1927 / *Poetry* 34:3 (June 1929).

See notes for "All the stars have filled the heavens" (340).

The title quotes from a well-known fifteenth-century carol, "I sing of a maiden": "He cam also stille / There his moder lay" (*A Test of Poetry* 13). LZ gives a reworked version of this carol in *Arise, Arise* (15-16, 22)

This is the first of four published sonnets LZ wrote during a single week that respond belatedly to the death of his mother on 29 January 1927. Two poems composed in the following month are probably related as well: "And human heart-beats; star-falling; engine-beats–" (155) and "A dying away as of trees" in *55 Poems* (*CSP* 27). See also note to "(Spinoza in a Winter Season)" (345).

"The silence of the good that you were wrought of"

10 March 1927 / *The Dial* 85:6 (Dec. 1928).

See notes for "'He Came Also Still'" (above).

"O lowering belts"

14 March 1927 / *The Left* 1:1 (Spring 1931).

"Someone said, 'earth, bowed with her death, we mourn'"

15 March 1927 / *The Dial* 85:6 (Dec. 1928).

See note for "'He Came Also Still.'" (346).

Two phrases from lines 1–2, "we mourn ourselves, our own earth selves," were incorporated into *Arise, Arise* (17).

"During lunch hour I shall stretch opposite"

15 March 1927 / *Poetry* 34:3 (June 1929).

See notes for "'He Came Also Still'" (346) and "All the stars have filled the heavens" (340).

"And human heart-beats; star-falling; engine-beats–"

8 April 1927 / *Blues* 8 (Spring 1930).

In *Blues*, l. 7 has "Star-falls"; emended according to MS.

Critique of Antheil

1927 / *The Exile* 4 (Autumn 1928).

There are minor variants and significant differences in layout from the TS sent to Pound (Yale), but the printed text is reproduced here (except for the elimination of a few wraparound lines, as indicated by the TS). There is a shorter MS version at HRC, which was also sent to Pound (Yale).

As LZ indicates, this verse-critique is a response to the American premier of George Antheil's *Ballet Méchanique* at Carnegie Hall, New York City, which both LZ and William Carlos Williams attended. The previous year, *Ballet Méchanique* caused an uproar at its world premiere in Paris, a response Antheil worked energetically to provoke. LZ apparently alludes to Antheil's staged disappearance in Africa as a publicity stunt leading up to that performance. Although the New York premiere was equally scandalous, it was widely derided by the New York media and Antheil retreated to Paris. For Williams' response, see "George Antheil and the Cantilene Critics" in *Selected Essays*.

(Awake!)

28 April 1927 / *Pagany* 2:1 (Jan.-March 1931).

LZ adapted several lines from this poem in *Arise, Arise*; see speech by Attendant D. (37).

Preface–1927

11 July 1927 / *The Exile* 4 (Autumn 1928).

(These States 1927)

11 July 1927 / Unpublished (MS HRC).

"Autumn, then autumn—what of it?"

13 Sept. 1927 / *Blues* 4 (May 1929).

"Finer was the dead artist's hand"

6 June 1928 / *Blues* 4 (May 1929).

"O autumn fields, if we should break, beyond"

31 Oct. 1928 / *Blues* 4 (May 1929).

University: Old-Time

1930 / *Poetry* 37:1 (Feb. 1931).

LZ explained the origin of this found poem in a letter to Pound dated 14 December 1931: "Napa—a kind of weed growing in Napa, Calif. I don't know why Persephone's husband, romanized [Dis, Roman god of the underworld, sometimes conflated with Pluto], shdn't be on the west coast now. I don't know that Napa has a university, but it might as well have. The literal meaning of this famous epigram was the bare statement in a letter of Roger Kaigh [Irving Kaplan] to Mr. L. Z.–D. (Dorothy his spouse, who was dispensing pensions to old folk) is in Napa trailing the sterilized. I added the title & lower-cased napa—which word you can find in Webster's international." LZ then adds some comical "allegorical" interpretations including the suggestion that he is Dis and napa is the University of Wisconsin, where he was teaching for a year (*Pound/Zukofsky: Selected Letters of Ezra Pound and Louis Zukofsky*, ed. Barry Ahearn. New Directions, 1987, 120-121). See also 22 March 1963 letter to Edmund Wilson (*Selected Letters*).

Song 11

27 May 1932 / Unpublished (MS HRC).

MS notes: "S.F. Calif."

The title suggests this was originally considered for inclusion among "29 Songs" in *55 Poems*.

(Collaboration)

10 Aug. 1932 / Unpublished (MS HRC).

In the MS, LZ specifies the spacing between stanzas: double, triple, double, triple.

LZ included a section of "collaborations" in *An "Objectivists" Anthology* (To, Publishers, 1932), which mostly consists of poems by Kenneth Rexroth, William Carlos Williams, and R. B. N. Warriston that LZ reworked by drastic reduction.

mirror fugue on "The Gnat" by Carl Rakosi

24 Nov. 1932 / *The Windsor Quarterly* 1.2 (Summer 1933).

LZ began corresponding with Carl Rakosi (1903–2004) regarding the "Objectivists" issue of *Poetry*, and the two wrote to each other fairly regularly through the early 1930s, until Rakosi moved to New York in 1935 where he remained for the latter half of the decade. Particularly during the two years immediately following the "Objectivists" issue, Rakosi regularly sent poems to LZ, who gave detailed feedback, much of which was incorporated into the final versions. The "mirror fugue" came out of the exchange of these years. Rakosi's "The Gnat" was itself a stripped down reworking of an earlier poem, "The January of a Gnat." Presumably it was Rakosi's idea to present the poems together with some contextualizing remarks from their letters in *The Windsor Quarterly*. Many years later, when Rakosi published *Amulet* (New Directions, 1967), which marked his return to poetry after a long hiatus, he reprinted "The Gnat" with the subtitle: A greeting to Louis Zukofsky.

LZ's side of the correspondence with Rakosi is held at the HRC; however, the letter in which LZ sent his "mirror fugue" is missing. LZ made a copy of Rakosi's poem and his response, with a slight difference in the final two stanzas of Rakosi's poem: "six rivers and six / wenches, the twelve // victories." Perhaps Rakosi decided to regularize the final stanza in the published version to better match LZ's response. LZ's final remark refers to what eventually became poem 5 of "A Journey Away," which has the lines: "She played a classical pianoforte / clef-wandering sweet pinna tremolo." See Carl Rakosi, *Poems 1923-1941*, ed. Andrew Crozier (Sun & Moon Press, 1995), 104.

"Of sleep where all your past goes on–"

May? 1934 / Unpublished (MS HRC).

LZ was closely involved in William Carlos Williams's protracted effort to compose an opera on George Washington, *The First President*, with music by their mutual friend Tibor Serly. The working relationship between Williams and Serly was difficult and eventually broke down, with LZ finding himself in the middle trying to mediate. A note on the MS indicates this poem was composed for Williams's opera but evidently not used. Marcella Booth quotes a letter LZ wrote her on 7 May 1969: "[Williams] wanted a song for Martha while Wash'n'ton sleeps [in the opening scene of the opera]—I was drafted to do it. . . . The whole business fell thru. But we stayed up all night" (*A Catalogue of the Louis Zukofsky Manuscript Collection* [Humanities Research Center, University of Texas at Austin, 1975] 63). LZ reworked the poem as "Alba (1952)" in *Some Time* (*CSP* 134).

"Sorrow! Sorrow little child"

The New Caravan (1936).

This song appears in William Carlos Williams' opera *The First* President (see preceding note) with an additional first line: "My baby! My baby!" A MS of this song among LZ's papers indicates he wrote it. See Williams, *Many Loves and Other Plays* (New Directions, 1961), 328.

"March Comrades"

New Masses 27:6 (3 May 1938).

LZ incorporated this song, without the title, into "A"-8, which was first published in *New Directions 1938* (97–98). However, when he revised this movement in 1957 in preparation for the publication of "A" 1-12, he cut out the more blatant political rhetoric, eliminating the first stanza altogether and severely trimming the last ("A" 48–49). The *New Masses* printing mistakenly adds a "was" in the final line of the third stanza that LZ never intended.

"Belly Lox Shnooks Oaky"

7 April 1941 / Unpublished (MS HRC).

This limerick is a spicier spin on *Anew* 38, "Belly Locks Shnooks Oakie" (*CSP* 97). Shnook is Yiddish for someone who is timid or gullible, a sad sack.

Cyclists

28 April 1941 (orig. 1 Jan. 1941) / Unpublished (TS Yale).

This poem is included in a 1943 *Anew* TS sent to Williams Carlos Williams (Yale). This TS represents an initial selection and arrangement for this planned collection, which would be significantly altered for the version published in 1946 by The Press of James A. Decker (Prairie City, Illinois). In a MS draft, the original title is "Bicyclers," then changed to "Cyclists," and finally to "Conversation."

This and the following poem are among a number of seemingly inconsequential squibs that were included in the early *Anew* TS but then withdrawn. However, several reappear in "Light," from *Some Time* (1956), the first of quite a few late serial poems that LZ assembled from discretely composed poems, not infrequently including bits of over-heard conversation.

"Eat the pie?"

1 May 1941 / Unpublished (TS Yale).

LZ sent an early, longer version of this poem as "Anew 25" to Lorine Niedecker on a postcard postmarked 5 May 1941: "Eat the pie? / Not I / Said the eye. // Spread the butter / Not / As I stutter. // Beef, pork, lamb? / Ham–/ As I am?" Another MS version in a folder of "discarded poems" consists of the first and third of these stanzas, with the latter further truncated as it appears in the 1943 *Anew* typescript (see preceding note).

"Can a mote of sunlight defeat its purpose"

15 Sept. 1942 / Unpublished (TS Yale/MS HRC).

This is an earlier version of what became *Anew* 21 (*CSP* 88), where it is truncated to just the first three lines with the addition of a word in the third.

What Passion for a Baby?

1–6 Dec. 1943 / Unpublished (MS HRC).

This is a longer version of a poem revised in 1948 and published as "Light 7" in *Some Time* (*CSP* 118).

Paul Zukofsky was born 22 October 1943, and Dinty was his nickname as a baby. See "To my baby Paul" (*CSP* 102).

Julia's Wild

13 Jan. 1960 / *Bottom: on Shakespeare* (Ark Press, 1963).

This poem and the circumstances of its composition became section J in "An Alphabet of Subjects," Part III of *Bottom: on Shakespeare* (393–394), which reproduces an exchange with the American poet and publisher, Cid Corman (1924-2004). Having just read *The Two Gentlemen of Verona*, Corman wrote that his favorite line was "Come, shadow, come, and take this shadow up" (IV, iv, 202) and urged LZ to "Ring a change on that for me? A dark valentine" (letter dated 9 Jan. 1960). The entire exchange, including Corman's answer to "Julia's Wild," became LZ's tribute to Corman, particularly for publishing *"A"* *1-12* (Origin Press, 1959). Although LZ did not include this poem in any of his collections of short poems, he performed it at readings and allowed it to be published on its own in a number of anthologies. It has had a curious history of being included in collections of concrete poetry. Charles Bernstein included the poem in *Selected Poems* of LZ (Library of America, 2006).

THE OVERWORLD

16 Jan. 1977 / Unpublished (MS HRC).

This poem was copied into LZ's notebook for *GAMUT: 90 Trees*, for which he was already collecting notes well before he completed *80 Flowers* (1978). "THE OVERWORLD" was originally composed as a possible epigraph for that volume, but LZ subsequently wrote a very different epigraph, "Much ado about trees lichen," which proved to be the only poem he finished for this projected collection before his death. "Much ado about trees lichen," incorrectly given the title "Gamut," was published in *CSP* (355).

"THE OVERWORLD" is a found poem, a radical condensation carved entirely out of the final "After Scene" of Thomas Hardy's *The Dynasts*, which, according to LZ's notation in his personal copy, he first read in 1922 and reread 6 December 1976-15 January 1977. Never one to waste anything, LZ incorporated or adapted bits of "THE OVERWORLD" into "Windflower" for *80 Flowers* (*CSP* 343), composed 27-31 May 1977.

The Greek line is from the Magnificat canticle or "Song of Mary" from the Gospel of Luke (1:52), and "echoes" Hardy's adaptation of it in line 6.

Translations (1930–1943)

André Salmon: An Arrangement from *Prikaz*

Nov.-Dec. 1930 / Unpublished (TS HRC).

The "Objectivists" issue of *Poetry* (Feb. 1931) included an essay on André Salmon by René Taupin and translated by LZ (the second half of the essay appeared in the following issue), which contained excerpts from Salmon's 1919 epic on the Russian

Revolution. LZ was interested in Salmon's "nominalism," which he compared with cinematic montage—a presentation of multiple discrete moments and perspectives without plot or recurring characters. LZ made this arrangement of a selection of the passages from *Prikaz* in Taupin's essay (slightly revised) as the final entry in *A Workers Anthology*, which he assembled in the mid-1930s. Although this anthology was never published, most of its selections ended up in *A Test for Poetry* (1948). The only complete copy of *A Workers Anthology* is a TS at the Basil Bunting Poetry Centre at Durham University.

Guillaume Apollinaire: The Gathering

Nov. 1931 / Unpublished (TS Yale).

Text based on a hand-corrected TS at Yale.

This translation was made while LZ was working on *Le Style Apollinaire* (1934) with René Taupin. Although LZ did not include this poem among the numerous quotations in that work, he did incorporate his translation, with slight deletions and differences in details, into *Arise, Arise* (14, 17). See next note.

Sequence from *The Writing of Guillaume Apollinaire*

7 April 1934 / *Columbia Review and Morningside* 15:4 (May 1934).

LZ made a few corrections in his copy of the printed text where the title is "From the Writings of Guillaume Apollinaire" and the roman numeral "X" in the first section is missing. On the back of his fair copy, LZ added the following note: "n.b. Use this sequence as a separate section to preface the English version of L. Z.'s and R. T's *The Writing of Guillaume Apollinaire* and the translation of 'The Gathering' as an appendix back-leaf colophon poem or what, at the end of the same volume." The French version of this book, translated by René Taupin, was published as *Le Style Apollinaire* by Les Presses Modernes (Paris, 1934). A complete English version of *The Writing of Guillaume Apollinaire* never appeared in LZ's lifetime, although the first and third parts were published in separate issues of *The Westminster Magazine* 22:4 (Winter 1933) and 23:1 (Spring 1934).

This assemblage consists entirely of translated snippets from Apollinaire's verse used in the book (the English version does not translate any of its numerous quotations and in effect is a dual-language work). See *The Writing of Guillaume Apollinaire/Le Style*

Apollinaire, ed. Serge Gavronsky (Wesleyan University Press, 2004), in sequence: 186/187, 220/221, 182/183, 194/195, 230/231, 228/229, 218/219, 233/234, 158/159. The MS fair copy date indicates this sequence was put together for publication in the *Columbia Review* a few years after LZ had completed the Apollinaire book. This was an alumni issue of the *Columbia Review* featuring past contributors to *The Morningside*, the university literary magazine to which LZ primarily contributed during his student years (1920-1923).

LZ made a different "arrangement" for the unpublished *A Workers Anthology* (1936) consisting of the last six sections as follows (without using the roman numerals): VII, VIII, V, VI, IV, IX. Sections IV, V and VI were incorporated into *Arise, Arise* (23, 20, 23).

LZ's notebook for "A"-23 indicates that the phrase "Histories dye the streets:" – appearing near the end of that poem ("*A*" 563)–is a summary allusion to the final selection in this Apollinaire sequence, which is a complete translation of the poem "Un Dernier Chapitre" from Philippe Soupault's *Guillaume Apollinaire ou Reflets de l'Incendie* (1927) (*The Writing of Guillaume Apollinaire* 158/159).

Alain Bosquet: The need to have you

16 Dec. 1942 / *View* 1:3 (Spring 1943).

LZ included this translation in the 1943 *Anew* TS sent to William Carlos Williams (Yale).

Alain Bosquet (1919-1998) spent the war years from 1942 in New York, and LZ probably met him in connection with the journal *La France en Liberté*, an ambitious but never realized literary journal to be co-edited with René Taupin in support of France. The four poems LZ translates are all from Bosquet's first book, *L'image impardonnable*, published in New York by the Collection Refuge (1942). Bosquet reciprocated by translating three of LZ's poems (HRC).

Alain Bosquet: Pluck the Cascade

Maryland Quarterly 1 (1944).

LZ included this translation in the 1943 *Anew* TS (Yale).

Alain Bosquet: To Begin Again With Your Body ("Recommencer avec ton corps")

2 Feb. 1943 / Unpublished (TS HRC).

Alain Bosquet: To Go On

Unpublished (TS HRC).

PART IV. Uncollected Prose

Uncollected Early Prose (1930–1936)

Charles Reznikoff: Sincerity and Objectification

4 Feb. 1930 / Unpublished (MS HRC).

This famous essay went through a number of permutations over the years:

1) The original version, presented here, was written as a comprehensive critical introduction to Reznikoff, which LZ intended for *The Menorah Journal*, but it was rejected.

2) When Harriet Monroe offered LZ the chance to edit an issue of *Poetry* (Feb. 1931), he stated a preference for using "American Poetry 1920-1930" as his key critical statement; however, he had already submitted that article to *The Symposium*. As LZ was unwilling and too busy to write something new for *Poetry*, he abridged "Sincerity and Objectification," following Monroe's suggestions, putting more emphasis on the theoretical or aesthetic discussion and cutting out the sections on Reznikoff's plays and fiction. Monroe also suggested altering the title to "Sincerity and Objectification: *With Special Reference to the Work of Charles Reznikoff*" (letter dated 18 Oct. 1930).

3) For An *"Objectivists" Anthology* (To, Publishers, 1932) LZ extracted a page and a half, primarily the definitions of "sincerity" and "objectification," for inclusion as an Appendix.

4) Later in the decade LZ put together a typescript collecting his major critical essays, to be entitled *Sincerity and Objectification*, which he hoped would be published

by New Directions (see note below on "Two Related Notes" for further details). Here he reproduced the *Poetry* version of "Sincerity and Objectification," adding abbreviated versions of the sections on Reznikoff's drama and fiction. This collection was never published.

5) The *Poetry* version was then reprinted, except for the deletion of a bibliographical endnote, in *5 Statements for Poetry* (1958), a mimeograph edition of his key statements on poetics put out when LZ taught a summer course at San Francisco State College. (This version is reproduced in the "Additional Prose" of *Prep.*)

6) For *Prepositions: The Collected Critical Essays* (1967), LZ drastically truncated the three main "Objectivists" statements—"Program: 'Objectivists' 1931," "Sincerity and Objectification," and "'Recencies' in Poetry," the preface to *An "Objectivists" Anthology*—and combined them under the title "An Objective." His purpose at this time was both to erase the historical relations with the "Objectivists" and to de-emphasize these documents in favor of "Poetry / For My Son When He Can Read" (1946), which he considered a more significant statement of his poetic position.

LZ always insisted there was no such thing as "Objectivism," only individual "Objectivists," and while he was resigned to the fact that "Sincerity and Objectification" would remain closely tied to his reputation, he had no interest in being read as belonging to any particular group or movement. At least on historical grounds, it seems worth presenting LZ's essay in its full original form, which was intended to draw attention to an unjustly ignored poet and friend, who himself was temperamentally averse to self-promotion.

LZ quotes Reznikoff's poetry from his published volumes, primarily *Five Groups of Verse* (1927), and from (presumably) typescripts of work that would appear in *Jerusalem the Golden* (The Objectivist Press, 1934). This presentation of the poems has been maintained here, including line and word breaks. Seamus Cooney's excellent collected edition of Reznikoff's poetry regularizes the presentation of his verse according to his later practice, in particular numbering all poems, dropping the convention of capitalizing each line, and obscuring Reznikoff's right justification of his prose poems.

Queen Esther said . . . : in the latter "stanza" of this poem LZ adds "hollowed out" for Reznikoff's "hollowed." Otherwise, LZ scrupulously reproduces the layout of this poem as it appears in *Rhythms* (1918).

not yet published: all the poems so designated appeared in *Jerusalem the Golden* (1934).

"stage where every subsidiary art . . . : although attributed to W. B. Yeats, this is from Pound's introduction to *'Noh' or Accomplishment* (1917), his second expanded edition of Noh drama from Ernest Fenollosa's notebooks. The earlier edition, *Certain Noble Plays of Japan* (1916), included an introduction by Yeats, but this was not reprinted in the subsequent volume.

"Passage at Arms": published in *The Menorah Journal* 19:1 (Nov.-Dec. 1930).

"Lot became one of the men that wander through the city . . . : from "Apocrypha," *The Menorah Journal* 14:2 (Feb. 1928).

By the Waters of Manhattan: the quotations from this novel are presumably from the then unfinished second part as published in *By the Waters of Manhattan: An Annual* (Charles Reznikoff, 1929), rather then the Boni version of the novel, which was published in the summer of 1930. The protagonist of this section of the novel was originally named Joel, apparently based on an acquaintance of Reznikoff's named Joel Stein. Reznikoff continued to refer to this as his Joel novel as he worked on it. However, for the published version of the novel he changed the name to Ezekiel, his own Hebrew name, although the narrative is not autobiographical.

I have run through a troop . . . : from part VIII of "King David," in "Editing and Glosses," *By the Waters of Manhattan: An Annual* (1929).

Imagisme

1930 / *The New Review* 2 (May 1931).

Review of René Taupin, *L'Influence du symbolisme français sur la poésie américaine (de 1910 à 1920)* (Librairie Honoré Champion, 1929).

LZ extracted the fourth and last paragraphs from this review for *Prepositions*, where they appear under the titles "Influence" and "Poetic Values" respectively (135-136).

"Moi, l'autre hiver, plus sourd que les cerveaux d'enfants": from Arthur Rimbaud's "The Drunken Boat" (*Bateau Ivre*): I, through the winter, emptier than children's minds.

American Poetry 1920-1930

2 June 1930 / *The Symposium* 2.1 (Jan. 1931).

LZ remarked several times that for the "Objectivists" issue of *Poetry* (Feb. 1931) he would have preferred to use this essay as his major critical statement, rather than "Sincerity and Objectification"; however, he had already submitted the essay to *The Symposium* when he received Harriet Monroe's invitation to edit the issue in October 1930. Decades later, when preparing this essay for inclusion in *Prepositions* (1967), LZ trimmed the more historical contextualizing elements, which blunted its polemic edge and purpose. LZ's numerous quotations from poems draw on various early sources that occasionally differ in some details from later standard editions.

McAlmon: LZ refers to two volumes of verse published by McAlmon's Contact Editions. The "Unfinished Poem" is *North America, Continent of Conjecture*.

unpublished "After Rain" (Reznikoff): published in revised form in *Jerusalem the Golden* (The Objectivist Press, 1934), which also includes the following poem, "The English in Virginia April 1607."

"Marina": LZ wrote Eliot requesting to include this poem in the "Objectivists" issue of *Poetry* (Feb. 1931) but did not receive a reply in time. However, the poem did appear in *An "Objectivists" Anthology* (To, Publishers, 1932).

Cowley: the quotation is from "The Streets of Air," *Blue Juniata* (Jonathan Cape & Harrison Smith, 1929).

Pound, Antheil: *Antheil and the Treatise on Harmony* (Three Mountains Press, 1924). See *Ezra Pound and Music*, ed. R. Murray Schafer (New Directions, 1977), 256-257.

unrhymed work in *transition*: LZ refers to a few poems later gathered in *Key West: An Island Sheaf*, most obviously "The Mango Tree" and "Moment Fugue."

Wylie: stanzas from "Address to My Soul," *Trivial Breath* (Alfred A Knopf, 1928).

Roger Kaigh's "Paper" (still unpublished): Kaigh is a pseudonym of LZ's friend and Columbia classmate Irving Kaplan. This essay eventually appeared, mistakenly attributed to Basil Bunting and given the title, "The Written Record...," in *Three Essays*, ed. Richard Caddel (Basil Bunting Poetry Centre, 1994).

"Botticellian Trees" (unpublished): LZ included Williams' poem in the "Objectivists" issue of *Poetry* (Feb. 1931).

Ezra Pound's *XXX Cantos*

7 Sept. 1930 / *Front* 4 (June 1931).
    Review of Ezra Pound, *A Draft of XXX Cantos* (Hours Press, 1930).
    In *Front*, this review is immediately followed by an almost page-length passage from the opening of Canto XVII. There is no indication that this is meant to be part of the review, but presumably was appended as an exemplar of the qualities of Pound's poetry LZ discusses.

Mr. T. S. Eliot has written . . . : in Eliot's *Ezra Pound: His Metric and Poetry* (Alfred A. Knopf, 1917).

"London or Troy?" "Adest"

Feb. 1931 / *Poetry* 38:3 (June 1931).
    Review of Basil Bunting, *Redimiculum Matellarum* (Milan: privately printed, 1930). This is the only known review of Bunting's first book.

"Against Memory": Ode I.5 in Bunting's later *Collected Poems*. In the fourth quoted line, the printed text has *savors* for *savour*.

"While Shepherds Watched": Ode I.8.

"Chorus of Furies—Overheard—*guarda, mi disse, le feroce Erine*": Ode I.10 quoted complete.

Lucretius' invocation to Venus: Overdrafts, "Darling of Gods and Men, beneath the gliding stars." LZ included this translation in *A Test of Poetry* (108-109).

French epigrams: opening and closing the main contents, Bunting added the following French quotations: "La même justesse d'esprit qui nous fait écrire de bonnes chôses nous fait appréhender qu'elles ne le soient pas assez pour mériter lues"—from Jean de La Bruyère, *Les Caractères ou Les Moeurs de ce siècle*, Chapitre Premier [The same common-sense which makes an author write good things, makes him dread they are not good enough to deserve reading. Trans. Henri Van Laun]. *"Bornons ici cette carrière, / Les longs ovrages me font peur"*—from La Fontaine *Fables* Book 6, Epilogue [Here we check our course, / Long works I greatly fear.]

Mr. Kagawa, Mr. Winters, Mr Blackmur

28 Feb. 1931 / Unpublished (TS Kansas State University).

Review of Bunichi Kagawa, *Hidden Flame*, with forward by Yvor Winters (Half Moon Press, 1930).

This review was intended for *Poetry* (letter to Ezra Pound dated 6 March 1931, see *Selected Letters*).

Bunichi Kagawa (1904–1981) immigrated from Japan in 1918 and studied at Stanford University, where he became a protégé of Yvor Winters. He is perhaps best remembered as a central figure in the literary activities at Tule Lake "relocation center" where Japanese Americans were incarcerated during World War II.

Both R. P. Blackmur and Winters were associate editors of the journal *Hound & Horn* at the time of this review. The Blackmur article LZ refers to is "Notes on E. E. Cummings' Language," *Hound & Horn* 4 (Jan.–March 1931), an influential essay later collected in *Form and Value in Modern Poetry* (1957), which took the opportunity to critique Cummings to make a blanket dismissal of the more experimental propensities of modernism as "anti-culture." The paragraph on Blackmur (without the reference to Kagawa) was originally drafted in immediate response to this article, and LZ asked that it be printed in *Hound & Horn* as a letter to the editors (letter to Alan M. Stroock dated 30 March 1931; Yale. See *Selected Letters*). Later in the same year when Winters published a long disparaging review of René Taupin's *L'Influence du symbolisme français sur la poésie américaine* ("The Symbolist Influence," *Hound & Horn* 4, July–Sept. 1931), Zukofsky promptly jumped to his friend's defense, and there was a sharp exchange of letters that the *Hound & Horn* planned to publish but was pulled at the last moment, much to LZ's exasperation (galleys edited by LZ are among the *Contempo* papers at the HRC). A little further down the road, Winters would testily dismiss *An "Objectivists" Anthology* (*Hound & Horn* 6, Oct.–Dec. 1932).

"prisms of sharp mind": from Cummings' "Song II" in *XLI Poems* (1925).

Prose Cantos XX–XXI

Nativity 2 (Spring 1931).

Reviews of Robert Hillyer, *The Gates of the Compass* (Viking Press, 1930), Leonora Speyer, *Naked Heel* (Alfred A. Knopf, 1931), and Kathleen Tankersley Young, *Ten Poems* (Parnassus Press, 1930).

Under the general title "Prose Cantos," *Nativity* included brief book reviews and commentary.

Robert Hillyer (1895-1961), Pulitzer Prize winner for his *Collected Verse* (1934), best remembered today as a busy opponent of modernist poetry and particularly for leading attacks on the awarding of the Bollingen Prize to Ezra Pound for *The Pisan Cantos* in 1948.

Leonora Speyer (1872-1956), violinist and poet, Pulitzer Prize winner for *Fiddler's Farewell* (1927).

Kathleen Tankersley Young (1902-1933), an editor of *Blues* with Charles Henri Ford and Parker Tyler, and founder of a pamphlet series, Modern Editions Press, which published Carl Rakosi's *Two Poems* (1933).

The first review ends with references to Speyer's "Ballad of Old Doc Higgins," which begins: "Old Doc Higgins shot a mermaid: / Vowed he'd ketch her, fish or woman, fiend or human. . . ."

"Completely and Accurately"

The New York Sun (10 Oct. 1931).

Review of Edward W. Naylor, *Shakespeare and Music*, new edition (E. P. Dutton & Co., 1931), Wilfred Owen, *The Poems*, new edition (Viking Press, 1931) and James Stephens, *Strict Joy and Other Poems* (Macmillan Co., 1931).

The Transition

19 May 1932 / *The Saturday Review of Literature* (30 July 1932).

Review of Wyndham Lewis, *The Doom of Youth* (Robert M. McBride & Co., 1932).

Since LZ highlights Lewis' extensive use of italics and single quotation marks, the quotations from Lewis have been lightly edited to conform with a TS held at Yale, which is closer to Lewis' printed text, although not exact in every detail. This TS also includes an additional paragraph following paragraph five:

> In this connexion, may be noted, as two examples, the expert, homogeneous writing of two social historians growing out of a dialectic hateful to Mr. Lewis, and not consciously on the side of genius—(Mr. Lewis—"if as a social historian I am unequalled, . . . The 'man of genius' in a communist state would of course hide his 'genius' as far as possible"): M. Ilin's *New Russia's Primer* [*The Story of the Five-Year Plan*] and M. Rubinstein's "Electrification as the Basis of Technical Reconstruction in the Soviet Union" (in *Science at the Cross Roads*—Kniga), both works of science,—and Mr. Lewis referring again to his own book. "This treatise is not a work of literature in any sense. It is a work of science, pure and simple. I merely bring in so much literary rhetorical artifice as is necessary to enable me to excite the reader's interest, arouse his attention, and direct it to what it has been my object to expose and explain."
> Mr. Lewis explains:

"The Open Mind"–Physiology and a Poem

The Lion and Crown (Fall 1932).

This piece was published anonymously, but in his own copy of *The Lion and Crown*, LZ hand-wrote a note: "L. Z. wrote (rather dictated extempore) this for J. R. [Jerry Reisman] who needed a student 'theme' at CCNY [City College New York]. Dec. 10/61"

Henry Adams: quoted "A"-8 (70).

André Breton, "Pour Dada": *La Nouvelle Revue Française* 83 (1 Aug. 1920), collected in *Les Pas perdus* (Gallimard, 1924), which LZ refers to several times in *The Writing of Guillaume Apollinaire*.

A Further Note on *XXX Cantos* by Ezra Pound

23 Feb. 1933 / *The Windsor Quarterly* 1:1 (Spring 1933).

An abridged version of this note was published in Ezra Pound's *Active Anthology* (Faber and Faber Ltd, 1933). A few details, particularly in the long quotation from Golding's Ovid, have been emended according to LZ's MS.

"Of the thinking gentleman's query: 'What does Mr. Pound believe?'": T. S. Eliot famously posed this question in a review of Pound's *Personae: The Collected Shorter Poems* (1926), "Isolated Superiority," *Dial* 84 (Jan. 1928). Pound responded by saying he believed in the Confucian *Ta Hio* in "Date Line," the introduction to *Make It New* (1934); *Literary Essays* (New Directions, 1954), 86.

One's Own Taste

1935? / Unpublished (TS HRC).

Review of L. H. Myers, *The Root and the Flower* (1935).

Leopold Hamilton Myers (1881-1944), British novelist. His trilogy, *The Root and the Flower* (1929-1935), is considered his major work. LZ reviews the third volume.

Different people, Marx noted . . . : this paraphrase of Marx on "equal right" appears in "A"-8 (45–46); the source is actually Lenin, *State and Revolution* (Progress Publishers, 1918), who quotes from and comments on Marx.

Muriel Rukeyser's Poems

1935? / Unpublished (TS HRC).

Review of Muriel Rukeyser, *Theory of Flight*, foreword by Stephen Vincent Benét (Yale University Press, 1935).

Rukeyser's first book was chosen as the winner of the Yale Younger Poets Series by Stephen Vincent Benét (1898-1943), the establishment poet and double Pulitzer Prize winner, which launched her career at age 22.

"expanding universe . . . : from "The Gyroscope."

"wave shocked to motion": from "Poem Out of Childhood."

"I give you cats? ...: all the quoted phrases in this paragraph from "Cats and a Cock."

"Ignatz among the jail,": referring to George Herriman's comic strip *Krazy Kat*, in which Krazy Kat and Ignatz were the cat and mouse protagonists. Ignatz often ends up in Officer Pupp's jail.

writing about the New York Public Library: "In the Dark House."

Sterling Brown, "Black Worker and White Worker": this poem was later given the title "Colloquy" with the earlier title as a subtitle. Apparently published in *International Literature* (International Union of Revolutionary Writers, 1935).

Tomorrow's Mayday ...: from "Cats and a Cock."

O, we are afflicted ...: from "The Blood Is Justified."

Matter That Thinks, or Notations towards Action

1936? / Unpublished (TS HRC).

  This TS is undated but includes several quotations incorporated into "A"-8, which LZ mainly worked on from the summer of 1936 through the following summer.

Lenin: both Lenin quotations are from *The Teachings of Karl Marx* (International Publishers Co., 1930).

"It is impossible to separate thought from matter that thinks ...: this quotation is actually from Marx as quoted in Engels' *Historical Materialism* (1892), the general introduction written for the English edition of *Socialism: Utopian or Scientific*, which was also published on its own under this title. Used in "A"-8 (46, 93).

"Now the present status musices ...: from a report Bach submitted to the Council of Leipzig. In "A"-8, LZ gives the full title, "A short and much-needed statement of the requirements of church music. With some general reflections on its decline," with various brief quotations including several from the passage quoted here (45).

Two Related Notes 1931 and 1936

1939 / Unpublished (TS HRC).

The first note simply extracts the essential elements of "Program: 'Objectivists' 1931," originally published in the "Objectivists" issue of *Poetry* (Feb. 1931) and again in *An "Objectivists" Anthology* (To, Publishers, 1932), but the second note was never published. In 1939, at a time when LZ was struggling to publish and somewhat desperate for money, he prepared a typescript of his critical prose under the title *Sincerity and Objectification*, which he hoped James Laughlin at New Directions would accept. For the most part this volume was made up of his major early essays: "Henry Adams," "Ezra Pound: His Cantos," a fuller version of "Sincerity and Objectification" (see note above to "Charles Reznikoff: Sincerity and Objectification"), "American Poetry 1920-1930," "Two Related Notes," the then unpublished *"Modern Times"* (on Charlie Chaplin) and finally, in a separate section, "Thanks to the Dictionary." There was a brief "Preface" as follows:

> The critical essays in this volume intend a form of analysis in which the words appear not only defined but entire like the art, or natural or conceptual thing,* discussed. This aim is perforce modified by subsequent information always affecting a new phase of the critic's judgment,—and the dates in the table of contents concede this fact.
>
> A similar awareness of it has been applied in *Thanks to the Dictionary* to the materials of a novel.
>
> *cf. *Le Style Apollinaire*, René Taupin et Louis Zukofsky, Les Presses Modernes, Paris, 1934.

Longinus: this quotation appears in both *The Writing of Guillaume Apollinaire* (164) and "A Statement for Poetry" (1950) (*Prep.* 21). Translation by W. Hamilton Fyfe from the Loeb Classical Library edition of *Aristotle: Poetics, Longinus: On the Sublime, Demetrius: On Style* (1902).

Engels: this remark at IV appears in "A"-8 (46). See note on "Matter That Thinks" above.

Uncollected Later Prose (1956–1973)

The Summing Up

The Pound Newsletter 10 (April 1956).

This title was given as a topic for the final issue of a mimeographed newsletter dedicated to Ezra Pound, edited by John H. Edwards and William Vasse, which solicited brief notes or comments in response from a range of writers and scholars.

A Preface?

7 April 1956 / Jonathan Williams, *Amen/Huzza/Selah–Black Mountain 1956-9* (Jargon 13(a), 1960).

After Robert Duncan and Robert Creeley, Jonathan Williams was one of the earliest of the younger poets to contact and support LZ from the mid-1950s, leading to LZ's remarkable public reemergence after a long period of obscurity throughout the 1940s and most of the 50s. The two corresponded frequently during the period 1955-1964. At the time LZ wrote this preface, Williams was in the process of publishing *Some Time* in a very handsome edition, which came out in September 1956. LZ's "A Preface?" was written as a letter responding to various points of mutual recognition and interest between the two poets.

Fifty-One High-Coup Syllables: Williams' poem has the parenthetical subtitle, "(or, Sight, Sound & Intellection)," quoting LZ's *A Test of Poetry* (1948), which at the time Williams was helping to distribute and would reprint in 1964.

Very good: Hymeneal: Williams' "Hymeneal to Leap-Year" reads in its entirety:

> Io! Io!—you
> yo-yo
>
> Go!

LZ associates this with Catullus, who wrote two marriage songs (Carmina 61, 62). Williams is presumably alluding to the former, which includes numerous instances of the interjection "io."

agite ite ad alta: quoted from Catullus' Carmina 63 meaning "Come away." ***Gai Valeri Catulli Veronensis Liber*** is the formal title of Catullus' collected poems (The Book of Catullus of Verona), which was used as the subtitle of LZ and Celia's *Catullus* (Cape Goliard, 1969). At this time LZ had not yet started on that project, although it was undoubtedly on his mind and the correspondence with Williams evidences the poets' mutual enthusiasm for Catullus.

In fair Verona: from second line of the prologue to Shakespeare's *Romeo and Juliet*, "...where we lay our scene."

Hark! how around the hills rejoice / And rocks reflected *ios* sing—: from William Congreve's "irregular ode," "To the King, On the Taking of Namur." LZ probably found these lines in his *Century Dictionary* under the entry for "io."

Buncombe: Buncombe county is in the Appalachian foothills of western North Carolina and includes both Asheville, where Williams was born, and Black Mountain College, which he attended in the early 1950s. Williams lived most of his life in this general area. This also explains the earlier reference to Cherokees, as there is a well-known Cherokee "reservation" in western North Carolina.

two of your friends: uncertain but quite possibly Robert Duncan and Robert Creeley.

Barely / and / widely: LZ quotes complete the title poem of *Barely and widely* (C.Z., 1958), composed the week before he wrote this "preface." LZ then quotes extracts from the beginning and end of the opening section of Part III of *Bottom* (97-99), "A-bomb and H-," also unpublished at this point; however, Williams apparently had seen this section when he visited LZ (letter to Williams dated 15 April 1956; see *Selected Letters*).

"What I Come To Do Is Partial"

15 Oct. 1957 / *Poetry* 92:2 (May 1958).

Review of Robert Creeley, *The Whip* (Migrant Books, 1957).

The Whip was a selection of early Creeley poems published by Gael Turnbull's Migrant Books and distributed in the U.S. through Jonathan Williams' Jargon Society.

Prose passages from *Autobiography*

1967 / *Autobiography* (Grossman Publishers, 1970).

Autobiography primarily consists of a selection of LZ's short poems with the scores of Celia's musical settings. These settings were all composed between 1940 and 1952 and in many cases appear to have been made as Christmas cards or gifts to LZ, just as LZ wrote annual valentine poems to Celia and Paul. As early as 1960, LZ proposed to Cid Corman to publish the poems with musical settings as a book (letter dated 11 May 1960), and the brief preface is dated 17 February 1962, indicating that he readied the volume for publication when the opportunity arose. In 1967, LZ was asked for a biographical statement for a reference volume, eventually published as *World Authors, 1950-1970: A Companion Volume to Twentieth Century Authors* (H. W. Wilson Co., 1975). His single page statement accompanies a more formal biographical entry. Perhaps wondering whether this statement would ever appear, LZ distributed his remarks in *Autobiography* among the poems and musical settings in Grossman's very handsomely designed edition.

Reply to Questionnaire: On Rhythm from America

Agenda 11:2-3 (1973).

PART V. Musical Adaptations of "A" (1964–1967)

"A" Libretto

29 Oct. 1964 / Unpublished (TS HRC).

    The draft version of this text is in Celia Zukofsky's hand, although the typed version simply credits LZ. This text uses passages from all the movements of "A" composed to date; that is, "A" 1-14, plus three movements written out of chronological sequence in 1963: "A"-16, "A"-17, and "A"-20.

    Little is known about what instigated this arrangement, although it may have been prompted by the prospect of the first performances of *Arise, Arise*, which took place in August 1965. There is a typed copy with a note that it was received from Jerry Benjamin, who directed *Arise* and may have arranged for the typing of the text for possible performance. However, there is no evidence that the *Libretto* was in fact performed.

"A" Cantata 13 v

The Journal of Creative Behavior, Poetry Supplement, 1:3 (Summer 1967).

    As the title indicates, this work consists of excerpts from the fifth cantata of "A"-13 with assigned voices (see "A" 309-313).

There exist copies of a further related text, *"A" 1-4* (Performing Edition), which was prepared in connection with the performance of *Autobiography* at the Library and Museum of the Performing Arts, New York City, on 31 March 1971. The creator of this arrangement is not clearly stated, but was probably David Stivender, then assistant chorus master of the New York Metropolitan Opera Company, who was the musical director and arranger for the performance of *Autobiography*. This text consists of the entirety of the first four movements of "A" with assigned vocal parts, which were to be recited except when the text quotes from Bach's *St. Matthew Passion*. The same five voices (Reader, Soprano, Alto, Tenor, Bass) are used as in the performance of *Autobiography* (in which LZ took the part of the Reader). There is no evidence that the *"A" 1-4* arrangement was performed.

INDEX OF TITLES AND FIRST LINES

INDEX OF SUBJECTS